AN INTRODUCTION TO PHILOSOPHY
by
GEORGE STUART FULLERTON

PREFACE

As there cannot be said to be a beaten path in philosophy, and as "Introductions" to the subject differ widely from one another, it is proper that I should give an indication of the scope of the present volume.

It undertakes:—

1. To point out what the word "philosophy" is made to cover in our universities and colleges at the present day, and to show why it is given this meaning.

2. To explain the nature of reflective or philosophical thinking, and to show how it differs from common thought and from science.

3. To give a general view of the main problems with which philosophers have felt called upon to deal.

4. To give an account of some of the more important types of philosophical doctrine which have arisen out of the consideration of such problems.

5. To indicate the relation of philosophy to the so-called philosophical sciences, and to the other sciences.

6. To show, finally, that the study of philosophy is of value to us all, and to give some practical admonitions on spirit and method. Had these admonitions been impressed upon me at a time when I was in especial need of guidance, I feel that they would have spared me no little anxiety and confusion of mind. For this reason, I recommend them to the attention of the reader.

Such is the scope of my book. It aims to tell what philosophy is. It is not its chief object to advocate a particular type of doctrine. At the same time, as it is impossible to treat of the problems of philosophy except from some point of view, it will be found that, in Chapters III to XI, a doctrine is presented. It is the same as that presented much more in detail, and with a greater wealth of reference, in my "System of Metaphysics," which was published a short time ago. In the Notes in the back of this volume, the reader will find references to those parts of the larger work which treat of the subjects more briefly discussed here. It will be helpful to the teacher to keep the larger work on hand, and to use more or less of the material there presented as his undergraduate classes discuss the chapters of this one. Other references are also given in the Notes, and it may be profitable to direct the attention of students to them.

The present book has been made as clear and simple as possible, that no unnecessary difficulties may be placed in the path of those who enter upon the thorny road of philosophical reflection. The subjects treated are deep enough to demand the serious attention of any one; and they are subjects of fascinating interest. That they are treated simply and clearly does not mean that they are treated superficially. Indeed, when a doctrine is presented in outline and in a brief and simple statement, its meaning may be more readily apparent than when it is treated more exhaustively. For this reason, I especially recommend, even to those who are well acquainted with philosophy, the account of the external world contained in Chapter IV.

For the doctrine I advocate I am inclined to ask especial consideration on the ground that it is, on the whole, a justification of the attitude taken by the plain man toward the world in which he finds himself. The experience of the race is not a thing that we may treat lightly.

Thus, it is maintained that there is a real external world presented in our experience—not a world which we have a right to regard as the sensations or ideas of any mind. It is maintained that we have evidence that there are minds in certain relations to that world, and that we can, within certain limits, determine these relations. It is pointed out that the plain man's belief in the activity of his mind and his notion of the significance of purposes and ends are not without justification. It is indicated that theism is a reasonable doctrine, and it is held that the human will is free in the only proper sense of the word "freedom." Throughout it is taken for granted that the philosopher has no private system of weights and measures, but must reason as other men reason, and must prove his conclusions in the same sober way.

I have written in hopes that the book may be of use to undergraduate students. They are often repelled by philosophy, and I cannot but think that this is in part due to the dry and abstract form in which philosophers have too often seen fit to express their thoughts. The same thoughts can be set forth in plain language, and their significance illustrated by a constant reference to experiences which we all have—experiences which must serve as the foundation to every theory of the mind and the world worthy of serious consideration.

But there are many persons who cannot attend formal courses of instruction, and who, nevertheless, are interested in philosophy. These, also, I have had in mind; and I have tried to be so clear that they could read the work with profit in the absence of a teacher.

Lastly, I invite the more learned, if they have found my "System of Metaphysics" difficult to understand in any part, to follow the simple statement contained in the chapters above alluded to, and then to return, if they will, to the more bulky volume.

GEORGE STUART FULLERTON.

New York, 1906.

AN INTRODUCTION TO PHILOSOPHY
I. INTRODUCTORY
CHAPTER I
THE MEANING OF THE WORD "PHILOSOPHY" IN THE PAST AND IN THE PRESENT

I must warn the reader at the outset that the title of this chapter seems to promise a great deal more than he will find carried out in the chapter itself. To tell all that philosophy has meant in the past, and all that it means to various classes of men in the present, would be a task of no small magnitude, and one quite beyond the scope of such a volume as this. But it is not impossible to give within small compass a brief indication, at least, of what the word once signified, to show how its signification has undergone changes, and to point out to what sort of a discipline or group of disciplines educated men are apt to apply the word, notwithstanding their differences of opinion as to the truth or falsity of this or that particular doctrine. Why certain subjects of investigation have come to be grouped together and to be regarded as falling within the province of the philosopher, rather than certain other subjects, will, I hope, be made clear in the body of the work. Only an indication can be given in this chapter.

1. THE BEGINNINGS OF PHILOSOPHY.—The Greek historian Herodotus (484-424 B.C.) appears to have been the first to use the verb "to philosophize." He makes Croesus tell Solon how he has heard that he "from a desire of knowledge has, philosophizing, journeyed through many lands." The word "philosophizing" seems to indicate that Solon pursued knowledge for its own sake, and was what we call an investigator. As for the word "philosopher" (etymologically, a lover of wisdom), a certain somewhat unreliable tradition traces it back to Pythagoras (about 582-500 B.C.). As told by Cicero, the story is that, in a conversation with Leon, the ruler of Phlius, in the Peloponnesus, he described himself as a philosopher, and said that his business was an investigation into the nature of things.

At any rate, both the words "philosopher" and "philosophy" are freely used in the writings of the disciples of Socrates (470-399 B.C.), and it is possible that he was the first to make use of them. The seeming modesty of the title philosopher—for etymologically it is a modest one, though it has managed to gather a very different signification with the lapse of time—the modesty of the title would naturally appeal to a man who claimed so much ignorance, as Socrates; and Plato represents him as distinguishing between the lover of wisdom and the wise, on the ground that God alone may be called wise. From that date to this the word "philosopher" has remained with us, and it has meant many things to many men. But for centuries the philosopher has not been simply the investigator, nor has he been simply the lover of wisdom.

An investigation into the origin of words, however interesting in itself, can tell us little of the uses to which words are put after they have come into being. If we turn from etymology to history, and review the labors of the men whom the world has agreed to call philosophers, we are struck by the fact that those who head the list chronologically appear to have been occupied with crude physical speculations, with attempts to guess what the world is made out of, rather than with that somewhat vague something that we call philosophy to-day.

Students of the history of philosophy usually begin their studies with the speculations of the Greek philosopher Thales (b. 624 B.C.). We are told that he assumed water to be the universal principle out of which all things are made, and that he maintained that "all things are full of gods." We find that Anaximander, the next in the list, assumed as the source out of which all things proceed and that to which they all return "the infinite and indeterminate"; and that Anaximenes, who was perhaps his pupil, took as his principle the all-embracing air.

This trio constitutes the Ionian school of philosophy, the earliest of the Greek schools; and one who reads for the first time the few vague statements which seem to constitute the sum of their contributions to human knowledge is impelled to wonder that so much has been made of the men.

This wonder disappears, however, when one realizes that the appearance of these thinkers was really a momentous thing. For these men turned their faces away from the poetical and mythologic way of accounting for things, which had obtained up to their time, and set their faces toward Science. Aristotle shows us how Thales may have been led to the formulation of his main thesis by an observation of the phenomena of nature. Anaximander saw in the world in which he lived the result of a process of evolution. Anaximenes explains the coming into being of fire, wind, clouds, water, and earth, as due to a condensation and expansion of the universal principle, air. The boldness of their speculations we may explain as due to a courage born of ignorance, but the explanations they offer are scientific in spirit, at least.

Moreover, these men do not stand alone. They are the advance guard of an army whose latest representatives are the men who are enlightening the world at the present day. The evolution of science—taking that word in the broad sense to mean organized and systematized knowledge—must be traced in the works of the Greek philosophers from Thales down. Here we have the source and the rivulet to which we can trace back the mighty stream which is flowing past our own doors. Apparently insignificant in its beginnings, it must still for a while seem insignificant to the man who follows with an unreflective eye the course of the current.

It would take me too far afield to give an account of the Greek schools which immediately succeeded the Ionic: to tell of the Pythagoreans, who held that all things were constituted by numbers; of the Eleatics, who held that "only Being is," and denied the possibility of change, thereby reducing the shifting panorama of the things about us to a mere delusive world of appearances; of Heraclitus, who was so impressed by the constant flux of things that he summed up his view of nature in the words: "Everything flows"; of Empedocles, who found his explanation of the world in the combination of the four elements, since become traditional, earth, water, fire, and air; of Democritus, who developed a materialistic atomism which reminds one strongly of the doctrine of atoms as it has appeared in modern science; of Anaxagoras, who traced the system of things to the setting in order of an infinite multiplicity of different elements,—"seeds of things,"—which setting in order was due to the activity of the finest of things, Mind.

It is a delight to discover the illuminating thoughts which came to the minds of these men; and, on the other hand, it is amusing to see how recklessly they launched themselves on boundless seas when they were unprovided with chart and compass. They were like brilliant children, who know little of the dangers of the great world, but are ready to undertake anything. These philosophers regarded all knowledge as their province, and did not despair of governing so great a realm. They were ready to explain the whole world and everything in it. Of course, this can only mean that they had little conception of how much there is to explain, and of what is meant by scientific explanation.

It is characteristic of this series of philosophers that their attention was directed very largely upon the external world. It was natural that this should be so. Both in the history of the race and in that of the individual, we find that the attention is seized first by material things, and that it is long before a clear conception of the mind and of its knowledge is arrived at. Observation precedes reflection. When we come to think definitely about the mind, we are all apt to make use of notions which we have derived from our experience of external things. The very words we use to denote mental operations are in many instances taken from this outer realm. We "direct" the attention; we speak of "apprehension," of "conception," of "intuition." Our knowledge is "clear" or "obscure"; an oration is "brilliant"; an emotion is "sweet" or "bitter." What wonder that, as we read over the fragments that have come down to us from the Pre-Socratic philosophers, we should be struck by the fact that they sometimes leave out altogether and sometimes touch lightly upon a number of those things that we regard to-day as peculiarly within the province of the philosopher. They busied themselves with the world as they saw it, and certain things had hardly as yet come definitely within their horizon.

2. THE GREEK PHILOSOPHY AT ITS HEIGHT.—The next succeeding period sees certain classes of questions emerge into prominence which had attracted comparatively little attention from the men of an earlier day. Democritus of Abdera, to whom reference has been made above, belongs chronologically to this latter period, but his way of thinking makes us class him with the earlier philosophers. It was characteristic of these latter that they assumed rather naïvely that man can look upon the world and can know it, and can by thinking about it succeed in giving a reasonable account of it. That there may be a difference between the world as it really is and the world as it appears to man, and that it may be impossible for man to attain to a knowledge of the absolute truth of things, does not seem to have occurred to them.

The fifth century before Christ was, in Greece, a time of intense intellectual ferment. One is reminded, in reading of it, of the splendid years of the Renaissance in Italy, of the awakening of the human mind to a vigorous life which cast off the bonds of tradition and insisted upon the right of free and unfettered development. Athens was the center of this intellectual activity.

In this century arose the Sophists, public teachers who busied themselves with all departments of human knowledge, but seemed to lay no little emphasis upon certain questions that touched very nearly the life of man. Can man attain to truth at all—to a truth that is more than a mere truth to him, a seeming truth? Whence do the laws derive their authority? Is there such a thing as justice, as right? It was with such questions as these that the Sophists occupied themselves, and such questions as these have held the attention of mankind ever since. When they make their appearance in the life of a people or of an individual man, it means that there has been a rebirth, a birth into the life of reflection.

When Socrates, that greatest of teachers, felt called upon to refute the arguments of these men, he met them, so to speak, on their own ground, recognizing that the subjects of which they discoursed were, indeed, matter for scientific investigation. His attitude seemed to many conservative persons in his day a dangerous one; he was regarded as an innovator; he taught men to think and to raise questions where, before, the traditions of the fathers had seemed a sufficient guide to men's actions.

And, indeed, he could not do otherwise. Men had learned to reflect, and there had come into existence at least the beginnings of what we now sometimes rather loosely call the mental and moral sciences. In the works of Socrates' disciple Plato (428-347 B.C.) and in those of Plato's disciple Aristotle (384-322 B.C.), abundant justice is done to these fields of human activity. These two, the greatest among the Greek philosophers, differ from each other in many things, but it is worthy of remark that they both seem to regard the whole sphere of human knowledge as their province.

Plato is much more interested in the moral sciences than in the physical, but he, nevertheless, feels called upon to give an account of how the world was made and out of what sort of elements. He evidently does not take his own account very seriously, and recognizes that he is on uncertain ground. But he does not consider the matter beyond his jurisdiction.

As for Aristotle, that wonderful man seems to have found it possible to represent worthily every science known to his time, and to have marked out several new fields for his successors to cultivate. His philosophy covers physics, cosmology, zoölogy, logic, metaphysics, ethics, psychology, politics and economics, rhetoric and poetics.

Thus we see that the task of the philosopher was much the same at the period of the highest development of the Greek philosophy that it had been earlier. He was supposed to give an account of the system of things. But the notion of what it means to give an account of the system of things had necessarily undergone some change. The philosopher had to be something more than a natural philosopher.

3. PHILOSOPHY AS A GUIDE TO LIFE.—At the close of the fourth century before Christ there arose the schools of the Stoics, the Epicureans, and the Skeptics. In them we seem to find a somewhat new conception of philosophy—philosophy appears as chiefly a guide to life. The Stoic emphasizes the necessity of living "according to nature," and dwells upon the character of the wise man; the Epicurean furnishes certain selfish maxims for getting through life as pleasantly as possible; the Skeptic counsels apathy, an indifference to all things,—blessed is he who expects nothing, for he shall not be disappointed.

And yet, when we examine more closely these systems, we find a conception of philosophy not really so very different from that which had obtained before. We do not find, it is true, that disinterested passion for the attainment of truth which is the glory of science. Man seems quite too much concerned with the problem of his own happiness or unhappiness; he has grown morbid. Nevertheless, the practical maxims which obtain in each of these systems are based upon a certain view of the system of things as a whole.

The Stoic tells us of what the world consists; what was the beginning and what will be the end of things; what is the relation of the system of things to God. He develops a physics and a logic as well as a system of ethics. The Epicurean informs us that the world originated in a rain of atoms through space; he examines into the foundations of human knowledge; and he proceeds to make himself comfortable in a world from which he has removed those disturbing elements, the gods. The Skeptic decides that there is no such thing as truth, before he enunciates the dogma that it is not worth while to worry about anything. The philosophy of each school includes a view of the system of things as a whole. The philosopher still regarded the universe of knowledge as his province.

4. PHILOSOPHY IN THE MIDDLE AGES.—I cannot do more than mention Neo-Platonism, that half Greek and half Oriental system of doctrine which arose in the third century after Christ, the first system of importance after the schools mentioned above. But I must not pass it by without pointing out that the Neo-Platonic philosopher undertook to give an account of the origin, development, and end of the whole system of things.

In the Middle Ages there gradually grew up rather a sharp distinction between those things that can be known through the unaided reason and those things that can only be known through a supernatural revelation. The term "philosophy" came to be synonymous with knowledge attained by the natural light of reason. This seems to imply some sort of a limitation to the task of the philosopher. Philosophy is not synonymous with all knowledge.

But we must not forget to take note of the fact that philosophy, even with this limitation, constitutes a pretty wide field. It covers both the physical and the moral sciences. Nor should we omit to notice that the scholastic philosopher was at the same time a theologian. Albert the Great and St. Thomas Aquinas, the famous scholastics of the thirteenth century, had to write a "*Summa Theologiae*," or system of theology, as well as to treat of the other departments of human knowledge.

Why were these men not overwhelmed with the task set them by the tradition of their time? It was because the task was not, after all, so great as a modern man might conceive it to be. Gil Blas, in Le Sage's famous romance, finds it possible to become a skilled physician in the twinkling of an eye, when Dr. Sangrado has imparted to him the secret that the remedy for all diseases is to be found in bleeding the patient and in making him drink copiously of hot water. When little is known about things, it does not seem impossible for one man to learn that little. During the Middle Ages and the centuries preceding, the physical sciences had a long sleep. Men were much more concerned in the thirteenth century to find out what Aristotle had said than they were to address questions to nature. The special sciences, as we now know them, had not been called into existence.

5. THE MODERN PHILOSOPHY.—The submission of men's minds to the authority of Aristotle and of the church gradually gave way. A revival of learning set in. Men turned first of all to a more independent choice of authorities, and then rose to the conception of a philosophy independent of authority, of a science based upon an observation of nature, of a science at first hand. The special sciences came into being.

But the old tradition of philosophy as universal knowledge remained. If we pass over the men of the transition period and turn our attention to Francis Bacon (1561-1626) and Rene Descartes (1596-1650), the two who are commonly regarded as heading the list of the modern philosophers, we find both of them assigning to the philosopher an almost unlimited field.

Bacon holds that philosophy has for its objects God, man, and nature, and he regards it as within his province to treat of "*philosophia prima*" (a sort of metaphysics, though he does not call it by this name), of logic, of physics and astronomy, of anthropology, in which he includes psychology, of ethics, and of politics. In short, he attempts to map out the whole field of human knowledge, and to tell those who work in this corner of it or in that how they should set about their task.

As for Descartes, he writes of the trustworthiness of human knowledge, of the existence of God, of the existence of an external world, of the human soul and its nature, of mathematics, physics, cosmology, physiology, and, in short, of nearly everything discussed by the men of his day. No man can accuse this extraordinary Frenchman of a lack of appreciation of the special sciences which were growing up. No one in his time had a better right to be called a scientist in the modern sense of the term. But it was not enough for him to be a mere mathematician, or even a worker in the physical sciences generally. He must be all that has been mentioned above.

The conception of philosophy as of a something that embraces all departments of human knowledge has not wholly passed away even in our day. I shall not dwell upon Spinoza (1632-1677), who believed it possible to deduce a world *a priori* with mathematical precision; upon Christian Wolff (1679-1754), who defined philosophy as the knowledge of the causes of what is or comes into being; upon Fichte (1762-1814), who believed that the philosopher, by mere thinking, could lay down the laws of all possible future experience; upon Schelling (1775-1854), who, without knowing anything worth mentioning about natural science, had the courage to develop a system of natural philosophy, and to condemn such investigators as Boyle and Newton; upon Hegel (1770-1831), who undertakes to construct the whole system of reality out of concepts, and who, with his immediate predecessors, brought philosophy for a while into more or less disrepute with men of a scientific turn of mind. I shall come down quite to our own times, and consider a man whose conception of philosophy has had and still has a good deal of influence, especially with the general public—with those to whom philosophy is a thing to be taken up in moments of leisure, and cannot be the serious pursuit of a life.

"Knowledge of the lowest kind," says Herbert Spencer, "is *un-unified* knowledge; Science is *partially-unified* knowledge; Philosophy is *completely-unified* knowledge." [1] Science, he argues, means merely the family of the Sciences—stands for nothing more than the sum of knowledge formed of their contributions. Philosophy is the fusion of these contributions into a whole; it is knowledge of the greatest generality. In harmony with this notion Spencer produced a system of philosophy which includes the following: A volume entitled "First Principles," which undertakes to show what man can and what man cannot know; a treatise on the principles of biology; another on the principles of psychology; still another on the principles of sociology; and finally one on the principles of morality. To complete the scheme it would have been necessary to give an account of inorganic nature before going on to the phenomena of life, but our philosopher found the task too great and left this out.

Now, Spencer was a man of genius, and one finds in his works many illuminating thoughts. But it is worthy of remark that those who praise his work in this or in that field are almost always men who have themselves worked in some other field and have an imperfect acquaintance with the particular field that they happen to be praising. The metaphysician finds the reasonings of the "First Principles" rather loose and inconclusive; the biologist pays little heed to the "Principles of Biology"; the sociologist finds Spencer not particularly accurate or careful in the field of his predilection. He has tried to be a professor of all the sciences, and it is too late in the world's history for him or for any man to cope with such a task. In the days of Plato a man might have hoped to accomplish it.

6. WHAT PHILOSOPHY MEANS IN OUR TIME.—It savors of temerity to write down such a title as that which heads the present section. There are men living to-day to whom philosophy means little else than the doctrine of Kant, or of Hegel, or of the brothers Caird, or of Herbert Spencer, or even of St. Thomas Aquinas, for we must not forget that many of the seminaries of learning in Europe and some in America still hold to the mediaeval church philosophy.

But let me gather up in a few words the purport of what has been said above. Philosophy once meant the whole body of scientific knowledge. Afterward it came to mean the whole body of knowledge which could be attained by the mere light of human reason, unaided by revelation. The several special sciences sprang up, and a multitude of men have for a long time past devoted themselves to definite limited fields of investigation with little attention to what has been done in other fields. Nevertheless, there has persisted the notion of a discipline which somehow concerns itself with the whole system of things, rather than with any limited division of that broad field. It is a notion not peculiar to the disciples of Spencer. There are many to whom philosophy is a "*Weltweisheit*," a world-wisdom. Shall we say that this is the meaning of the word philosophy now? And if we do, how shall we draw a line between philosophy and the body of the special sciences?

Perhaps the most just way to get a preliminary idea of what philosophy means to the men of our time is to turn away for the time being from the definition of any one man or group of men, and to ask ourselves what a professor of philosophy in an American or European university is actually supposed to teach.

It is quite clear that he is not supposed to be an Aristotle. He does not represent all the sciences, and no one expects him to lecture on mathematics, mechanics, physics, chemistry, zoölogy, botany, economics, politics, and various other disciplines. There was a time when he might have been expected to teach all that men could know, but that time is long past.

Nevertheless, there is quite a group of sciences which are regarded as belonging especially to his province; and although a man may devote a large part of his attention to some one portion of the field, he would certainly be thought remiss if he wholly neglected the rest. This group of sciences includes logic, psychology, ethics and aesthetics, metaphysics, and the history of philosophy. I have not included epistemology or the "theory of knowledge" as a separate discipline, for reasons which will appear later (Chapter XIX); and I have included the history of philosophy, because, whether we care to call this a special science or not, it constitutes a very important part of the work of the teacher of philosophy in our day.

Of this group of subjects the student who goes to the university to study philosophy is supposed to know something before he leaves its walls, whatever else he may or may not know.

It should be remarked, again, that there is commonly supposed to be a peculiarly close relation between philosophy and religion. Certainly, if any one about a university undertakes to give a course of lectures on theism, it is much more apt to be the professor of philosophy than the professor of mathematics or of chemistry. The man who has written an "Introduction to Philosophy," a "Psychology," a "Logic," and an "Outlines of Metaphysics" is very apt to regard it as his duty to add to the list a "Philosophy of Religion." The students in the theological seminaries of Europe and America are usually encouraged, if not compelled, to attend courses in philosophy.

Finally, it appears to be definitely accepted that even the disciplines that we never think of classing among the philosophical sciences are not wholly cut off from a connection with philosophy. When we are occupied, not with adding to the stock of knowledge embraced within the sphere of any special science, but with an examination of the methods of the science, with, so to speak, a criticism of the foundations upon which the science rests, our work is generally recognized as philosophical. It strikes no one as odd in our day that there should be established a "Journal of Philosophy, Psychology, and Scientific Methods," but we should think it strange if some one announced the intention to publish a "Journal of Philosophy and Comparative Anatomy." It is not without its significance that, when Mach, who had been professor of physics at Prague, was called (in 1895) to the University of Vienna to lecture on the history and theory of the inductive sciences, he was made, not professor of physics, but professor of philosophy.

The case, then, stands thus: a certain group of disciplines is regarded as falling peculiarly within the province of the professor of philosophy, and the sciences which constitute it are frequently called the philosophical sciences; moreover, it is regarded as quite proper that the teacher of philosophy should concern himself with the problems of religion, and should pry into the methods and fundamental assumptions of special sciences in all of which it is impossible that he should be an adept. The question naturally arises: Why has his task come to be circumscribed as it is? Why should he teach just these things and no others?

To this question certain persons are at once ready to give an answer. There was a time, they argue, when it seemed possible for one man to embrace the whole field of human knowledge. But human knowledge grew; the special sciences were born; each concerned itself with a definite class of facts and developed its own methods. It became possible and necessary for a man to be, not a scientist at large, but a chemist, a physicist, a biologist, an economist. But in certain portions of the great field men have met with peculiar difficulties; here it cannot be said that we have sciences, but rather that we have attempts at science. The philosopher is the man to whom is committed what is left when we have taken away what has been definitely established or is undergoing investigation according to approved scientific methods. He is Lord of the Uncleared Ground, and may wander through it in his compassless, irresponsible way, never feeling that he is lost, for he has never had any definite bearings to lose.

Those who argue in this way support their case by pointing to the lack of a general consensus of opinion which obtains in many parts of the field which the philosopher regards as his own; and also by pointing out that, even within this field, there is a growing tendency on the part of certain sciences to separate themselves from philosophy and become independent. Thus the psychologist and the logician are sometimes very anxious to have it understood that they belong among the scientists and not among the philosophers.

Now, this answer to the question that we have raised undoubtedly contains some truth. As we have seen from the sketch contained in the preceding pages, the word philosophy was once a synonym for the whole sum of the sciences or what stood for such; gradually the several sciences have become independent and the field of the philosopher has been circumscribed. We must admit, moreover, that there is to be found in a number of the special sciences a body of accepted facts which is without its analogue in philosophy. In much of his work the philosopher certainly seems to be walking upon more uncertain ground than his neighbors; and if he is unaware of that fact, it must be either because he has not a very nice sense of what constitutes scientific evidence, or because he is carried away by his enthusiasm for some particular form of doctrine.

Nevertheless, it is just to maintain that the answer we are discussing is not a satisfactory one. For one thing, we find in it no indication of the reason why the particular group of disciplines with which the philosopher occupies himself has been left to him, when so many sciences have announced their independence. Why have not these, also, separated off and set up for themselves? Is it more difficult to work in these fields than in others? and, if so, what reason can be assigned for the fact?

Take psychology as an instance. How does it happen that the physicist calmly develops his doctrine without finding it necessary to make his bow to philosophy at all, while the psychologist is at pains to explain that his book is to treat psychology as "a natural science," and will avoid metaphysics as much as possible? For centuries men have been interested in the phenomena of the human mind. Can anything be more open to observation than what passes in a man's own consciousness? Why, then, should the science of psychology lag behind? and why these endless disputes as to whether it can really be treated as a "natural science" at all?

Again. May we assume that, because certain disciplines have taken a position of relative independence, therefore all the rest of the field will surely come to be divided up in the same way, and that there will be many special sciences, but no such thing as philosophy? It is hasty to assume this on no better evidence than that which has so far been presented. Before making up one's mind upon this point, one should take a careful look at the problems with which the philosopher occupies himself.

A complete answer to the questions raised above can only be given in the course of the book, where the main problems of philosophy are discussed, and the several philosophical sciences are taken up and examined. But I may say, in anticipation, as much as this:—

(1) Philosophy is reflective knowledge. What is meant by reflective knowledge will be explained at length in the next chapter.

(2) The sciences which are grouped together as philosophical are those in which we are forced back upon the problems of reflective thought, and cannot simply put them aside.

(3) The peculiar difficulties of reflective thought may account for the fact that these sciences are, more than others, a field in which we may expect to find disputes and differences of opinion.

(4) We need not be afraid that the whole field of human knowledge will come to be so divided up into special sciences that philosophy will disappear. The problems with which the philosopher occupies himself are real problems, which present themselves unavoidably to the thoughtful mind, and it is not convenient to divide these up among the several sciences. This will become clearer as we proceed.

7

CHAPTER II

COMMON THOUGHT, SCIENCE, AND REFLECTIVE THOUGHT

7. COMMON THOUGHT.—Those who have given little attention to the study of the human mind are apt to suppose that, when the infant opens its eyes upon the new world of objects surrounding its small body, it sees things much as they do themselves. They are ready to admit that it does not know much *about* things, but it strikes them as absurd for any one to go so far as to say that it does not see things—the things out there in space before its eyes.

Nevertheless, the psychologist tells us that it requires quite a course of education to enable us to see things—not to have vague and unmeaning sensations, but to see things, things that are known to be touchable as well as seeable, things that are recognized as having size and shape and position in space. And he aims a still severer blow at our respect for the infant when he goes on to inform us that the little creature is as ignorant of itself as it is of things; that in its small world of as yet unorganized experiences there is no self that is distinguished from other things; that it may cry vociferously without knowing who is uncomfortable, and may stop its noise without knowing who has been taken up into the nurse's arms and has experienced an agreeable change.

This chaotic little world of the dawning life is not our world, the world of common thought, the world in which we all live and move in maturer years; nor can we go back to it on the wings of memory. We seem to ourselves to have always lived in a world of things,—things in time and space, material things. Among these things there is one of peculiar interest, and which we have not placed upon a par with the rest, our own body, which sees, tastes, touches, other things. We cannot remember a time when we did not know that with this body are somehow bound up many experiences which interest us acutely; for example, experiences of pleasure and pain. Moreover, we seem always to have known that certain of the bodies which surround our own rather resemble our own, and are in important particulars to be distinguished from the general mass of bodies.

Thus, we seem always to have been living in a world of *things* and to have recognized in that world the existence of ourselves and of other people. When we now think of "ourselves" and of "other people," we think of each of the objects referred to as possessing a *mind*. May we say that, as far back as we can remember, we have thought of ourselves and of other persons as possessing minds?

Hardly. The young child does not seem to distinguish between mind and body, and, in the vague and fragmentary pictures which come back to us from our early life, certainly this distinction does not stand out. The child may be the completest of egoists, it may be absorbed in itself and all that directly concerns this particular self, and yet it may make no conscious distinction between a bodily self and a mental, between mind and body. It does not explicitly recognize its world as a world that contains minds as well as bodies.

But, however it may be with the child in the earlier stages of its development, we must all admit that the mature man does consciously recognize that the world in which he finds himself is a world that contains minds as well as bodies. It never occurs to him to doubt that there are bodies, and it never occurs to him to doubt that there are minds.

Does he not perceive that he has a body and a mind? Has he not abundant evidence that his mind is intimately related to his body? When he shuts his eyes, he no longer sees, and when he stops his ears, he no longer hears; when his body is bruised, he feels pain; when he wills to raise his hand, his body carries out the mental decree. Other men act very much as he does; they walk and they talk, they laugh and they cry, they work and they play, just as he does. In short, they act precisely as though they had minds like his own. What more natural than to assume that, as he himself gives expression, by the actions of his body, to the thoughts and emotions in his mind, so his neighbor does the same?

We must not allow ourselves to underrate the plain man's knowledge either of bodies or of minds. It seems, when one reflects upon it, a sufficiently wonderful thing that a few fragmentary sensations should automatically receive an interpretation which conjures up before the mind a world of real things; that, for example, the little patch of color sensation which I experience when I turn my eyes toward the window should seem to introduce me at once to a world of material objects lying in space, clearly defined in magnitude, distance, and direction; that an experience no more complex should be the key which should unlock for me the secret storehouse of another mind, and lay before me a wealth of thoughts and emotions not my own. From the poor, bare, meaningless world of the dawning intelligence to the world of common thought, a world in which real things with their manifold properties, things material and things mental, bear their part, is indeed a long step.

And we should never forget that he who would go farther, he who would strive to gain a better knowledge of matter and of mind by the aid of science and of philosophical reflection,

8

must begin his labors on this foundation which is common to us all. How else can he begin than by accepting and more critically examining the world as it seems revealed in the experience of the race?

8. SCIENTIFIC KNOWLEDGE.—Still, the knowledge of the world which we have been discussing is rather indefinite, inaccurate, and unsystematic. It is a sufficient guide for common life, but its deficiencies may be made apparent. He who wishes to know matter and mind better cannot afford to neglect the sciences.

Now, it is important to observe that although, when the plain man grows scientific, great changes take place in his knowledge of things, yet his way of looking at the mind and the world remains in general much what it was before. To prevent this statement from being misunderstood, I must explain it at some length.

Let us suppose that the man in question takes up the study of botany. Need he do anything very different from what is done more imperfectly by every intelligent man who interests himself in plants? There in the real material world before him are the same plants that he observed somewhat carelessly before. He must collect his information more systematically and must arrange it more critically, but his task is not so much to do something different as it is to do the same thing much better.

The same is evidently true of various other sciences, such as geology, zoölogy, physiology, sociology. Some men have much accurate information regarding rocks, animals, the functions of the bodily organs, the development of a given form of society, and other things of the sort, and other men have but little; and yet it is usually not difficult for the man who knows much to make the man who knows little understand, at least, what he is talking about. He is busying himself with *things*—the same things that interest the plain man, and of which the plain man knows something. He has collected information touching their properties, their changes, their relationships; but to him, as to his less scientific neighbor, they are the same things they always were,—things that he has known from the days of childhood.

Perhaps it will be admitted that this is true of such sciences as those above indicated, but doubted whether it is true of all the sciences, even of all the sciences which are directly concerned with *things* of *some* sort. For example, to the plain man the world of material things consists of things that can be seen and touched. Many of these seem to fill space continuously. They may be divided, but the parts into which they may be divided are conceived as fragments of the things, and as of the same general nature as the wholes of which they are parts. Yet the chemist and the physicist tell us that these same extended things are not really continuous, as they seem to us to be, but consist of swarms of imperceptible atoms, in rapid motion, at considerable distances from one another in space, and grouped in various ways.

What has now become of the world of realities to which the plain man pinned his faith? It has come to be looked upon as a world of appearances, of phenomena, of manifestations, under which the real things, themselves imperceptible, make their presence evident to our senses. Is this new, real world the world of things in which the plain man finds himself, and in which he has felt so much at home?

A closer scrutiny reveals that the world of atoms and molecules into which the man of science resolves the system of material things is not, after all, so very different in kind from the world to which the plain man is accustomed. He can understand without difficulty the language in which it is described to him, and he can readily see how a man may be led to assume its existence.

The atom is not, it is true, directly perceivable by sense, but it is conceived as though it and its motions were thus perceivable. The plain man has long known that things consist of parts which remain, under some circumstances, invisible. When he approaches an object from a distance, he sees parts which he could not see before; and what appears to the naked eye a mere speck without perceptible parts is found under the microscope to be an insect with its full complement of members. Moreover, he has often observed that objects which appear continuous when seen from a distance are evidently far from continuous when seen close at hand. As we walk toward a tree we can see the indefinite mass of color break up into discontinuous patches; a fabric, which presents the appearance of an unbroken surface when viewed in certain ways may be seen to be riddled with holes when held between the eye and the light. There is no man who has not some acquaintance with the distinction between appearance and reality, and who does not make use of the distinction in common life.

Nor can it seem a surprising fact that different combinations of atoms should exhibit different properties. Have we not always known that things in combination are apt to have different properties from the same things taken separately? He who does not know so much as this is not fit even to be a cook.

9

No, the imperceptible world of atoms and molecules is not by any means totally different from the world of things in which the plain man lives. These little objects and groups of objects are discussed very much as we discuss the larger objects and groups of objects to which we are accustomed. We are still concerned with *things* which exist in space and move about in space; and even if these things are small and are not very familiarly known, no intellectual revolution is demanded to enable a man to understand the words of the scientist who is talking about them, and to understand as well the sort of reasonings upon which the doctrine is based.

9. MATHEMATICS.—Let us now turn to take a glance at the mathematical sciences. Of course, these have to do with things sooner or later, for our mathematical reasonings would be absolutely useless to us if they could not be applied to the world of things; but in mathematical reasonings we abstract from things for the time being, confident that we can come back to them when we want to do so, and can make use of the results obtained in our operations.

Now, every civilized man who is not mentally deficient can perform the fundamental operations of arithmetic. He can add and subtract, multiply and divide. In other words, he can use *numbers*. The man who has become an accomplished mathematician can use numbers much better; but if we are capable of following intelligently the intricate series of operations that he carries out on the paper before us, and can see the significance of the system of signs which he uses as an aid, we shall realize that he is only doing in more complicated ways what we have been accustomed to do almost from our childhood.

If we are interested, not so much in performing the operations, as in inquiring into what really takes place in a mind when several units are grasped together and made into a new unit,— for example, when twelve units are thought as one dozen,—the mathematician has a right to say: I leave all that to the psychologist or to the metaphysician; every one knows in a general way what is meant by a unit, and knows that units can be added and subtracted, grouped and separated; I only undertake to show how one may avoid error in doing these things.

It is with geometry as it is with arithmetic. No man is wholly ignorant of points, lines, surfaces, and solids. We are all aware that a short line is not a point, a narrow surface is not a line, and a thin solid is not a mere surface. A door so thin as to have only one side would be repudiated by every man of sense as a monstrosity. When the geometrician defines for us the point, the line, the surface, and the solid, and when he sets before us an array of axioms, or self-evident truths, we follow him with confidence because he seems to be telling us things that we can directly see to be reasonable; indeed, to be telling us things that we have always known.

The truth is that the geometrician does not introduce us to a new world at all. He merely gives us a fuller and a more exact account than was before within our reach of the space relations which obtain in the world of external objects, a world we already know pretty well.

Suppose that we say to him: You have spent many years in dividing up space and in scrutinizing the relations that are to be discovered in that realm; now tell us, what is space? Is it real? Is it a thing, or a quality of a thing, or merely a relation between things? And how can any man think space, when the ideas through which he must think it are supposed to be themselves non-extended? The space itself is not supposed to be in the mind; how can a collection of non-extended ideas give any inkling of what is meant by extension?

Would any teacher of mathematics dream of discussing these questions with his class before proceeding to the proof of his propositions? It is generally admitted that, if such questions are to be answered at all, it is not with the aid of geometrical reasonings that they will be answered.

10. THE SCIENCE OF PSYCHOLOGY.—Now let us come back to a science which has to do directly with things. We have seen that the plain man has some knowledge of minds as well as of material things. Every one admits that the psychologist knows minds better. May we say that his knowledge of minds differs from that of the plain man about as the knowledge of plants possessed by the botanist differs from that of all intelligent persons who have cared to notice them? Or is it a knowledge of a quite different kind?

Those who are familiar with the development of the sciences within recent years have had occasion to remark the fact that psychology has been coming more and more to take its place as an independent science. Formerly it was regarded as part of the duty of the philosopher to treat of the mind and its knowledge; but the psychologist who pretends to be no more than a psychologist is a product of recent times. This tendency toward specialization is a natural thing, and is quite in line with what has taken place in other fields of investigation.

When any science becomes an independent discipline, it is recognized that it is a more or less limited field in which work of a certain kind is done in a certain way. Other fields and other kinds of work are to some extent ignored. But it is quite to be expected that there should be some dispute, especially at first, as to what does or does not properly fall within the limits of a given science. Where these limits shall be placed is, after all, a matter of convenience; and sometimes it is not well to be too strict in marking off one field from another. It is well to watch the actual development of a science, and to note the direction instinctively taken by investigators in that particular field.

If we compare the psychology of a generation or so ago with that of the present day, we cannot but be struck with the fact that there is an increasing tendency to treat psychology as a *natural science*. By this is not meant, of course, that there is no difference between psychology and the sciences that concern themselves with the world of material things—psychology has to do primarily with minds and not with bodies. But it is meant that, as the other sciences improve upon the knowledge of the plain man without wholly recasting it, as they accept the world in which he finds himself and merely attempt to give us a better account of it, so the psychologist may accept the world of matter and of minds recognized by common thought, and may devote himself to the study of minds, without attempting to solve a class of problems discussed by the metaphysician. For example, he may refuse to discuss the question whether the mind can really know that there is an external world with which it stands in relation, and from which it receives messages along the avenues of the senses. He may claim that it is no more his business to treat of this than it is the business of the mathematician to treat of the ultimate nature of space.

Thus the psychologist assumes without question the existence of an external real world, a world of matter and motion. He finds in this world certain organized bodies that present phenomena which he regards as indicative of the presence of minds. He accepts it as a fact that each mind knows its own states directly, and knows everything else by inference from those states, receiving messages from the outer world along one set of nerves and reacting along another set. He conceives of minds as wholly dependent upon messages thus conveyed to them from without. He tells us how a mind, by the aid of such messages, gradually builds up for itself the notion of the external world and of the other minds which are connected with bodies to be found in that world.

We may fairly say that all this is merely a development of and an improvement upon the plain man's knowledge of minds and of bodies. There is no normal man who does not know that his mind is more intimately related to his body than it is to other bodies. We all distinguish between our ideas of things and the external things they represent, and we believe that our knowledge of things comes to us through the avenues of the senses. Must we not open our eyes to see, and unstop our ears to hear? We all know that we do not perceive other minds directly, but must infer their contents from what takes place in the bodies to which they are referred—from words and actions. Moreover, we know that a knowledge of the outer world and of other minds is built up gradually, and we never think of an infant as knowing what a man knows, much as we are inclined to overrate the minds of infants.

The fact that the plain man and the psychologist do not greatly differ in their point of view must impress every one who is charged with the task of introducing students to the study of psychology and philosophy. It is rather an easy thing to make them follow the reasonings of the psychologist, so long as he avoids metaphysical reflections. The assumptions which he makes seem to them not unreasonable; and, as for his methods of investigation, there is not one of them which they have not already employed themselves in a more or less blundering way. They have had recourse to *introspection, i.e.* they have noticed the phenomena of their own minds; they have made use of the *objective method*, i.e. they have observed the signs of mind exhibited by other persons and by the brutes; they have sometimes *experimented*—this is done by the schoolgirl who tries to find out how best to tease her roommate, and by the boy who covers and uncovers his ears in church to make the preacher sing a tune.

It may not be easy to make men good psychologists, but it is certainly not difficult to make them understand what the psychologist is doing and to make them realize the value of his work. He, like the workers in the other natural sciences, takes for granted the world of the plain man, the world of material things in space and time and of minds related to those material things. But when it is a question of introducing the student to the reflections of the philosophers the case is very different. We seem to be enticing him into a new and a strange world, and he is apt to be filled with suspicion and distrust. The most familiar things take on an unfamiliar aspect, and questions are raised which it strikes the unreflective man as highly absurd even to propose. Of this world of reflective thought I shall say just a word in what follows.

11. REFLECTIVE THOUGHT.—If we ask our neighbor to meet us somewhere at a given hour, he has no difficulty in understanding what we have requested him to do. If he wishes to do so, he can be on the spot at the proper moment. He may never have asked himself in his whole life what he means by space and by time. He may be quite ignorant that thoughtful men have disputed concerning the nature of these for centuries past.

And a man may go through the world avoiding disaster year after year by distinguishing with some success between what is real and what is not real, and yet he may be quite unable to tell us what, in general, it means for a thing to be real. Some things are real and some are not; as a rule he seems to be able to discover the difference; of his method of procedure he has never tried to give an account to himself.

That he has a mind he cannot doubt, and he has some idea of the difference between it and certain other minds; but even the most ardent champion of the plain man must admit that he has the most hazy of notions touching the nature of his mind. He seems to be more doubtful concerning the nature of the mind and its knowledge than he is concerning the nature of external things. Certainly he appears to be more willing to admit his ignorance in this realm.

And yet the man can hold his own in the world of real things. He can distinguish between this thing and that, this place and that, this time and that. He can think out a plan and carry it into execution; he can guess at the contents of other minds and allow this knowledge to find its place in his plan.

All of which proves that our knowledge is not necessarily useless because it is rather dim and vague. It is one thing to use a mental state; it is another to have a clear comprehension of just what it is and of what elements it may be made up. The plain man does much of his thinking as we all tie our shoes and button our buttons. It would be difficult for us to describe these operations, but we may perform them very easily nevertheless. When we say that we *know* how to tie our shoes, we only mean that we can tie them.

Now, enough has been said in the preceding sections to make clear that the vagueness which characterizes many notions which constantly recur in common thought is not wholly dispelled by the study of the several sciences. The man of science, like the plain man, may be able to use very well for certain purposes concepts which he is not able to analyze satisfactorily. For example, he speaks of space and time, cause and effect, substance and qualities, matter and mind, reality and unreality. He certainly is in a position to add to our knowledge of the things covered by these terms. But we should never overlook the fact that the new knowledge which he gives us is a knowledge of the same kind as that which we had before. He measures for us spaces and times; he does not tell us what space and time are. He points out the causes of a multitude of occurrences; he does not tell us what we mean whenever we use the word "cause." He informs us what we should accept as real and what we should repudiate as unreal; he does not try to show us what it is to be real and what it is to be unreal.

In other words, the man of science *extends* our knowledge and makes it more accurate; he does not *analyze* certain fundamental conceptions, which we all use, but of which we can usually give a very poor account.

On the other hand, it is the task of *reflective thought*, not in the first instance, to extend the limits of our knowledge of the world of matter and of minds, but rather *to make us more clearly conscious of what that knowledge really is*. Philosophical reflection takes up and tries to analyze complex thoughts that men use daily without caring to analyze them, indeed, without even realizing that they may be subjected to analysis.

It is to be expected that it should impress many of those who are introduced to it for the first time as rather a fantastic creation of problems that do not present themselves naturally to the healthy mind. There is no thoughtful man who does not reflect sometimes and about some things; but there are few who feel impelled to go over the whole edifice of their knowledge and examine it with a critical eye from its turrets to its foundations. In a sense, we may say that philosophical thought is not natural, for he who is examining the assumptions upon which all our ordinary thought about the world rests is no longer in the world of the plain man. He is treating things as men do not commonly treat them, and it is perhaps natural that it should appear to some that, in the solvent which he uses, the real world in which we all rejoice should seem to dissolve and disappear.

I have said that it is not the task of reflective thought, *in the first instance*, to extend the limits of our knowledge of the world of matter and of minds. This is true. But this does not mean that, as a result of a careful reflective analysis, some errors which may creep into the thought both of the plain man and of the scientist may not be exploded; nor does it mean that some new extensions of our knowledge may not be suggested.

In the chapters to follow I shall take up and examine some of the problems of reflective thought. And I shall consider first those problems that present themselves to those who try to subject to a careful scrutiny our knowledge of the external world. It is well to begin with this, for, even in our common experience, it seems to be revealed that the knowledge of material things is a something less vague and indefinite than the knowledge of minds.

II. PROBLEMS TOUCHING THE EXTERNAL WORLD
CHAPTER III

IS THERE AN EXTERNAL WORLD?

12. HOW THE PLAIN MAN THINKS HE KNOWS THE WORLD.—As schoolboys we enjoyed Cicero's joke at the expense of the "minute philosophers." They denied the immortality of the soul; he affirmed it; and he congratulated himself upon the fact that, if they were right, they would not survive to discover it and to triumph over him.

At the close of the seventeenth century the philosopher John Locke was guilty of a joke of somewhat the same kind. "I think," said he, "nobody can, in earnest, be so skeptical as to be uncertain of the existence of those things which he sees and feels. At least, he that can doubt so far (whatever he may have with his own thoughts) will never have any controversy with me; since he can never be sure I say anything contrary to his own opinion."

Now, in this chapter and in certain chapters to follow, I am going to take up and turn over, so that we may get a good look at them, some of the problems that have presented themselves to those who have reflected upon the world and the mind as they seem given in our experience. I shall begin by asking whether it is not possible to doubt that there is an external world at all.

The question cannot best be answered by a jest. It may, of course, be absurd to maintain that there is no external world; but surely he, too, is in an absurd position who maintains dogmatically that there is one, and is yet quite unable to find any flaw in the reasonings of the man who seems to be able to show that this belief has no solid foundation. And we must not forget that the men who have thought it worth while to raise just such questions as this, during the last twenty centuries, have been among the most brilliant intellects of the race. We must not assume too hastily that they have occupied themselves with mere trivialities.

Since, therefore, so many thoughtful men have found it worth while to ask themselves seriously whether there is an external world, or, at least, how we can know that there is an external world, it is not unreasonable to expect that, by looking for it, we may find in our common experience or in science some difficulty sufficient to suggest the doubt which at first strikes the average man as preposterous. In what can such a doubt take its rise? Let us see.

I think it is scarcely too much to say that the plain man believes that he *does not* directly perceive an external world, and that he, at the same time, believes that he *does* directly perceive one. It is quite possible to believe contradictory things, when one's thought of them is somewhat vague, and when one does not consciously bring them together.

As to the first-mentioned belief. Does not the plain man distinguish between his ideas of things and the things themselves? Does he not believe that his ideas come to him through the avenues of the senses? Is he not aware of the fact that, when a sense is disordered, the thing as he perceives it is not like the thing "as it is"? A blind man does not see things when they are there; a color-blind man sees them as others do not see them; a man suffering under certain abnormal conditions of the nervous system sees things when they are not there at all, *i.e.* he has hallucinations. The thing itself, as it seems, is not in the man's mind; it is the idea that is in the man's mind, and that represents the thing. Sometimes it appears to give a true account of it; sometimes it seems to give a garbled account; sometimes it is a false representative throughout— there is no reality behind it. It is, then, the *idea* that is immediately known, and not the *thing*; the thing is merely*inferred* to exist.

I do not mean to say that the plain man is conscious of drawing this conclusion. I only maintain that it seems a natural conclusion to draw from the facts which he recognizes, and that sometimes he seems to draw the conclusion half-consciously.

On the other hand, we must all admit that when the plain man is not thinking about the distinction between ideas and things, but is looking at some material object before him, is touching it with his fingers and turning it about to get a good look at it, it never occurs to him that he is not directly conscious of the thing itself.

He seems to himself to perceive the thing immediately; to perceive it *as* it is and *where* it is; to perceive it as a really extended thing, out there in space before his body. He does not think of himself as occupied with mere images, representations of the object. He may be willing to admit that his mind is in his head, but he cannot think that what he sees is in his head. Is not the object *there*? does he not *see* and *feel* it? Why doubt such evidence as this? He who tells him that the external world does not exist seems to be denying what is immediately given in his experience.

The man who looks at things in this way assumes, of course, that the external object is known directly, and is not a something merely inferred to exist from the presence of a representative image. May one embrace this belief and abandon the other one? If we elect to do this, we appear to be in difficulties at once. All the considerations which made us distinguish so carefully between our ideas of things and the things themselves crowd in upon us. Can it be that we know things independently of the avenues of the senses? Would a man with different senses know things just as we do? How can any man suffer from an hallucination, if things are not inferred from images, but are known independently?

The difficulties encountered appear sufficiently serious even if we keep to that knowledge of things which seems to be given in common experience. But even the plain man has heard of atoms and molecules; and if he accepts the extension of knowledge offered him by the man of science, he must admit that, whatever this apparently immediately perceived external thing may be, it cannot be the external thing that science assures him is out there in space beyond his body, and which must be a very different sort of thing from the thing he seems to perceive. The thing he perceives must, then, be *appearance*; and where can that appearance be if not in his own mind?

The man who has made no study of philosophy at all does not usually think these things out; but surely there are interrogation marks written all over his experience, and he misses them only because he does not see clearly. By judiciously asking questions one may often lead him either to affirm or to deny that he has an immediate knowledge of the external world, pretty much as one pleases. If he affirms it, his position does not seem to be a wholly satisfactory one, as we have seen; and if he denies it, he makes the existence of the external world wholly a matter of inference from the presence of ideas in the mind, and he must stand ready to justify this inference.

To many men it has seemed that the inference is not an easy one to justify. One may say: We could have no ideas of things, no sensations, if real things did not exist and make an impression upon our senses. But to this it may be answered: How is that statement to be proved? Is it to be proved by observing that, when things are present and affect the senses, there come into being ideas which represent the things? Evidently such a proof as this is out of the question, for, if it is true that we know external things only by inference and never immediately, then we can never prove by observation that ideas and things are thus connected. And if it is not to be proved by observation, how shall it be proved? Shall we just assume it dogmatically and pass on to something else? Surely there is enough in the experience of the plain man to justify him in raising the question whether he can certainly know that there is an external world.

13. THE PSYCHOLOGIST AND THE EXTERNAL WORLD.—We have seen just above that the doubt regarding the existence of the world seems to have its root in the familiar distinction between ideas and things, appearances and the realities which they are supposed to represent. The psychologist has much to say about ideas; and if sharpening and making clear this distinction has anything to do with stirring up doubts, it is natural to suppose that they should become more insistent when one has exchanged the ignorance of everyday life for the knowledge of the psychologist.

Now, when the psychologist asks how a given mind comes to have a knowledge of any external thing, he finds his answer in the messages which have been brought to the mind by means of the bodily senses. He describes the sense-organs and the nervous connections between these and the brain, and tells us that when certain nervous impulses have traveled, let us say, from the eye or the ear to the brain, one has sensations of sight or sound.

He describes for us in detail how, out of such sensations and the memories of such sensations, we frame mental images of external things. Between the mental image and the thing that it represents he distinguishes sharply, and he informs us that the mind knows no more about the external thing than is contained in such images. That a thing is present can be known only by the fact that a message from the thing is sent along the nerves, and what the thing is must be determined from the character of the message. Given the image in the absence of the thing,— that is to say, an hallucination,—the mind will naturally suppose that the thing is present. This false supposition cannot be corrected by a direct inspection of the thing, for such a direct inspection of things is out of the question. The only way in which the mind concerned can discover that the thing is absent is by referring to its other experiences. This image is compared with other images and is discovered to be in some way abnormal. We decide that it is a false representative and has no corresponding reality behind it.

This doctrine taken as it stands seems to cut the mind off from the external world very completely; and the most curious thing about it is that it seems to be built up on the assumption that it is not really true. How can one know certainly that there is a world of material things, including human bodies with their sense-organs and nerves, if no mind has ever been able to inspect directly anything of the sort? How can we tell that a sensation arises when a nervous impulse has been carried along a sensory nerve and has reached the brain, if every mind is shut up to the charmed circle of its own ideas? The anatomist and the physiologist give us very detailed accounts of the sense-organs and of the brain; the physiologist even undertakes to measure the speed with which the impulse passes along a nerve; the psychologist accepts and uses the results of their labors. But can all this be done in the absence of any first-hand knowledge of the things of which one is talking? Remember that, if the psychologist is right, any

14

external object, eye, ear, nerve, or brain, which we can perceive directly, is a mental complex, a something in the mind and not external at all. How shall we prove that there are objects, ears, eyes, nerves, and brains,—in short, all the requisite mechanism for the calling into existence of sensations,—in an outer world which is not immediately perceived but is only inferred to exist?

I do not wish to be regarded as impugning the right of the psychologist to make the assumptions which he does, and to work as he does. He has a right to assume, with the plain man, that there is an external world and that we know it. But a very little reflection must make it manifest that he seems, at least, to be guilty of an inconsistency, and that he who wishes to think clearly should strive to see just where the trouble lies.

So much, at least, is evident: the man who is inclined to doubt whether there is, after all, any real external world, appears to find in the psychologist's distinction between ideas and things something like an excuse for his doubt. To get to the bottom of the matter and to dissipate his doubt one has to go rather deeply into metaphysics. I merely wish to show just here that the doubt is not a gratuitous one, but is really suggested to the thoughtful mind by a reflection upon our experience of things. And, as we are all apt to think that the man of science is less given to busying himself with useless subtleties than is the philosopher, I shall, before closing this chapter, present some paragraphs upon the subject from the pen of a professor of mathematics and mechanics.

14. THE "TELEPHONE EXCHANGE."—"We are accustomed to talk," writes Professor Karl Pearson,[1] "of the 'external world,' of the 'reality' outside us. We speak of individual objects having an existence independent of our own. The store of past sense-impressions, our thoughts and memories, although most probably they have beside their psychical element a close correspondence with some physical change or impress in the brain, are yet spoken of as *inside* ourselves. On the other hand, although if a sensory nerve be divided anywhere short of the brain, we lose the corresponding class of sense impression, we yet speak of many sense-impressions, such as form and texture, as existing outside ourselves. How close then can we actually get to this supposed world outside ourselves? Just as near but no nearer than the brain terminals of the sensory nerves. We are like the clerk in the central telephone exchange who cannot get nearer to his customers than his end of the telephone wires. We are indeed worse off than the clerk, for to carry out the analogy properly we must suppose him *never to have been outside the telephone exchange, never to have seen a customer or any one like a customer—in short, never, except through the telephone wire, to have come in contact with the outside universe.* Of that 'real' universe outside himself he would be able to form no direct impression; the real universe for him would be the aggregate of his constructs from the messages which were caused by the telephone wires in his office. About those messages and the ideas raised in his mind by them he might reason and draw his inferences; and his conclusions would be correct—for what? For the world of telephonic messages, for the type of messages that go through the telephone. Something definite and valuable he might know with regard to the spheres of action and of thought of his telephonic subscribers, but outside those spheres he could have no experience. Pent up in his office he could never have seen or touched even a telephonic subscriber *in himself.* Very much in the position of such a telephone clerk is the conscious *ego* of each one of us seated at the brain terminals of the sensory nerves. Not a step nearer than those terminals can the *ego* get to the 'outer world,' and what in and for themselves are the subscribers to its nerve exchange it has no means of ascertaining. Messages in the form of sense-impressions come flowing in from that 'outside world,' and these we analyze, classify, store up, and reason about. But of the nature of 'things-in-themselves,' of what may exist at the other end of our system of telephone wires, we know nothing at all.

"But the reader, perhaps, remarks, 'I not only see an object, but I can *touch* it. I can trace the nerve from the tip of my finger to the brain. I am not like the telephone clerk, I can follow my network of wires to their terminals and find what is at the other end of them.' Can you, reader? Think for a moment whether your *ego* has for one moment got away from his brain exchange. The sense-impression that you call touch was just as much as sight felt only at the brain end of a sensory nerve. What has told you also of the nerve from the tip of your finger to your brain? Why, sense-impressions also, messages conveyed along optic or tactile sensory nerves. In truth, all you have been doing is to employ one subscriber to your telephone exchange to tell you about the wire that goes to a second, but you are just as far as ever from tracing out for yourself the telephone wires to the individual subscriber and ascertaining what his nature is in and for himself. The immediate sense-impression is just as far removed from what you term the 'outside world' as the store of impresses. If our telephone clerk had recorded by aid of a phonograph certain of the messages from the outside world on past occasions, then if any telephonic message on its receipt set several phonographs repeating past messages, we have an image analogous to what goes on in the brain. Both telephone and phonograph are equally

15

removed from what the clerk might call the 'real outside world,' but they enable him through their sounds to construct a universe; he projects those sounds, which are really inside his office, outside his office, and speaks of them as the external universe. This outside world is constructed by him from the contents of the inside sounds, which differ as widely from things-in-themselves as language, the symbol, must always differ from the thing it symbolizes. For our telephone clerk sounds would be the real world, and yet we can see how conditioned and limited it would be by the range of his particular telephone subscribers and by the contents of their messages.

"So it is with our brain; the sounds from telephone and phonograph correspond to immediate and stored sense-impressions. These sense-impressions we project as it were outwards and term the real world outside ourselves. But the things-in-themselves which the sense-impressions symbolize, the 'reality,' as the metaphysicians wish to call it, at the other end of the nerve, remains unknown and is unknowable. Reality of the external world lies for science and for us in combinations of form and color and touch—sense-impressions as widely divergent from the thing 'at the other end of the nerve' as the sound of the telephone from the subscriber at the other end of the wire. We are cribbed and confined in this world of sense-impressions like the exchange clerk in his world of sounds, and not a step beyond can we get. As his world is conditioned and limited by his particular network of wires, so ours is conditioned by our nervous system, by our organs of sense. Their peculiarities determine what is the nature of the outside world which we construct. It is the similarity in the organs of sense and in the perceptive faculty of all normal human beings which makes the outside world the same, or *practically* the same, for them all. To return to the old analogy, it is as if two telephone exchanges had very nearly identical groups of subscribers. In this case a wire between the two exchanges would soon convince the imprisoned clerks that they had something in common and peculiar to themselves. That conviction corresponds in our comparison to the recognition of other consciousness."

I suggest that this extract be read over carefully, not once but several times, and that the reader try to make quite clear to himself the position of the clerk in the telephone exchange, *i.e.* the position of the mind in the body, as depicted by Professor Pearson, before recourse is had to the criticisms of any one else. One cannot find anywhere better material for critical philosophical reflection.

As has been seen, our author accepts without question, the psychological doctrine that the mind is shut up within the circle of the messages that are conducted to it along the sensory nerves, and that it cannot directly perceive anything truly external. He carries his doctrine out to the bitter end in the conclusion that, since we have never had experience of anything beyond sense-impressions, and have no ground for an inference to anything beyond, we must recognize that the only external world of which we know anything is an external world built up out of sense-impressions. It is, thus, in the mind, and is not external at all; it is only "projected outwards," *thought of* as though it were beyond us. Shall we leave the inconsistent position of the plain man and of the psychologist and take our refuge in this world of projected mental constructs?

Before the reader makes up his mind to do this, I beg him to consider the following:—

(1) If the only external world of which we have a right to speak at all is a construct in the mind or *ego*, we may certainly affirm that the world is in the *ego*, but does it sound sensible to say that the *ego* is somewhere in the world?

(2) If all external things are really inside the mind, and are only "projected" outwards, of course our own bodies, sense-organs, nerves, and brains, are really inside and are merely projected outwards. Now, do the sense-impressions of which everything is to be constructed "come flowing in" along these nerves that are really inside?

(3) Can we say, when a nerve lies entirely within the mind or *ego*, that this same mind or *ego* is nearer to one end of the nerve than it is to the other? How shall we picture to ourselves "the conscious *ego* of each one of us seated at the brain terminals of the sensory nerves"? How can the *ego* place the whole of itself at the end of a nerve which it has constructed within itself? And why is it more difficult for it to get to one end of a nerve like this than it is to get to the other?

(4) Why should the thing "at the other end of the nerve" remain unknown and unknowable? Since the nerve is entirely in the mind, is purely a mental construct, can anything whatever be at the end of it without being in the mind? And if the thing in question is not in the mind, how are we going to prove that it is any nearer to one end of a nerve which is inside the mind than it is to the other? If it may really be said to be at the end of the nerve, why may we not know it quite as well as we do the end of the nerve, or any other mental construct?

It must be clear to the careful reader of Professor Pearson's paragraphs, that he does not confine himself strictly to the world of mere "projections," to an outer world which is really *inner*. If he did this, the distinction between inner and outer would disappear. Let us consider for a

16

moment the imprisoned clerk. He is in a telephone exchange, about him are wires and subscribers. He gets only sounds and must build up his whole universe of things out of sounds. Now we are supposing him to be in a telephone exchange, to be receiving messages, to be building up a world out of these messages. Do we for a moment think of him as building up, out of the messages which came along the wires, those identical wires which carried the messages and the subscribers which sent them? Never! we distinguish between the exchange, with its wires and subscribers, and the messages received and worked up into a world. In picturing to ourselves the telephone exchange, we are doing what the plain man and the psychologist do when they distinguish between mind and body,—they never suppose that the messages which come through the senses are identical with the senses through which they come.

But suppose we maintain that there is no such thing as a telephone exchange, with its wires and subscribers, which is not to be found within some clerk. Suppose the real external world is something *inner* and only "projected" without, mistakenly supposed by the unthinking to be without. Suppose it is nonsense to speak of a wire which is not in the mind of a clerk. May we under such circumstances describe any clerk as *in a telephone exchange?* as *receiving messages?* as *no nearer* to his subscribers than his end of the wire? May we say that sense-impressions *come flowing in* to him? The whole figure of the telephone exchange becomes an absurdity when we have once placed the exchange within the clerk. Nor can we think of two clerks as connected by a wire, when it is affirmed that every wire must "really" be in some clerk.

The truth is, that, in the extracts which I have given above and in many other passages in the same volume, the real external world, the world which does not exist in the mind but*without* it, is much discredited, and is yet not actually discarded. The ego is placed at the brain terminals of the sensory nerves, and it receives messages which *flow in; i.e.* the clerk is actually placed in an exchange. That the existence of the exchange is afterward denied in so many words does not mean that it has not played and does not continue to play an important part in the thought of the author.

It is interesting to see how a man of science, whose reflections compel him to deny the existence of the external world that we all seem to perceive and that we somehow recognize as distinct from anything in our minds, is *nevertheless compelled to admit the existence of this world at every turn.*

But if we do admit it, what shall we make of it? Shall we deny the truth of what the psychologist has to tell us about a knowledge of things only through the sensations to which they give rise? We cannot, surely, do that. Shall we affirm that we know the external world directly, and at the same time that we do not know it directly, but only indirectly, and through the images which arise in our minds? That seems inconsistent. Certainly there is material for reflection here.

Nevertheless the more we reflect on that material, the more evident does it become that the plain man cannot be wrong in believing in the external world which seems revealed in his experiences. We find that all attempts to discredit it rest upon the implicit assumption of its existence, and fall to the ground when that existence is honestly denied. So our problem changes its form. We no longer ask: Is there an external world? but rather: *What* is the external world, and how does it differ from the world of mere ideas?

[1] "The Grammar of Science," 2d Ed., London, 1900, pp. 60-63.

CHAPTER IV

SENSATIONS AND "THINGS"

15. SENSE AND IMAGINATION.—Every one distinguishes between things perceived and things only imagined. With open eyes I see the desk before me; with eyes closed, I can imagine it. I lay my hand on it and feel it; I can, without laying my hand on it, imagine that I feel it. I raise my eyes, and see the pictures on the wall opposite me; I can sit here and call before my mind the image of the door by which the house is entered.

What is the difference between sense and imagination? It must be a difference of which we are all somehow conscious, for we unhesitatingly distinguish between the things we perceive and the things we merely imagine.

It is well to remember at the outset that the two classes of experiences are not wholly different. The blue color that I imagine seems blue. It does not lose this quality because it is only imaginary. The horse that I imagine seems to have four legs, like a horse perceived. As I call it before my mind, it seems as large as the real horse. Neither the color, nor the size, nor the distribution of parts, nor any other attribute of the sort appears to be different in the imaginary object from what it is in the object as given in sensation.

The two experiences are, nevertheless, not the same; and every one knows that they are not the same. One difference that roughly marks out the two classes of experiences from one another is that, as a rule, our sense-experiences are more vivid than are the images that exist in the imagination.

I say, as a rule, for we cannot always remark this difference. Sensations may be very clear and unmistakable, but they may also be very faint and indefinite. When a man lays his hand firmly on my shoulder, I may be in little doubt whether I feel a sensation or do not; but when he touches my back very lightly, I may easily be in doubt, and may ask myself in perplexity whether I have really been touched or whether I have merely imagined it. As a vessel recedes and becomes a mere speck upon the horizon, I may well wonder, before I feel sure that it is really quite out of sight, whether I still see the dim little point, or whether I merely imagine that I see it.

On the other hand, things merely imagined may sometimes be very vivid and insistent. To some persons, what exists in the imagination is dim and indefinite in the extreme. Others imagine things vividly, and can describe what is present only to the imagination almost as though it were something seen. Finally, we know that an image may become so vivid and insistent as to be mistaken for an external thing. That is to say, there are such things as hallucinations.

The criterion of vividness will not, therefore, always serve to distinguish between what is given in the sense and what is only imagined. And, indeed, it becomes evident, upon reflection, that we do not actually make it our ultimate test. We may be quite willing to admit that faint sensations may come to be confused with what is imagined, with "ideas," but we always regard such a confusion as somebody's error. We are not ready to admit that things perceived faintly are things imagined, or that vivid "ideas" are things perceived by sense.

Let us come back to the illustrations with which we started. How do I know that I perceive the desk before me; and how do I know that, sitting here, I imagine, and do not see, the front door of the house?

My criterion is this: when I have the experience I call "seeing my desk," the bit of experience which presents itself as my desk is in a certain setting. That is to say, the desk seen must be in a certain relation to my body, and this body, as I know it, also consists of experiences. Thus, if I am to know that I see the desk, I must realize that my eyes are open, that the object is in front of me and not behind me, etc.

The desk as seen varies with the relation to the body in certain ways that we regard as natural and explicable. When I am near it, the visual experience is not just what it is when I recede from it. But how can I know that I am near the desk or far from it? What do these expressions mean? Their full meaning will become clearer in the next chapter, but here I may say that nearness and remoteness must be measured for me in experiences of some sort, or I would never know anything as near to or far from my body.

Thus, all our sensory experiences are experiences that fall into a certain system or order. It is a system which we all recognize implicitly, for we all reject as merely imaginary those experiences which lack this setting. If my eyes are shut—I am speaking now of the eyes as experienced, as felt or perceived, as given in sensation—I never say; "I see my desk," no matter how vivid the image of the object. Those who believe in "second sight" sometimes talk of seeing things not in this setting, but the very name they give to the supposed experience indicates that there is something abnormal about it. No one thinks it remarkable that I see the desk before which I perceive myself to be sitting with open eyes. Every one would think it strange if I could see and describe the table in the next room, now shut away from me. When a man thinks he hears his name pronounced, and, turning his head, seeks in vain for the speaker, he sets his experience down as a hallucination. He says, I did not really hear that; I merely imagined it.

May one not, with open eyes, have a hallucination of vision, just as one may seem to hear one's name pronounced when no one is by? Certainly. But in each case the experience may be proved to be a hallucination, nevertheless. It may be recognized that the sensory setting is incomplete, though it may not, at first, seem so. Thus the unreal object which seems to be seen may be found to be a thing that cannot be touched. Or, when one has attained to a relatively complete knowledge of the system of experiences recognized as sensory, one may make use of roundabout methods of ascertaining that the experience in question does not really have the right setting. Thus, the ghost which is seen by the terrified peasant at midnight, but which cannot be photographed, we may unhesitatingly set down as something imagined and not really seen.

All our sensations are, therefore, experiences which take their place in a certain setting. This is our ultimate criterion. We need not take the word of the philosopher for it. We need only reflect, and ask ourselves how we know that, in a given case, we are seeing or hearing or touching something, and are not merely imagining it. In every case, we shall find that we come back to the same test. In common life, we apply the test instinctively, and with little realization of what we are doing.

And if we turn to the psychologist, whose business it is to be more exact and scientific, we find that he gives us only a refinement of this same criterion. It is important to him to distinguish between what is given in sensation and what is furnished by memory or imagination, and he tells us that sensation is the result of a message conducted along a sensory nerve to the brain.

Here we see emphasized the relation to the body which has been mentioned above. If we ask the psychologist how he knows that the body he is talking about is a real body, and not merely an imagined one, he has to fall back upon the test which is common to us all. A real hand is one which we see with the eyes open, and which we touch with the other hand. If our experiences of our own body had not the setting which marks all sensory experiences, we could never say: I *perceive* that my body is near the desk. When we call our body real, as contrasted with things imaginary, we recognize that this group of experiences belongs to the class described; it is given in sensation, and is not merely thought of.

It will be observed that, in distinguishing between sensations and things imaginary, we never go beyond the circle of our experiences. We do not reach out to a something*beyond* or *behind* experiences, and say: When such a reality is present, we may affirm that we have a sensation, and when it is not, we may call the experience imaginary. If there were such a reality as this, it would do us little good, for since it is not supposed to be perceived directly, we should have to depend upon the sensations to prove the presence of the reality, and could not turn to the reality and ask it whether we were or were not experiencing a sensation. The distinction between sensations and what is imaginary is an *observed* distinction. It can be *proved* that some experiences are sensory and that some are not. This means that, in drawing the distinction, we remain within the circle of our experiences.

There has been much unnecessary mystification touching this supposed reality behind experiences. In the next chapter we shall see in what senses the word "reality" may properly be used, and in what sense it may not. There is a danger in using it loosely and vaguely.

16. MAY WE CALL "THINGS" GROUPS OF SENSATIONS?—Now, the external world seems to the plain man to be directly given in his sense experiences. He is willing to admit that the table in the next room, of which he is merely thinking, is known at one remove, so to speak. But this desk here before him: is it not known directly? Not the mental image, the mere representative, but the desk itself, a something that is physical and not mental?

And the psychologist, whatever his theory of the relation between the mind and the world, seems to support him, at least, in so far as to maintain that in sensation the external world is known as directly as it is possible for the external world to be known, and that one can get no more of it than is presented in sensation. If a sense is lacking, an aspect of the world as given is also lacking; if a sense is defective, as in the color-blind, the defect is reflected in the world upon which one gazes.

Such considerations, especially when taken together with what has been said at the close of the last section about the futility of looking for a reality behind our sensations, may easily suggest rather a startling possibility. May it not be, if we really are shut up to the circle of our experiences, that the physical things, which we have been accustomed to look upon as non-mental, are nothing more than complexes of sensations? Granted that there seems to be presented in our experience a material world as well as a mind, may it not be that this material world is a mental thing of a certain kind—a mental thing contrasted with other mental things, such as imaginary things?

This question has always been answered in the affirmative by the idealists, who claim that all existence must be regarded as psychical existence. Their doctrine we shall consider later (sections 49 and 53). It will be noticed that we seem to be back again with Professor Pearson in the last chapter.

To this question I make the following answer: In the first place, I remark that even the plain man distinguishes somehow between his sensations and external things. He thinks that he has reason to believe that things do not cease to exist when he no longer has sensations. Moreover, he believes that things do not always appear to his senses as they really are. If we tell him that his sensations *are* the things, it shocks his common sense. He answers: Do you mean to tell me that complexes of sensation can be on a shelf or in a drawer? can be cut with a knife or broken with the hands? He feels that there must be some real distinction between sensations and the things without him.

Now, the notions of the plain man on such matters as these are not very clear, and what he says about sensations and things is not always edifying. But it is clear that he feels strongly that the man who would identify them is obliterating a distinction to which his experience testifies unequivocally. We must not hastily disregard his protest. He is sometimes right in his feeling that things are not identical, even when he cannot prove it.

In the second place, I remark that, in this instance, the plain man is in the right, and can be shown to be in the right. "Things" are not groups of sensations. The distinction between them will be explained in the next section.

17. THE DISTINCTION BETWEEN SENSATIONS AND "THINGS"—Suppose that I stand in my study and look at the fire in the grate. I am experiencing sensations, and am not

busied merely with an imaginary fire. But may my whole experience of the fire be summed up as an experience of sensations and their changes? Let us see.

If I shut my eyes, the fire disappears. Does any one suppose that the fire has been annihilated? No. We say, I no longer see it, but nothing has happened to the fire.

Again, I may keep my eyes open, and simply turn my head. The fire disappears once more. Does any one suppose that my turning my head has done anything to the fire? We say unhesitatingly, my sensations have changed, but the fire has remained as it was.

Still, again, I may withdraw from the fire. Its heat seems to be diminished. Has the fire really grown less hot? And if I could withdraw to a sufficient distance, I know that the fire would appear to me smaller and less bright. Could I get far enough away to make it seem the faintest speck in the field of vision, would I be tempted to claim that the fire shrunk and grew faint merely because I walked away from it? Surely not.

Now, suppose that I stand on the same spot and look at the fire without turning my head. The stick at which I am gazing catches the flame, blazes up, turns red, and finally falls together, a little mass of gray ashes. Shall I describe this by saying that my sensations have changed, or may I say that the fire itself has changed? The plain man and the philosopher alike use the latter expression in such a case as this.

Let us take another illustration. I walk towards the distant house on the plain before me. What I see as my goal seems to grow larger and brighter. It does not occur to me to maintain that the house changes as I advance. But, at a given instant, changes of a different sort make their appearance. Smoke arises, and flames burst from the roof. Now I have no hesitation in saying that changes are taking place in the house. It would seem foolish to describe the occurrence as a mere change in my sensations. Before it was my sensations that changed; now it is the house itself.

We are drawing this distinction between changes in our sensations and changes in things at every hour in the day. I cannot move without making things appear and disappear. If I wag my head, the furniture seems to dance, and I regard it as a mere seeming. I count on the clock's going when I no longer look upon its face. It would be absurd to hold that the distinction is a mere blunder, and has no foundation in our experience. The rôle it plays is too important for that. If we obliterate it, the real world of material things which seems to be revealed in our experience melts into a chaos of fantastic experiences whose appearances and disappearances seem to be subject to no law.

And it is worthy of remark that it is not merely in common life that the distinction is drawn. Every man of science must give heed to it. The psychologist does, it is true, pay much attention to sensations; but even he distinguishes between the sensations which he is studying and the material things to which he relates them, such as brains and sense-organs. And those who cultivate the physical sciences strive, when they give an account of things and their behavior, to lay before us a history of changes analogous to the burning of the stick and of the house, excluding mere changes in sensations.

There is no physicist or botanist or zoölogist who has not our common experience that things as perceived by us—our experiences of things—appear or disappear or change their character when we open or shut our eyes or move about. But nothing of all this appears in their books. What they are concerned with is things and their changes, and they do not consider such matters as these as falling within their province. If a botanist could not distinguish between the changes which take place in a plant, and the changes which take place in his sensations as he is occupied in studying the plant, but should tell us that the plant grows smaller as one recedes from it, we should set him down as weak-minded.

That the distinction is everywhere drawn, and that we must not obliterate it, is very evident. But we are in the presence of what has seemed to many men a grave difficulty. Are not things presented in our experience only as we have sensations? what is it to perceive a thing? is it not to have sensations? how, then, can we distinguish between sensations and things? We certainly do so all the time, in spite of the protest of the philosopher; but many of us do so with a haunting sense that our behavior can scarcely be justified by the reason.

Our difficulty, however, springs out of an error of our own. Grasping imperfectly the full significance of the word "sensation," we extend its use beyond what is legitimate, and we call by that name experiences which are not sensations at all. Thus the external world comes to seem to us to be not really a something contrasted with the mental, but a part of the mental world. We accord to it the attributes of the latter, and rob it of those distinguishing attributes which belong to it by right. When we have done this, we may feel impelled to say, as did Professor Pearson, that things are not really "outside" of us, as they seem to be, but are merely "projected" outside— thought of as if they were "outside." All this I must explain at length.

Let us come back to the first of the illustrations given above, the case of the fire in my study. As I stand and look at it, what shall I call the red glow which I observe? Shall I call it a *quality of a thing*, or shall I call it a *sensation*?

To this I answer: *I may call it either the one or the other, according to its setting among other experiences.*

We have seen (section 15) that sensations and things merely imaginary are distinguished from one another by their setting. With open eyes we see things; with our eyes closed we can imagine them: we see what is before us; we imagine what lies behind our backs. If we confine our attention to the bit of experience itself, we have no means of determining whether it is sensory or imaginary. Only its setting can decide that point. Here, we have come to another distinction of much the same sort. That red glow, that bit of experience, taken by itself and abstracted from all other experiences, cannot be called either a sensation or the quality of a thing. Only its context can give us the right to call it the one or the other.

This ought to become clear when we reflect upon the illustration of the fire. We have seen that one whole series of changes has been unhesitatingly described as a series of changes in my sensations. Why was this? Because it was observed to depend upon changes in the relations of my body, my senses (a certain group of experiences), to the bit of experience I call the fire. Another series was described as a series of changes in the fire. Why? Because, the relation to my senses remaining unchanged, changes still took place, and had to be accounted for in other ways.

It is a matter of common knowledge that they can be accounted for in other ways. This is not a discovery of the philosopher. He can only invite us to think over the matter and see what the unlearned and the learned are doing at every moment. Sometimes they are noticing that experiences change as they turn their heads or walk toward or away from objects; sometimes they abstract from this, and consider the series of changes that take place independently of this.

That bit of experience, that red glow, is not related only to my body. Such experiences are related also to each other; they stand in a vast independent system of relations, which, as we have seen, the man of science can study without troubling himself to consider sensations at all. This system is the external world—the external world as known or as knowable, the only external world that it means anything for us to talk about. As having its place in this system, a bit of experience is not a sensation, but is a quality or aspect of a thing.

Sensations, then, to be sensations, must be bits of experience considered in their relation to some organ of sense. They should never be confused with qualities of things, which are experiences in a different setting. It is as unpardonable to confound the two as it is to confound sensations with things imaginary.

We may not, therefore, say that "things" are groups of sensations. We may, if we please, describe them as complexes of qualities. And we may not say that the "things" we perceive are really "inside" of us and are merely "projected outside."

What can "inside" and "outside" mean? Only this. We recognize in our experience two distinct orders, the *objective order*, the system of phenomena which constitutes the material world, and the *subjective order*, the order of things mental, to which belong sensations and "ideas." That is "outside" which belongs to the objective order. The word has no other meaning when used in this connection. That is "inside" which belongs to the subjective order, and is contrasted with the former.

If we deny that there is an objective order, an external world, and say that everything is "inside," we lose our distinction, and even the word "inside" becomes meaningless. It indicates no contrast. When men fall into the error of talking in this way, what they do is to *keep* the external world and gain the distinction, and at the same time to *deny* the existence of the world which has furnished it. In other words, they put the clerk into a telephone exchange, and then tell us that the exchange does not really exist. He is inside—of what? He is inside of nothing. Then, can he really be inside?

We see, thus, that the plain man and the man of science are quite right in accepting the external world. The objective order is known as directly as is the subjective order. Both are orders of experiences; they are open to observation, and we have, in general, little difficulty in distinguishing between them, as the illustrations given above amply prove.

18. THE EXISTENCE OF MATERIAL THINGS.—One difficulty seems to remain and to call for a solution. We all believe that material things exist when we no longer perceive them. We believe that they existed before they came within the field of our observation.

In these positions the man of science supports us. The astronomer has no hesitation in saying that the comet, which has sailed away through space, exists, and will return. The geologist describes for us the world as it was in past ages, when no eye was opened upon it.

But has it not been stated above that the material world is an order of *experiences?* and can there be such a thing as an experience that is not *experienced* by somebody? In other words, can the world exist, except as it is *perceived to exist?*

This seeming difficulty has occasioned much trouble to philosophers in the past. Bishop Berkeley (1684-1753) said, "To exist is to be perceived." There are those who agree with him at the present day.

Their difficulty would have disappeared had they examined with sufficient care the meaning of the word "exist." We have no right to pass over the actual uses of such words, and to give them a meaning of our own. If one thing seems as certain as any other, it is that material things exist when we do not perceive them. On what ground may the philosopher combat the universal opinion, the dictum of common sense and of science? When we look into his reasonings, we find that he is influenced by the error discussed at length in the last section—he has confused the phenomena of the two orders of experience.

I have said that, when we concern ourselves with the objective order, we abstract or should abstract, from the relations which things bear to our senses. We account for phenomena by referring to other phenomena which we have reason to accept as their physical conditions or causes. We do not consider that a physical cause is effective only while we perceive it. When we come back to this notion of our perceiving a thing or not perceiving it, we have left the objective order and passed over to the subjective. We have left the consideration of "things" and have turned to sensations.

There is no reason why we should do this. The physical order is an independent order, as we have seen. The man of science, when he is endeavoring to discover whether some thing or quality of a thing really existed at some time in the past, is not in the least concerned to establish the fact that some one saw it. No one ever saw the primitive fire-mist from which, as we are told, the world came into being. But the scientist cares little for that. He is concerned only to prove that the phenomena he is investigating really have a place in the objective order. If he decides that they have, he is satisfied; he has proved something to exist. *To belong to the objective order is to exist as a physical thing or quality.*

When the plain man and the man of science maintain that a physical thing exists, they use the word in precisely the same sense. The meaning they give to it is the proper meaning of the word. It is justified by immemorial usage, and it marks a real distinction. Shall we allow the philosopher to tell us that we must not use it in this sense, but must say that only sensations and ideas exist? Surely not. This would mean that we permit him to obliterate for us the distinction between the external world and what is mental.

But is it right to use the word "experience" to indicate the phenomena which have a place in the objective order? Can an experience be anything but mental?

There can be no doubt that the suggestions of the word are unfortunate—it has what we may call a subjective flavor. It suggests that, after all, the things we perceive are sensations or percepts, and must, to exist at all, exist in a mind. As we have seen, this is an error, and an error which we all avoid in actual practice. We do not take sensations for things, and we recognize clearly enough that it is one thing for a material object to exist and another for it to be perceived.

Why, then, use the word "experience"? Simply because we have no better word. We must use it, and not be misled by the associations which cling to it. The word has this great advantage: it brings out clearly the fact that all our knowledge of the external world rests ultimately upon those phenomena which, when we consider them in relation to our senses, we recognize as sensations. We cannot start out from mere imaginings to discover what the world was like in the ages past.

It is this truth that is recognized by the plain man, when he maintains that, in the last resort, we can know things only in so far as we see, touch, hear, taste, and smell them; and by the psychologist, when he tells us that, in sensation, the external world is revealed as directly as it is possible that it could be revealed. But it is a travesty on this truth to say that we do not know things, but know only our sensations of sight, touch, taste, hearing, and the like.[1]

[1] See the note on this chapter at the close of the volume.

CHAPTER V

APPEARANCES AND REALITIES

19. THINGS AND THEIR APPEARANCES.—We have seen in the last chapter that there is an external world and that it is given in our experience. There is an objective order, and we are all capable of distinguishing between it and the subjective. He who says that we perceive only sensations and ideas flies in the face of the common experience of mankind.

But we are not yet through with the subject. We all make a distinction between things as they *appear* and things as they *really are.*

If we ask the plain man, What is the real external world? the first answer that seems to present itself to his mind is this: Whatever we can see, hear, touch, taste, or smell may be regarded as belonging to the real world. What we merely imagine does not belong to it.

That this answer is not a very satisfactory one occurred to men's minds very early in the history of reflective thought. The ancient skeptic said to himself: The colors of objects vary according to the light, and according to the position and distance of the objects; can we say that any object has a real color of its own? A staff stuck into water looks bent, but feels straight to the touch; why believe the testimony of one sense rather than that of another?

Such questionings led to far-reaching consequences. They resulted in a forlorn distrust of the testimony of the senses, and to a doubt as to our ability to know anything as it really is.

Now, the distinction between appearances and realities exists for us as well as for the ancient skeptic, and without being tempted to make such extravagant statements as that there is no such thing as truth, and that every appearance is as real as any other, we may admit that it is not very easy to see the full significance of the distinction, although we are referring to it constantly.

For example, we look from our window and see, as we say, a tree at a distance. What we are conscious of is a small bluish patch of color. Now, a small bluish patch of color is not, strictly speaking, a tree; but for us it represents the tree. Suppose that we walk toward the tree. Do we continue to see what we saw before? Of course, we say that we continue to see the same tree; but it is plain that what we immediately perceive, what is given in consciousness, does not remain the same as we move. Our blue patch of color grows larger and larger; it ceases to be blue and faint; at the last it has been replaced by an expanse of vivid green, and we see the tree just before us.

During our whole walk we have been seeing the tree. This appears to mean that we have been having a whole series of visual experiences, no two of which were just alike, and each of which was taken as a representative of the tree. Which of these representatives is most like the tree? Is the tree *really* a faint blue, or is it *really* a vivid green? Or is it of some intermediate color?

Probably most persons will be inclined to maintain that the tree only seems blue at a distance, but that it really is green, as it appears when one is close to it. In a sense, the statement is just; yet some of those who make it would be puzzled to tell by what right they pick out of the whole series of experiences, each of which represents the tree as seen from some particular position, one individual experience, which they claim not only represents the tree as seen from a given point but also represents it as it is. Does this particular experience bear some peculiar earmark which tells us that it is like the real tree while the others are unlike it?

20. REAL THINGS.—And what is this *real tree* that we are supposed to see as it is when we are close to it?

About two hundred years ago the philosopher Berkeley pointed out that the distinction commonly made between things as they look, the apparent, and things as they are, the real, is at bottom the distinction between things as presented to the sense of sight and things as presented to the sense of touch. The acute analysis which he made has held its own ever since.

We have seen that, in walking towards the tree, we have a long series of visual experiences, each of which differs more or less from all of the others. Nevertheless, from the beginning of our progress to the end, we say that we are looking at the same tree. The images change color and grow larger. We do not say that the tree changes color and grows larger. Why do we speak as we do? It is because, all along the line, we mean by the real tree, not what is given to the sense of sight, but something for which this stands as a sign. This something must be given in our experience somewhere, we must be able to perceive it under some circumstances or other, or it would never occur to us to recognize the visual experiences as *signs*, and we should never say that in being conscious of them in succession we are looking at the same tree. They are certainly not the same with each other; how can we know that they all stand for the same thing, unless we have had experience of a connection of the whole series with one thing?

This thing for which so many different visual experiences may serve as signs is the thing revealed in experiences of touch. When we ask: In what direction is the tree? How far away is the tree? How big is the tree? we are always referring to the tree revealed in touch. It is nonsense to say that *what we see* is far away, if by what we see we mean the visual experience itself. As soon as we move we lose that visual experience and get another, and to recover the one we lost we must go back where we were before. When we say we see a tree at a distance, we must mean, then, that we know from certain visual experiences which we have that by moving a certain distance we will be able to touch a tree. And what does it mean to move a certain distance? In the last analysis it means to us to have a certain quantity of movement sensations.

Thus the real world of things, for which experiences of sight serve as signs, is a world revealed in experiences of touch and movement, and when we speak of real positions, distances, and magnitudes, we are always referring to this world. But this is a world revealed in our experience, and it does not seem a hopeless task to discover what may properly be called real and what should be described as merely apparent, when both the real and the apparent are open to our inspection.

Can we not find in this analysis a satisfactory explanation of the plain man's claim that under certain circumstances he sees the tree as it is and under others he does not? What he is really asserting is that one visual experience gives him better information regarding the real thing, the touch thing, than does another.

But what shall we say of his claim that the tree is really green, and only looks blue under certain circumstances? Is it not just as true that the tree only looks green under certain circumstances? Is color any part of the touch thing? Is it ever more than a sign of the touch thing? How can one color be more real than another?

Now, we may hold to Berkeley's analysis and maintain that, in general, the real world, as contrasted with the apparent, means to us the world that is revealed in experiences of touch and movement; and yet we may admit that the word "real" is sometimes used in rather different senses.

It does not seem absurd for a woman to Say: This piece of silk really is yellow; it only looks white under this light. We all admit that a white house may look pink under the rays of the setting sun, and we never call it a pink house. We have seen that it is not unnatural to say: That tree is really green; it is only its distance that makes it look blue.

When one reflects upon these uses of the word "real," one recognizes the fact that, among all the experiences in which things are revealed to us, certain experiences impress us as being more prominent or important or serviceable than certain others, and they come to be called *real*. Things are not commonly seen by artificial light; the sun is not always setting; the tree looks green when it is seen most satisfactorily. In each case, the real color of the thing is the color that it has under circumstances that strike us as normal or as important. We cannot say that we always regard as most real that aspect under which we most commonly perceive things, for if a more unusual experience is more serviceable and really gives us more information about the thing, we give the preference to that. Thus we look with the naked eye at a moving speck on the table before us, and we are unable to distinguish its parts. We place a microscope over the speck and perceive an insect with all its members. The second experience is the more unusual one, but would not every one say: Now we perceive the thing *as it is*?

21. ULTIMATE REAL THINGS.—Let us turn away from the senses of the word "real," which recognize one color or taste or odor as more real than another, and come back to the real world of things presented in sensations of touch. All other classes of sensations may be regarded as related to this as the series of visual experiences above mentioned was related to the one tree which was spoken of as revealed in them all, the touch tree of which they gave information.

Can we say that this world is always to be regarded as reality and never as appearance? We have already seen (section 8) that science does not regard as anything more than appearance the real things which seem to be directly presented in our experience.

This pen that I hold in my hand seems, as I pass my fingers over it, to be continuously extended. It does not appear to present an alternation of filled spaces and empty spaces. I am told that it is composed of molecules in rapid motion and at considerable distances from one another. I am further told that each molecule is composed of atoms, and is, in its turn, not a continuous thing, but, so to speak, a group of little things.

If I accept this doctrine, as it seems I must, am I not forced to conclude that the reality which is given in my experience, the reality with which I have contrasted appearances and to which I have referred them, is, after all, itself only an appearance? The touch things which I have hitherto regarded as the real things that make up the external world, the touch things for which all my visual experiences have served as signs, are, then, not themselves real external things, but only the appearances under which real external things, themselves imperceptible, manifest themselves to me.

It seems, then, that I do not directly perceive any real thing, or, at least, anything that can be regarded as more than an appearance. What, then, is the external world? What are things really like? Can we give any true account of them, or are we forced to say with the skeptics that we only know how things seem to us, and must abandon the attempt to tell what they are really like?

Now, before one sets out to answer a question it is well to find out whether it is a sensible question to ask and a sensible question to try to answer. He who asks: Where is the middle of an infinite line? When did all time begin? Where is space as a whole? does not deserve a serious answer to his questions. And it is well to remember that he who asks: What is the external world like? must keep his question a significant one, if he is to retain his right to look for an answer at all. He has manifestly no right to ask us: How does the external world look when no one is

24

looking? How do things feel when no one feels them? How shall I think of things, not as I think of them, but as they are?

If we are to give an account of the external world at all, it must evidently be *an account* of the external world; *i.e.* it must be given in terms of our experience of things. The only legitimate problem is to give a true account instead of a false one, to distinguish between what only appears and is not real and what both appears and is real.

Bearing this in mind, let us come back to the plain man's experience of the world. He certainly seems to himself to perceive a real world of things, and he constantly distinguishes, in a way very serviceable to himself, between the merely apparent and the real. There is, of course, a sense in which every experience is real; it is, at least, an experience; but when he contrasts real and apparent he means something more than this. Experiences are not relegated to this class or to that merely at random, but the final decision is the outcome of a long experience of the differences which characterize different individual experiences and is an expression of the relations which are observed to hold between them. Certain experiences are accepted as signs, and certain others come to take the more dignified position of thing signified; the mind rests in them and regards them as the real.

We have seen above that the world of real things in which the plain man finds himself is a world of objects revealed in experiences of touch. When he asks regarding anything: How far away is it? How big is it? In what direction is it? it is always the touch thing that interests him. What is given to the other senses is only a sign of this.

We have also seen (section 8) that the world of atoms and molecules of which the man of science tells us is nothing more than a further development of the world of the plain man. The real things with which science concerns itself are, after all, only minute touch things, conceived just as are the things with which the plain man is familiar. They exist in space and move about in space, as the things about us are perceived to exist in space and move about in space. They have size and position, and are separated by distances. We do not *perceive* them, it is true; but we *conceive* them after the analogy of the things that we do perceive, and it is not inconceivable that, if our senses were vastly more acute, we might perceive them directly.

Now, when we conclude that the things directly perceptible to the sense of touch are to be regarded as appearances, as signs of the presence of these minuter things, do we draw such a conclusion arbitrarily? By no means. The distinction between appearance and reality is drawn here just as it is drawn in the world of our common everyday experiences. The great majority of the touch things about us we are not actually touching at any given moment. We only *see* the things, *i.e.* we have certain *signs* of their presence. None the less we believe that the things exist all the time. And in the same way the man of science does not doubt the existence of the real things of which he speaks; he perceives their *signs*. That certain experiences are to be taken as signs of such realities he has established by innumerable observations and careful deductions from those observations. To see the full force of his reasonings one must read some work setting forth the history of the atomic theory.

If, then, we ask the question: What is the real external world? it is clear that we cannot answer it satisfactorily without taking into consideration the somewhat shifting senses of the word "real." What is the real external world to the plain man? It is the world of touch things, of objects upon which he can lay his hands. What is the real external world to the man of science? It is the world of atoms and molecules, of minuter touch things that he cannot actually touch, but which he conceives as though he could touch them.

It should be observed that the man of science has no right to deny the real world which is revealed in the experience of the plain man. In all his dealings with the things which interest him in common life, he refers to this world just as the plain man does. He sees a tree and walks towards it, and distinguishes between its real and its apparent color, its real and its apparent size. He talks about seeing things as they are, or not seeing things as they are. These distinctions in his experience of things remain even after he has come to believe in atoms and molecules.

Thus, the touch object, the tree as he feels it under his hand, may come to be regarded as the sign of the presence of those entities that science seems, at present, to regard as ultimate. Does this prevent it from being the object which has stood as the interpreter of all those diverse visual sensations that we have called different views of the tree? They are still the appearances, and it, relatively to them, is the reality. Now we find that it, in its turn, can be used as a sign of something else, can be regarded as an appearance of a reality more ultimate. It is clear, then, that the same thing may be regarded both as appearance and as reality—appearance as contrasted with one thing, and reality as contrasted with another.

But suppose one says: *I do not want to know what the real external world is to this man or to that man; I want to know what the real external world is.* What shall we say to such a demand?

There is a sense in which such a demand is not purely meaningless, though it may not be a very sensible demand to make. We have seen that an increase of knowledge about things compels a man to pass from the real things of common life to the real things of science, and to look upon the former as appearance. Now, a man may arbitrarily decide that he will use the word "reality" to indicate only that which can never in its turn be regarded as appearance, a reality which must remain an ultimate reality; and he may insist upon our telling him about that. How a man not a soothsayer can tell when he has come to ultimate reality, it is not easy to see.

Suppose, however, that we could give any one such information. We should then be telling him about things *as they are*, it is true, but his knowledge of things would not be different in *kind* from what it was before. The only difference between such a knowledge of things and a knowledge of things not known to be ultimate would be that, in the former case, it would be recognized that no further extension of knowledge was possible. The distinction between appearance and reality would remain just what it was in the experience of the plain man.

22. THE BUGBEAR OF THE "UNKNOWABLE."—It is very important to recognize that we must not go on talking about appearance and reality, as if our words really meant something, when we have quite turned our backs upon our experience of appearances and the realities which they represent.

That appearances and realities are connected we know very well, for we perceive them to be connected. What we see, we can touch. And we not only know that appearances and realities are connected, but we know with much detail what appearances are to be taken as signs of what realities. The visual experience which I call the house as seen from a distance I never think of taking for a representative of the hat which I hold in my hand. This visual experience I refer to its own appropriate touch thing, and not to another. If what *looks like* a beefsteak could *really be* a fork or a mountain or a kitten indifferently,—but I must not even finish the sentence, for the words "look like" and "could really be" lose all significance when we loosen the bond between appearances and the realities to which they are properly referred.

Each appearance, then, must be referred to some particular real thing and not to any other. This is true of the appearances which we recognize as such in common life, and it is equally true of the appearances recognized as such in science. The pen which I feel between my fingers I may regard as appearance and refer to a swarm of moving atoms. But it would be silly for me to refer it to atoms "in general." The reality to which I refer the appearance in question is a particular group of atoms existing at a particular point in space. The chemist never supposes that the atoms within the walls of his test-tube are identical with those in the vial on the shelf. Neither in common life nor in science would the distinction between appearances and real things be of the smallest service were it not possible to distinguish between this appearance and that, and this reality and that, and to refer each appearance to its appropriate reality. Indeed, it is inconceivable that, under such circumstances, the distinction should have been drawn at all.

These points ought to be strongly insisted upon, for we find certain philosophic writers falling constantly into a very curious abuse of the distinction and making much capital of it. It is argued that what we see, what we touch, what we conceive as a result of scientific observation and reflection—all is, in the last analysis, material which is given us in sensation. The various senses furnish us with different classes of sensations; we work these up into certain complexes. But sensations are only the impressions which something outside of us makes upon us. Hence, although we seem to ourselves to know the external world as it is, our knowledge can never extend beyond the impressions made upon us. Thus, we are absolutely shut up to *appearances*, and can know nothing about the *reality* to which they must be referred.

Touching this matter Herbert Spencer writes[1] as follows: "When we are taught that a piece of matter, regarded by us as existing externally, cannot be really known, but that we can know only certain impressions produced on us, we are yet, by the relativity of thought, compelled to think of these in relation to a cause—the notion of a real existence which generated these impressions becomes nascent. If it be proved that every notion of a real existence which we can frame is inconsistent with itself,—that matter, however conceived by us, cannot be matter as it actually is,—our conception, though transfigured, is not destroyed: there remains the sense of reality, dissociated as far as possible from those special forms under which it was before represented in thought."

This means, in plain language, that we must regard everything we know and can know as appearance and must refer it to an unknown reality. Sometimes Mr. Spencer calls this reality the Unknowable, sometimes he calls it the Absolute, and sometimes he allows it to pass by a variety of other names, such as Power, Cause, etc. He wishes us to think of it as "lying behind appearances" or as "underlying appearances."

Probably it has already been remarked that this Unknowable has brought us around again to that amusing "telephone exchange" discussed in the third chapter. But if the reader feels

26

within himself the least weakness for the Unknowable, I beg him to consider carefully, before he pins his faith to it, the following:—

(1) If we do perceive external bodies, our own bodies and others, then it is conceivable that we may have evidence from observation to the effect that other bodies affecting our bodies may give rise to sensations. In this case we cannot say that we know nothing but sensations; we know real bodies as well as sensations, and we may refer the sensations to the real bodies.

(2) If we do not perceive that we have bodies, and that our bodies are acted upon by others, we have no evidence that what we call our sensations are due to messages which come from "external things" and are conducted along the nerves. It is then, absurd to talk of such "external things" as though they existed, and to call them the reality to which sensations, as appearances, must be referred,

(3) In other words, if there is perceived to be a telephone exchange with its wires and subscribers, we may refer the messages received to the subscribers, and call this, if we choose, a reference of appearance to reality.

But if there is perceived no telephone exchange, and if it is concluded that any wires or subscribers of which it means anything to speak must be composed of what we have heretofore called "messages," then it is palpably absurd to refer the "messages" as a whole to subscribers not supposed to be composed of "messages"; and it is a blunder to go on calling the things that we know "messages," as though we had evidence that they came from, and must be referred to, something beyond themselves.

We must recognize that, with the general demolition of the exchange, we lose not only known subscribers, but the very notion of a subscriber. It will not do to try to save from this wreck some "unknowable" subscriber, and still pin our faith to him.

(4) We have seen that the relation of appearance to reality is that of certain experiences to certain other experiences. When we take the liberty of calling the Unknowable a *reality*, we blunder in our use of the word. The Unknowable cannot be an experience either actual, possible, or conceived as possible, and it cannot possibly hold the relation to any of our experiences that a real thing of any kind holds to the appearances that stand as its signs.

(5) Finally, no man has ever made an assumption more perfectly useless and purposeless than the assumption of the Unknowable. We have seen that the distinction between appearance and reality is a serviceable one, and it has been pointed out that it would be of no service whatever if it were not possible to refer particular appearances to their own appropriate realities. The realities to which we actually refer appearances serve to explain them. Thus, when I ask: Why do I perceive that tree now as faint and blue and now as vivid and green? the answer to the question is found in the notion of distance and position in space; it is found, in other words, in a reference to the real world of touch things, for which visual experiences serve as signs. Under certain circumstances, the mountain *ought* to be robed in its azure hue, and, under certain circumstances, it *ought not*. The circumstances in each case are open to investigation.

Now, let us substitute for the real world of touch things, which furnishes the explanation of given visual experiences, that philosophic fiction, that pseudo-real nonentity, the Unknowable. Now I perceive a tree as faint and blue, now as bright and green; will a reference to the Unknowable explain why the experiences differed? Was the Unknowable in the one instance farther off in an unknowable space, and in the other nearer? This, even if it means anything, must remain unknowable. And when the chemist puts together a volume of chlorine gas and a volume of hydrogen gas to get two volumes of hydrochloric acid gas, shall we explain the change which has taken place by a reference to the Unknowable, or shall we turn to the doctrine of atoms and their combinations?

The fact is that no man in his senses tries to account for any individual fact by turning for an explanation to the Unknowable. It is a life-preserver by which some set great store, but which no man dreams of using when he really falls into the water.

If, then, we have any reason to believe that there is a real external world at all, we have reason to believe that we know what it is. That some know it imperfectly, that others know it better, and that we may hope that some day it will be known still more perfectly, is surely no good reason for concluding that we do not know it at all.

[1] "First Principles," Part I, Chapter IV, section 26.

CHAPTER VI
OF SPACE

23. WHAT ARE WE SUPPOSED TO KNOW ABOUT IT.—The plain man may admit that he is not ready to hazard a definition of space, but he is certainly not willing to admit that he is wholly ignorant of space and of its attributes. He knows that it is something in which material objects have position and in which they move about; he knows that it has not merely length, like a line, nor length and breadth, like a surface, but has the three dimensions of length, breadth, and

depth; he knows that, except in the one circumstance of its position, every part of space is exactly like every other part, and that, although objects may move about in space, it is incredible that the spaces themselves should be shifted about.

Those who are familiar with the literature of the subject know that it has long been customary to make regarding space certain other statements to which the plain man does not usually make serious objection when he is introduced to them. Thus it is said:—

(1) The idea of space is *necessary*. We can think of objects in space as annihilated, but we cannot conceive space to be annihilated. We can clear space of things, but we cannot clear away space itself, even in thought.

(2) Space must be *infinite*. We cannot conceive that we should come to the end of space.

(3) Every space, however small, is *infinitely divisible*. That is to say, even the most minute space must be composed of spaces. We cannot, even theoretically, split a solid into mere surfaces, a surface into mere lines, or a line into mere points.

Against such statements the plain man is not impelled to rise in rebellion, for he can see that there seems to be some ground for making them. He can conceive of any particular material object as annihilated, and of the place which it occupied as standing empty; but he cannot go on and conceive of the annihilation of this bit of empty space. Its annihilation would not leave a gap, for a gap means a bit of empty space; nor could it bring the surrounding spaces into juxtaposition, for one cannot shift spaces, and, in any case, a shifting that is not a shifting through space is an absurdity.

Again, he cannot conceive of any journey that would bring him to the end of space. There is no more reason for stopping at one point than at another; why not go on? What could end space?

As to the infinite divisibility of space, have we not, in addition to the seeming reasonableness of the doctrine, the testimony of all the mathematicians? Does any one of them ever dream of a line so short that it cannot be divided into two shorter lines, or of an angle so small that it cannot be bisected?

24. SPACE AS NECESSARY AND SPACE AS INFINITE.—That these statements about space contain truth one should not be in haste to deny. It seems silly to say that space can be annihilated, or that one can travel "over the mountains of the moon" in the hope of reaching the end of it. And certainly no prudent man wishes to quarrel with that coldly rational creature the mathematician.

But it is well worth while to examine the statements carefully and to see whether there is not some danger that they may be understood in such a way as to lead to error. Let us begin with the doctrine that space is necessary and cannot be "thought away."

As we have seen above, it is manifestly impossible to annihilate in thought a certain portion of space and leave the other portions intact. There are many things in the same case. We cannot annihilate in thought one side of a door and leave the other side; we cannot rob a man of the outside of his hat and leave him the inside. But we can conceive of a whole door as annihilated, and of a man as losing a whole hat. May we or may we not conceive of space as a whole as nonexistent?

I do not say, be it observed, can we conceive of something as attacking and annihilating space? Whatever space may be, we none of us think of it as a something that may be threatened and demolished. I only say, may we not think of a system of things—not a world such as ours, of course, but still a system of things of some sort—in which space relations have no part? May we not conceive such to be possible?

It should be remarked that space relations are by no means the only ones in which we think of things as existing. We attribute to them time relations as well. Now, when we think of occurrences as related to each other in time, we do, in so far as we concentrate our attention upon these relations, turn our attention away from space and contemplate another aspect of the system of things. Space is not such a necessity of thought that we must keep thinking of space when we have turned our attention to something else. And is it, indeed, inconceivable that there should be a system of things (not extended things in space, of course), characterized by time relations and perhaps other relations, but not by space relations?

It goes without saying that we cannot go on thinking of space and at the same time not think of space. Those who keep insisting upon space as a necessity of thought seem to set us such a task as this, and to found their conclusion upon our failure to accomplish it. "We can never represent to ourselves the nonexistence of space," says the German philosopher Kant (1724-1804), "although we can easily conceive that there are no objects in space."

It would, perhaps, be fairer to translate the first half of this sentence as follows: "We can never picture to ourselves the nonexistence of space." Kant says we cannot make of it a *Vorstellung*, a representation. This we may freely admit, for what does one try to do when one makes the effort to imagine the nonexistence of space? Does not one first clear space of objects, and then try to clear space of space in much the same way? We try to "think space away," *i.e. to remove it from the place where it was and yet keep that place.*

What does it mean to imagine or represent to oneself the nonexistence of material objects? Is it not to represent to oneself the objects as no longer in space, *i.e.* to imagine the space as empty, as cleared of the objects? It means something in this case to speak of a *Vorstellung*, or representation. We can call before our minds the empty space. But if we are to think of space as nonexistent, what shall we call before our minds? Our procedure must not be analogous to what it was before; we must not try to picture to our minds *the absence of space*, as though that were in itself a something that could be pictured; we must turn our attention to other relations, such as time relations, and ask whether it is not conceivable that such should be the only relations obtaining within a given system.

Those who insist upon the fact that we cannot but conceive space as infinite employ a very similar argument to prove their point. They set us a self-contradictory task, and regard our failure to accomplish it as proof of their position. Thus, Sir William Hamilton (1788-1856) argues: "We are altogether unable to conceive space as bounded—as finite; that is, as a whole beyond which there is no further space." And Herbert Spencer echoes approvingly: "We find ourselves totally unable to imagine bounds beyond which there is no space."

Now, whatever one may be inclined to think about the infinity of space, it is clear that this argument is an absurd one. Let me write it out more at length: "We are altogether unable to conceive space as bounded—as finite; that is, as a whole *in the space* beyond which there is no further space." "We find ourselves totally unable to imagine bounds, *in the space* beyond which there is no further space." The words which I have added were already present implicitly. What can the word "beyond" mean if it does not signify space beyond? What Sir William and Mr. Spencer have asked us to do is to imagine a limited space with a *beyond* and yet *no beyond.*

There is undoubtedly some reason why men are so ready to affirm that space is infinite, even while they admit that they do not know that the world of material things is infinite. To this we shall come back again later. But if one wishes to affirm it, it is better to do so without giving a reason than it is to present such arguments as the above.

25. SPACE AS INFINITELY DIVISIBLE.—For more than two thousand years men have been aware that certain very grave difficulties seem to attach to the idea of motion, when we once admit that space is infinitely divisible. To maintain that we can divide any portion of space up into ultimate elements which are not themselves spaces, and which have no extension, seems repugnant to the idea we all have of space. And if we refuse to admit this possibility there seems to be nothing left to us but to hold that every space, however small, may theoretically be divided up into smaller spaces, and that there is no limit whatever to the possible subdivision of spaces. Nevertheless, if we take this most natural position, we appear to find ourselves plunged into the most hopeless of labyrinths, every turn of which brings us face to face with a flat self-contradiction.

To bring the difficulties referred to clearly before our minds, let us suppose a point to move uniformly over a line an inch long, and to accomplish its journey in a second. At first glance, there appears to be nothing abnormal about this proceeding. But if we admit that this line is infinitely divisible, and reflect upon this property of the line, the ground seems to sink from beneath our feet at once.

For it is possible to argue that, under the conditions given, the point must move over one half of the line in half a second; over one half of the remainder, or one fourth of the line, in one fourth of a second; over one eighth of the line, in one eighth of a second, etc. Thus the portions of line moved over successively by the point may be represented by the descending series:

1/2, 1/4, 1/8, 1/16, . . . [Greek omicron symbol]

Now, it is quite true that the motion of the point can be described in a number of different ways; but the important thing to remark here is that, if the motion really is uniform, and if the line really is infinitely divisible, this series must, as satisfactorily as any other, describe the motion of the point. And it would be absurd to maintain that *a part* of the series can describe the whole motion. We cannot say, for example, that, when the point has moved over one half, one fourth, and one eighth of the line, it has completed its motion. If even a single member of the series is left out, the whole line has not been passed over; and this is equally true whether the omitted member represent a large bit of line or a small one.

The whole series, then, represents the whole line, as definite parts of the series represent definite parts of the line. The line can only be completed when the series is completed. But when and how can this series be completed? In general, a series is completed when we reach the final term, but here there appears to be no final term. We cannot make zero the final term, for it does not belong to the series at all. It does not obey the law of the series, for it is not one half as large as the term preceding it—what space is so small that dividing it by 2 gives us [omicron]? On the other hand, some term just before zero cannot be the final term; for if it really represents a little bit of the line, however small, it must, by hypothesis, be made up of lesser bits, and a smaller term must be conceivable. There can, then, be no last term to the series; *i.e.* what the point is doing at the very last is absolutely indescribable; it is inconceivable that there should be a *very last*.

It was pointed out many centuries ago that it is equally inconceivable that there should be a *very first*. How can a point even begin to move along an infinitely divisible line? Must it not before it can move over any distance, however short, first move over half that distance? And before it can move over that half, must it not move over the half of that? Can it find something to move over that has no halves? And if not, how shall it even start to move? To move at all, it must begin somewhere; it cannot begin with what has no halves, for then it is not moving over any part of the line, as all parts have halves; and it cannot begin with what has halves, for that is not the beginning. *What does the point do first?* that is the question. Those who tell us about points and lines usually leave us to call upon gentle echo for an answer.

The perplexities of this moving point seem to grow worse and worse the longer one reflects upon them. They do not harass it merely at the beginning and at the end of its journey. This is admirably brought out by Professor W. K. Clifford (1845-1879), an excellent mathematician, who never had the faintest intention of denying the possibility of motion, and who did not desire to magnify the perplexities in the path of a moving point. He writes:—

"When a point moves along a line, we know that between any two positions of it there is an infinite number . . . of intermediate positions. That is because the motion is continuous. Each of those positions is where the point was at some instant or other. Between the two end positions on the line, the point where the motion began and the point where it stopped, there is no point of the line which does not belong to that series. We have thus an infinite series of successive positions of a continuously moving point, and in that series are included all the points of a certain piece of line-room." [1]

Thus, we are told that, when a point moves along a line, between any two positions of it there is an infinite number of intermediate positions. Clifford does not play with the word "infinite"; he takes it seriously and tells us that it means without any end: "*Infinite*; it is a dreadful word, I know, until you find out that you are familiar with the thing which it expresses. In this place it means that between any two positions there is some intermediate position; between that and either of the others, again, there is some other intermediate; and so on *without any end*. Infinite means without any end."

But really, if the case is as stated, the point in question must be at a desperate pass. I beg the reader to consider the following, and ask himself whether he would like to change places with it:—

(1) If the series of positions is really endless, the point must complete one by one the members of an endless series, and reach a nonexistent final term, for a really endless series cannot have a final term.

(2) The series of positions is supposed to be "an infinite series of successive positions." The moving point must take them one after another. But how can it? *Between any two positions of the point there is an infinite number of intermediate positions.* That is to say, no two of these successive positions must be regarded as *next to* each other; every position is separated from every other by an infinite number of intermediate ones. How, then, shall the point move? It cannot possibly move from one position to the next, for there is no next. Shall it move first to some position that is not the next? Or shall it in despair refuse to move at all?

Evidently there is either something wrong with this doctrine of the infinite divisibility of space, or there is something wrong with our understanding of it, if such absurdities as these refuse to be cleared away. Let us see where the trouble lies.

26. WHAT IS REAL SPACE?—It is plain that men are willing to make a number of statements about space, the ground for making which is not at once apparent. It is a bold man who will undertake to say that the universe of matter is infinite in extent. We feel that we have the right to ask him how he knows that it is. But most men are ready enough to affirm that space is and must be infinite. How do they know that it is? They certainly do not directly perceive all space, and such arguments as the one offered by Hamilton and Spencer are easily seen to be poor proofs.

Men are equally ready to affirm that space is infinitely divisible. Has any man ever looked upon a line and perceived directly that it has an infinite number of parts? Did any one ever succeed in dividing a space up infinitely? When we try to make clear to ourselves how a point moves along an infinitely divisible line, do we not seem to land in sheer absurdities? On what sort of evidence does a man base his statements regarding space? They are certainly very bold statements.

30

A careful reflection reveals the fact that men do not speak as they do about space for no reason at all. When they are properly understood, their statements can be seen to be justified, and it can be seen also that the difficulties which we have been considering can be avoided. The subject is a deep one, and it can scarcely be discussed exhaustively in an introductory volume of this sort, but one can, at least, indicate the direction in which it seems most reasonable to look for an answer to the questions which have been raised. How do we come to a knowledge of space, and what do we mean by space? This is the problem to solve; and if we can solve this, we have the key which will unlock many doors.

Now, we saw in the last chapter that we have reason to believe that we know what the real external world is. It is a world of things which we perceive, or can perceive, or, not arbitrarily but as a result of careful observation and deductions therefrom, conceive as though we did perceive it—a world, say, of atoms and molecules. It is not an Unknowable behind or beyond everything that we perceive, or can perceive, or conceive in the manner stated.

And the space with which we are concerned is real space, the space in which real things exist and move about, the real things which we can directly know or of which we can definitely know something. In some sense it must be given in our experience, if the things which are in it, and are known to be in it, are given in our experience. How must we think of this real space?

Suppose we look at a tree at a distance. We are conscious of a certain complex of color. We can distinguish the kind of color; in this case, we call it blue. But the quality of the color is not the only thing that we can distinguish in the experience. In two experiences of color the quality may be the same, and yet the experiences may be different from each other. In the one case we may have more of the same color—we may, so to speak, be conscious of a larger patch; but even if there is not actually more of it, there may be such a difference that we can know from the visual experience alone that the touch object before us is, in the one case, of the one shape, and, in the other case, of another. Thus we may distinguish between the *stuff* given in our experience and the *arrangement* of that stuff. This is the distinction which philosophers have marked as that between "matter" and "form." It is, of course, understood that both of these words, so used, have a special sense not to be confounded with their usual one.

This distinction between "matter" and "form" obtains in all our experiences. I have spoken just above of the shape of the touch object for which our visual experiences stand as signs. What do we mean by its shape? To the plain man real things are the touch things of which he has experience, and these touch things are very clearly distinguishable from one another in shape, in size, in position, nor are the different parts | of the things to be confounded with each other. Suppose that, as we pass our hand over a table, all the sensations of touch and movement which we experience fused into an undistinguishable mass. Would we have any notion of size or shape? It is because our experiences of touch and movement do not fuse, but remain distinguishable from each other, and we are conscious of them as *arranged*, as constituting a system, that we can distinguish between this part of a thing and that, this thing and that.

This arrangement, this order, of what is revealed by touch and movement, we may call the "form" of the touch world. Leaving out of consideration, for the present, time relations, we may say that the "form" of the touch world is the whole system of actual and possible relations of arrangement between the elements which make it up. It is because there is such a system of relations that we can speak of things as of this shape or of that, as great or small, as near or far, as here or there.

Now, I ask, is there any reason to believe that, when the plain man speaks of *space*, the word means to him anything more than this system of actual and possible relations of arrangement among the touch things that constitute his real world? He may talk sometimes as though space were some kind of a *thing*, but he does not really think of it as a thing.

This is evident from the mere fact that he is so ready to make about it affirmations that he would not venture to make about things. It does not strike him as inconceivable that a given material object should be annihilated; it does strike him as inconceivable that a portion of space should be blotted out of existence. Why this difference? Is it not explained when we recognize that space is but a name for all the actual and possible relations of arrangement in which things in the touch world may stand? We cannot drop out some of these relations and yet keep *space*, *i.e.* the system of relations which we had before. That this is what space means, the plain man may not recognize explicitly, but he certainly seems to recognize it implicitly in what he says about space. Men are rarely inclined to admit that space is a *thing* of any kind, nor are they much more inclined to regard it as a quality of a thing. Of what could it be the quality?

And if space really were a thing of any sort, would it not be the height of presumption for a man, in the absence of any direct evidence from observation, to say how much there is of it—to declare it infinite? Men do not hesitate to say that space must be infinite. But when we realize that we do not mean by space merely the actual relations which exist between the touch things

31

that make up the world, but also the *possible* relations, *i.e.* that we mean the whole *plan* of the world system, we can see that it is not unreasonable to speak of space as infinite.

The material universe may, for aught we know, be limited in extent. The actual space relations in which things stand to each other may not be limitless. But these actual space relations taken alone do not constitute space. Men have often asked themselves whether they should conceive of the universe as limited and surrounded by void space. It is not nonsense to speak of such a state of things. It would, indeed, appear to be nonsense to say that, if the universe is limited, it does not lie in void space. What can we mean by void space but the system of possible relations in which things, if they exist, must stand? To say that, beyond a certain point, no further relations are possible, seems absurd.

Hence, when a man has come to understand what we have a right to mean by space, it does not imply a boundless conceit on his part to hazard the statement that space is infinite. When he has said this, he has said very little. What shall we say to the statement that space is infinitely divisible?

To understand the significance of this statement we must come back to the distinction between appearances and the real things for which they stand as signs, the distinction discussed at length in the last chapter.

When I see a tree from a distance, the visual experience which I have is, as we have seen, not an indivisible unit, but is a complex experience; it has parts, and these parts are related to each other; in other words, it has both "matter" and "form." It is, however, one thing to say that this experience has parts, and it is another to say that it has an infinite number of parts. No man is conscious of perceiving an infinite number of parts in the patch of color which represents to him a tree at a distance; to say that it is constituted of such strikes us in our moments of sober reflection as a monstrous statement.

Now, this visual experience is to us the sign of the reality, the real tree; it is not taken as the tree itself. When we speak of the size, the shape, the number of parts, of the tree, we do not have in mind the size, the shape, the number of parts, of just this experience. We pass from the sign to the thing signified, and we may lay our hand upon this thing, thus gaining a direct experience of the size and shape of the touch object.

We must recognize, however, that just as no man is conscious of an infinite number of parts in what he sees, so no man is conscious of an infinite number of parts in what he touches. He who tells me that, when I pass my finger along my paper cutter, *what I perceive* has an infinite number of parts, tells me what seems palpably untrue. When an object is very small, I can see it, and I cannot see that it is composed of parts; similarly, when an object is very small, I can feel it with my finger, but I cannot distinguish its parts by the sense of touch. There seem to be limits beyond which I cannot go in either case.

Nevertheless, men often speak of thousandths of an inch, or of millionths of an inch, or of distances even shorter. Have such fractions of the magnitudes that we do know and can perceive any real existence? The touch world of real things as it is revealed in our experience does not appear to be divisible into such; it does not appear to be divisible even so far, and much less does it appear to be infinitely divisible.

But have we not seen that the touch world given in our experience must be taken by the thoughtful man as itself the sign or appearance of a reality more ultimate? The speck which appears to the naked eye to have no parts is seen under the microscope to have parts; that is to say, an experience apparently not extended has become the sign of something that is seen to have part out of part. We have as yet invented no instrument that will make directly perceptible to the finger tip an atom of hydrogen or of oxygen, but the man of science conceives of these little things as though they could be perceived. They and the space in which they move—the system of actual and possible relations between them—seem to be related to the world revealed in touch very much as the space revealed in the field of the microscope is related to the space of the speck looked at with the naked eye.

Thus, when the thoughtful man speaks of *real space*, he cannot mean by the word only the actual and possible relations of arrangement among the things and the parts of things directly revealed to his sense of touch. He may speak of real things too small to be thus perceived, and of their motion as through spaces too small to be perceptible at all. What limit shall he set to the possible subdivision of *real* things? Unless he can find an ultimate reality which cannot in its turn become the appearance or sign of a further reality, it seems absurd to speak of a limit at all.

We may, then, say that real space is infinitely divisible. By this statement we should mean that certain experiences may be represented by others, and that we may carry on our division in the case of the latter, when a further subdivision of the former seems out of the question. But it should not mean that any single experience furnished us by any sense, or anything that we can represent in the imagination, is composed of an infinite number of parts.

When we realize this, do we not free ourselves from the difficulties which seemed to make the motion of a point over a line an impossible absurdity? The line as revealed in a single experience either of sight or of touch is not composed of an infinite number of parts. It is composed of points seen or touched—least experiences of sight or touch, *minima sensibilia.* These are next to each other, and the point, in moving, takes them one by one.

But such a single experience is not what we call a line. It is but one experience of a line. Though the experience is not infinitely divisible, the line may be. This only means that the visual or tactual point of the single experience may stand for, may represent, what is not a mere point but has parts, and is, hence, divisible. Who can set a limit to such possible substitutions? in other words, who can set a limit to the divisibility of a *real line?*

It is only when we confuse the single experience with the real line that we fall into absurdities. What the mathematician tells us about real points and real lines has no bearing on the constitution of the single experience and its parts. Thus, when he tells us that between any two points on a line there are an infinite number of other points, he only means that we may expand the line indefinitely by the system of substitutions described above. We do this for ourselves within limits every time that we approach from a distance a line drawn on a blackboard. The mathematician has generalized our experience for us, and that is all he has done. We should try to get at his real meaning, and not quote him as supporting an absurdity.

[1] "Seeing and Thinking," p. 149.

CHAPTER VII

OF TIME

27. TIME AS NECESSARY, INFINITE, AND INFINITELY DIVISIBLE.—Of course, we all know something about time; we know it as past, present, and future; we know it as divisible into parts, all of which are successive; we know that whatever happens must happen in time. Those who have thought a good deal about the matter are apt to tell us that time is a necessity of thought, we cannot but think it; that time is and must be infinite; and that it is infinitely divisible.

These are the same statements that were made regarding space, and, as they have to be criticised in just the same way, it is not necessary to dwell upon them at great length. However, we must not pass them over altogether.

As to the statement that time is a *necessary* idea, we may freely admit that we cannot in thought *annihilate* time, or *think it away.* It does not seem to mean anything to attempt such a task. Whatever time may be, it does not appear to be a something of such a nature that we can demolish it or clear it away from something else. But is it necessarily absurd to speak of a system of things—not, of course, a system of things in which there is change, succession, an earlier and a later, but still a system of things of some sort—in which there obtain no time relations? The problem is, to be sure, one of theoretical interest merely, for such a system of things is not the world we know.

And as for the infinity of time, may we not ask on what ground any one ventures to assert that time is infinite? No man can say that infinite time is directly given in his experience. If one does not directly perceive it to be infinite, must one not seek for some proof of the fact? The only proof which appears to be offered us is contained in the statement that we cannot conceive of a time before which there was no time, nor of a time after which there will be no time; a proof which is no proof, for written out at length it reads as follows: we cannot conceive of a time *in the time* before which there was no time, nor of a time *in the time* after which there will be no time. As well say: We cannot conceive of a number the number before which was no number, nor of a number the number after which will be no number. Whatever may be said for the conclusion arrived at, the argument is a very poor one.

When we turn to the consideration of time as infinitely divisible, we seem to find ourselves confronted with the same difficulties which presented themselves when we thought of space as infinitely divisible. Certainly no man was immediately conscious of an infinite number of parts in the minute which just slipped by. Shall he assert that it did, nevertheless, contain an infinite number of parts? Then how did it succeed in passing? how did it even *begin* to pass away? It is infinitely divisible, that is, there is no end to the number of parts into which it may be divided; those parts and parts of parts are all successive, no two can pass at once, they must all do it in a certain order, one after the other.

Thus, something must pass *first.* What can it be? If that something has parts, is divisible, the whole of it cannot pass first. It must itself pass bit by bit, as must the whole minute; and if it is infinitely divisible we have precisely the problem that we had at the outset. Whatever passes first cannot, then, have parts.

Let us assume that it has no parts, and bid it Godspeed! Has the minute begun? Our minute is, by hypothesis, infinitely divisible; it is composed of parts, and those parts of other parts, and so on without end. We cannot by subdivision come to any part which is itself not composed of smaller parts. The partless thing that passed, then, is no part of the minute. That is all still waiting at the gate, and no member of its troop can prove that it has a right to lead the rest. In the same outer darkness is waiting the point on the line that misbehaved itself in the last chapter.

28. THE PROBLEM OF PAST, PRESENT, AND FUTURE.—It seems bad enough to have on our hands a minute which must pass away in successive bits, and to discover that no bit of it can possibly pass first. But if we follow with approval the reflections of certain thinkers, we may find ourselves at such a pass that we would be glad to be able to prove that we may have on our hands a minute of any sort. Men sometimes are so bold as to maintain that they know time to be infinite; would it not be well for them to prove first that they can know time at all?

The trouble is this; as was pointed out long ago by Saint Augustine (354-430) in his famous "Confessions," [1] the parts of time are successive, and of the three divisions, past, present, and future, only one can be regarded as existing: "Those two times, past and future, how can they be, when the past is not now, and the future is not yet?" The present is, it seems, the only existent; how long is the present?

"Even a single hour passes in fleeting moments; as much of it as has taken flight is past, what remains is future. If we can comprehend any time that is divisible into no parts at all, or perhaps into the minutest parts of moments, this alone let us call present; yet this speeds so hurriedly from the future to the past that it does not endure even for a little space. If it has duration, it is divided into a past and a future; but the present has no duration.

"Where, then, is the time that we may call long? Is it future? We do not say of the future: it *is* long; for as yet there exists nothing to be long. We say: it *will be* long. But when? If while yet future it will not be long, for nothing will yet exist to be long. And if it will be long, when, from a future as yet nonexistent, it has become a present, and has begun to be, that it may be something that is long, then present time cries out in the words of the preceding paragraph that it cannot be long."

Augustine's way of presenting the difficulty is a quaint one, but the problem is as real at the beginning of the twentieth century as it was at the beginning of the fifth. Past time does not exist now, future time does not exist yet, and present time, it seems, has no duration. Can a man be said to be conscious of time as past, present, and future? Who can be conscious of the nonexistent? And the existent is not *time*, it has no duration, there is no before and after in a mere limiting point.

Augustine's way out of the difficulty is the suggestion that, although we cannot, strictly speaking, measure time, we can measure *memory* and *expectation*. Before he begins to repeat a psalm, his expectation extends over the whole of it. After a little a part of it must be referred to expectation and a part of it to memory. Finally, the whole psalm is "extended along" the memory. We can measure this, at least.

But how is the psalm in question "extended along" the memory or the expectation? Are the parts of it successive, or do they exist simultaneously? If everything in the memory image exists at once, if all belongs to the punctual present, to the mere point that divides past from future, how can a man get from it a consciousness of time, of a something whose parts cannot exist together but must follow each other?

Augustine appears to overlook the fact that on his own hypothesis, the present, the only existent, the only thing a man can be conscious of, is an indivisible instant. In such there can be no change; the man who is shut up to such cannot be aware that the past is growing and the future diminishing. Any such change as this implies at least two instants, an earlier and a later. He who has never experienced a change of any sort, who has never been conscious of the relation of earlier and later, of succession, cannot think of the varied content of memory as of *that which has been present*. It cannot mean to him what memory certainly means to us; he cannot be conscious of a past, a present, and a future. To extract the notion of time, of past, present, and future, from an experience which contains no element of succession, from an indivisible instant, is as hopeless a task as to extract a line from a mathematical point.

It appears, then, that, if we are to be conscious of time at all, if we are to have the least conception of it, we must have some direct experience of change. We cannot really be shut up to that punctual present, that mere point or limit between past and future, that the present has been described as being. But does this not imply that we can be directly conscious of what is not present, that we can *now* perceive what does *not now* exist? How is this possible?

It is not easy for one whose reading has been somewhat limited in any given field to see the full significance of the problems which present themselves in that field. Those who read much in the history of modern philosophy will see that this ancient difficulty touching our consciousness of time has given rise to some exceedingly curious speculations, and some strange conclusions touching the nature of the mind.

Thus, it has been argued that, since the experience of each moment is something quite distinct from the experience of the next, a something that passes away to give place to its successor, we cannot explain the consciousness of time, of a whole in which successive moments are recognized as having their appropriate place, unless we assume a something that knows each moment and knits it, so to speak, to its successor. This something is the self or consciousness, which is independent of time, and does not exist in time, as do the various experiences that fill the successive moments. It is assumed to be *timelessly* present *at all times*, and thus to connect the nonexistent past with the existent present.

I do not ask the reader to try to make clear to himself how anything can be timelessly present at all times, for I do not believe that the words can be made to represent any clear thought whatever. Nor do I ask him to try to conceive how this timeless something can join past and present. I merely wish to point out that these modern speculations, which still influence the minds of many distinguished men, have their origin in a difficulty which suggested itself early in the history of reflective thought, and are by no means to be regarded as a gratuitous and useless exercise of the ingenuity. They are serious attempts to solve a real problem, though they may be unsuccessful ones, and they are worthy of attention even from those who incline to a different solution.

29. WHAT IS REAL TIME?—From the thin air of such speculations as we have been discussing let us come back to the world of the plain man, the world in which we all habitually live. It is from this that we must start out upon all our journeys, and it is good to come back to it from time to time to make sure of our bearings.

We have seen (Chapter V) that we distinguish between the real and the apparent, and that we recognize as the real world the objects revealed to the sense of touch. These objects stand to each other in certain relations of arrangement; that is to say, they exist in space. And just as we may distinguish between the object as it appears and the object as it is, so we may distinguish between apparent space and real space, *i.e.* between the relations of arrangement, actual and possible, which obtain among the parts of the object as it appears, and those which obtain among the parts of the object as it really is.

But our experience does not present us only with objects in space relations; it presents us with a succession of changes in those objects. And if we will reason about those changes as we have reasoned about space relations, many of our difficulties regarding the nature of time may, as it seems, be made to disappear.

Thus we may recognize that we are directly conscious of duration, of succession, and may yet hold that this crude and immediate experience of duration is not what we mean by real time. Every one distinguishes between apparent time and real time now and then. We all know that a sermon may _seem _long and not *be* long; that the ten years that we live over in a dream are not ten real years; that the swallowing of certain drugs may be followed by the illusion of the lapse of vast spaces of time, when really very little time has elapsed. What is this *real* time?

It is nothing else than the order of the changes which take place or may take place in real things. In the last chapter I spoke of space as the "form" of the real world; it would be better to call it *a* "form" of the real world, and to give the same name also to time.

It is very clear that, when we inquire concerning the real time of any occurrence, or ask how long a series of such lasted, we always look for our answer to something that has happened in the external world. The passage of a star over the meridian, the position of the sun above the horizon, the arc which the moon has described since our last observation, the movement of the hands of a clock, the amount of sand which has fallen in the hourglass, these things and such as these are the indicators of real time. There may be indicators of a different sort; we may decide that it is noon because we are hungry, or midnight because we are tired; we may argue that the preacher must have spoken more than an hour because he quite wore out the patience of the congregation. These are more or less uncertain signs of the lapse of time, but they cannot be regarded as experiences of the passing of time either apparent or real.

Thus, we see that real space and real time are the *plan* of the world system. They are not*things* of any sort, and they should not be mistaken for things. They are not known independently of things, though, when we have once had an experience of things and their changes, we can by abstraction from the things themselves fix our attention upon their arrangement and upon the order of their changes. We can divide and subdivide spaces and times without much reference to the things. But we should never forget that it would never have occurred to us to do this, indeed, that the whole procedure would be absolutely meaningless to us, were not a real world revealed in our experience as it is.

He who has attained to this insight into the nature of time is in a position to offer what seem to be satisfactory solutions to the problems which have been brought forward above.

(1) He can see, thus, why it is absurd to speak of any portion of time as becoming nonexistent. Time is nothing else than an order, a great system of relations. One cannot drop out certain of these and leave the rest unchanged, for the latter imply the former. Day-after-to-morrow would not be day-after-to-morrow, if to-morrow did not lie between it and to-day. To speak of dropping out to-morrow and leaving it the time it was conceived to be is mere nonsense.

(2) He can see why it does not indicate a measureless conceit for a man to be willing to say that time is infinite. One who says this need not be supposed to be acquainted with the whole past and future history of the real world, of which time is an aspect. We constantly abstract from things, and consider only the order of their changes, and in this order itself there is no reason why one should set a limit at some point; indeed, to set such a limit seems a gratuitous absurdity. He who says that time is infinite does not say much; he is not affirming the existence of some sort of a thing; he is merely affirming a theoretical possibility, and is it not a theoretical possibility that there may be an endless succession of real changes in a real world?

(3) It is evident, furthermore, that, when one has grasped firmly the significance of the distinction between apparent time and real time, one may with a clear conscience speak of time as infinitely divisible. Of course, the time directly given in any single experience, the minute or the second of which we are conscious as it passes, cannot be regarded as composed of an infinite number of parts. We are not directly conscious of these subdivisions, and it is a monstrous assumption to maintain that they must be present in the minute or second as perceived.

But no such single experience of duration constitutes what we mean by real time. We have seen that real time is the time occupied by the changes in real things, and the question is, How far can one go in the subdivision of this time?

Now, the touch thing which usually is for us in common life the real thing is not the real thing for science; it is the appearance under which the real world of atoms and molecules reveals itself. The atom is not directly perceivable, and we may assign to its motions a space so small that no one could possibly perceive it as space, as a something with part out of part, a something with a here and a there. But, as has been before pointed out (section 26), this does not prevent us from believing the atom and the space in which it moves to be real, and we can *represent* them to ourselves as we can the things and the spaces with which we have to do in common life.

It is with time just as it is with space. We can perceive an inch to have parts; we cannot perceive a thousandth of an inch to have parts, if we can perceive it at all; but we can represent it to ourselves as extended, that is, we can let an experience which is extended stand for it, and can dwell upon the parts of that. We can perceive a second to have duration; we cannot perceive a thousandth of a second to have duration; but we can conceive it as having duration, *i.e.* we can let some experience of duration stand for it and serve as its representative.

It is, then, reasonable to speak of the space covered by the vibration of an atom, and it is equally reasonable to speak of the time taken up by its vibration. It is not necessary to believe that the duration that we actually experience as a second must itself be capable of being divided up into the number of parts indicated by the denominator of the fraction that we use in indicating such a time, and that each of these parts must be perceived as duration.

There is, then, a sense in which we may affirm that time is infinitely divisible. But we must remember that apparent time—the time presented in any single experience of duration—is never infinitely divisible; and that real time, in any save a relative sense of the word, is not a single experience of duration at all. It is a recognition of the fact that experiences of duration may be substituted for each other without assignable limit.

(4) But what shall we say to the last problem—to the question how we can be conscious of time at all, when the parts of time are all successive? How can we even have a consciousness of "crude" time, of apparent time, of duration in any sense of the word, when duration must be made up of moments no two of which can exist together and no one of which alone can constitute time? The past is not now, the future is not yet, the present is a mere point, as we are told, and cannot have parts. If we are conscious of time as past, present, and future, must we not be conscious of a series as a series when every member of it save one is nonexistent? Can a man be conscious of the nonexistent?

The difficulty does seem a serious one, and yet I venture to affirm that, if we examine it carefully, we shall see that it is a difficulty of our own devising. The argument quietly makes an assumption—and makes it gratuitously—with which any consciousness of duration is incompatible, and then asks us how there can be such a thing as a consciousness of duration.

The assumption is that *we can be conscious only of the existent*, and this, written out a little more at length, reads as follows: *we can be conscious only of the now existent*, or, in other words *of the present.*

Of course, this determines from the outset that we cannot be conscious of the past and the future, of duration.

The past and the future are, to be sure, nonexistent from the point of view of the present; but it should be remarked as well that the present is nonexistent from the point of view of the past or the future. If we are talking of time at all we are talking of that no two parts of which are simultaneous; it would be absurd to speak of a past that existed simultaneously with the present, just as it would be absurd to speak of a present existing simultaneously with the past. But we should not deny to past, present, and future, respectively, their appropriate existence; nor is it by any means self-evident that there cannot be a consciousness of past, present, and future as such.

We fall in with the assumption, it seems, because we know very well that we are not directly conscious of a remote past and a remote future. We represent these to ourselves by means of some proxy—we have present memories of times long past and present anticipations of what will be in the time to come. Moreover, we use the word "present" very loosely; we say the present year, the present day, the present hour, the present minute, or the present second. When we use the word thus loosely, there seems no reason for believing that there should be such a thing as a direct consciousness that extends beyond the present. It appears reasonable to say: No one can be conscious save of the present.

It should be remembered, however, that the generous present of common discourse is by no means identical with the ideal point between past and future dealt with in the argument under discussion. We all say: I now see that the cloud is moving; I now see that the snow is falling. But there can be no moving, no falling, no change, in the timeless "now" with which we have been concerned. Is there any evidence whatever that we are shut up, for all our immediate knowledge, to such a "now"? There is none whatever.

The fact is that this timeless "now" is a product of reflective thought and not a something of which we are directly conscious. It is an ideal point in the real time of which this chapter has treated, the time that is in a certain sense infinitely divisible. It is first cousin to the ideal mathematical point, the mere limit between two lines, a something not perceptible to any sense. We have a tendency to carry over to it what we recognize to be true of the very different present of common discourse, a present which we distinguish from past and future in a somewhat loose way, but a present in which there certainly is the consciousness of change, of duration. And when we do this, we dig for ourselves a pit into which we proceed to fall.

We may, then, conclude that we are directly conscious of more than the present, in the sense in which Augustine used the word. We are conscious of *time*, of "crude" time, and from this we can pass to a knowledge of real time, and can determine its parts with precision.

[1] Book XI, Chapters 14 and 15.

III. PROBLEMS TOUCHING THE MIND
CHAPTER VIII
WHAT IS THE MIND?

30. PRIMITIVE NOTIONS OF MIND.—The soul or mind, that something to which we refer sensations and ideas of all sorts, is an object that men do not seem to know very clearly and definitely, though they feel so sure of its existence that they regard it as the height of folly to call it in question. That he has a mind, no man doubts; what his mind is, he may be quite unable to say.

We have seen (section 7) that children, when quite young, can hardly be said to recognize that they have minds at all. This does not mean that what is mental is not given in their experience. They know that they must open their eyes to see things, and must lay their hands upon them to feel them; they have had pains and pleasures, memories and fancies. In short, they have within their reach all the materials needed in framing a conception of the mind, and in drawing clearly the distinction between their minds and external things. Nevertheless, they are incapable of using these materials; their attention is engrossed with what is physical,—with their own bodies and the bodies of others, with the things that they can eat, with the toys with which they can play, and the like. It is only later that there emerges even a tolerably clear conception of a self or mind different from the physical and contrasted with it.

Primitive man is almost as material in his thinking as is the young child. Of this we have traces in many of the words which have come to be applied to the mind. Our word "spirit" is from the Latin *spiritus*, originally a breeze. The Latin word for the soul, the word used by the great philosophers all through the Middle Ages, *anima* (Greek, anemos), has the same significance. In the Greek New Testament, the word used for spirit (pneuma) carries a similar suggestion. When we are told in the Book of Genesis that "man became a living soul," we may read the word literally "a breath."

37

What more natural than that the man who is just awakening to a consciousness of that elusive entity the mind should confuse it with that breath which is the most striking outward and visible sign that distinguishes a living man from a dead one?

That those who first tried to give some scientific account of the soul or mind conceived it as a material thing, and that it was sufficiently common to identify it with the breath, we know from direct evidence. A glance at the Greek philosophy, to which we owe so much that is of value in our intellectual life, is sufficient to disclose how difficult it was for thinking men to attain to a higher conception.

Thus, Anaximenes of Miletus, who lived in the sixth century before Christ, says that "our soul, which is air, rules us." A little later, Heraclitus, a man much admired for the depth of his reflections, maintains that the soul is a fiery vapor, evidently identifying it with the warm breath of the living creature. In the fifth century, B.C., Anaxagoras, who accounts for the ordering of the elements into a system of things by referring to the activity of Mind or Reason, calls mind "the finest of things," and it seems clear that he did not conceive of it as very different in nature from the other elements which enter into the constitution of the world.

Democritus of Abdera (between 460 and 360 B.C.), that great investigator of nature and brilliant writer, developed a materialistic doctrine that admits the existence of nothing save atoms and empty space. He conceived the soul to consist of fine, smooth, round atoms, which are also atoms of fire. These atoms are distributed through the whole body, but function differently in different places—in the brain they give us thought, in the heart, anger, and in the liver, desire. Life lasts just so long as we breathe in and breathe out such atoms.

The doctrine of Democritus was taken up by Epicurus, who founded his school three hundred years before Christ—a school which lived and prospered for a very long time. Those who are interested in seeing how a materialistic psychology can be carried out in detail by an ingenious mind should read the curious account of the mind presented in his great poem, "On Nature," by the Roman poet Lucretius, an ardent Epicurean, who wrote in the first century B.C.

The school which we commonly think of contrasting with the Epicurean, and one which was founded at about the same time, is that of the Stoics. Certainly the Stoics differed in many things from the Epicureans; their view of the world, and of the life of man, was a much nobler one; but they were uncompromising materialists, nevertheless, and identified the soul with the warm breath that animates man.

31. THE MIND AS IMMATERIAL.—It is scarcely too much to say that the Greek philosophy as a whole impresses the modern mind as representing the thought of a people to whom it was not unnatural to think of the mind as being a breath, a fire, a collection of atoms, a something material. To be sure, we cannot accuse those twin stars that must ever remain the glory of literature and science, Plato and Aristotle, of being materialists. Plato (427-347, B.C.) distributes, it is true, the three-fold soul, which he allows man, in various parts of the human body, in a way that at least suggests the Democritean distribution of mind-atoms. The lowest soul is confined beneath the diaphragm; the one next in rank has its seat in the chest; and the highest, the rational soul, is enthroned in the head. However, he has said quite enough about this last to indicate clearly that he conceived it to be free from all taint of materiality.

As for Aristotle (384-322, B.C.), who also distinguished between the lower psychical functions and the higher, we find him sometimes speaking of soul and body in such a way as to lead men to ask themselves whether he is really speaking of two things at all; but when he specifically treats of the *nous* or reason, he insists upon its complete detachment from everything material. Man's reason is not subjected to the fate of the lower psychical functions, which, as the "form" of the body, perish with the body; it enters from without, and it endures after the body has passed away. It is interesting to note, however, an occasional lapse even in Aristotle. When he comes to speak of the relation to the world of the Divine Mind, the First Cause of Motion, which he conceives as pure Reason, he represents it as *touching* the world, although it remains itself*untouched*. We seem to find here just a flavor—an inconsistent one—of the material.

Such reflections as those of Plato and Aristotle bore fruit in later ages. When we come down to Plotinus the Neo-Platonist (204-269, A.D.), we have left the conception of the soul as a warm breath, or as composed of fine round atoms, far behind. It has become curiously abstract and incomprehensible. It is described as an immaterial substance This substance is, in a sense, in the body, or, at least, it is present to the body. But it is not in the body as material things are in this place or in that. *It is as a whole in the whole body, and it is as a whole in every part of the body.* Thus the soul may be regarded as divisible, since it is distributed throughout the body; but it must also be regarded as indivisible, since it is wholly in every part.

Let the man to whom such sentences as these mean anything rejoice in the meaning that he is able to read into them! If he can go as far as Plotinus, perhaps he can go as far as

Cassiodorus (477-570, A.D.), and maintain that the soul is not merely as a whole in every part of the body, but is wholly in each of its own parts.

Upon reading such statements one's first impulse is to exclaim: How is it possible that men of sense should be led to speak in this irresponsible way? and when they do speak thus, is it conceivable that other men should seriously occupy themselves with what they say?

But if one has the historic sense, and knows something of the setting in which such doctrines come to the birth, one cannot regard it as remarkable that men of sense should urge them. No one coins them independently out of his own brain; little by little men are impelled along the path that leads to such conclusions. Plotinus was a careful student of the philosophers that preceded him. He saw that mind must be distinguished from matter, and he saw that what is given a location in space, in the usual sense of the words, is treated like a material thing. On the other hand, he had the common experience that we all have of a relation between mind and body. How do justice to this relation, and yet not materialize mind?

What he tried to do is clear, and it seems equally clear that he had good reason for trying to do it. But it appears to us now that what he actually did was to make of the mind or soul a something very like an inconsistent bit of matter, that is somehow in space, and yet not exactly in space, a something that can be in two places at once, a logical monstrosity. That his doctrine did not meet with instant rejection was due to the fact, already alluded to, that our experience of the mind is something rather dim and elusive. It is not easy for a man to say what it is, and, hence, it is not easy for a man to say what it is not.

The doctrine of Plotinus passed over to Saint Augustine, and from him it passed to the philosophers of the Middle Ages. How extremely difficult it has been for the world to get away from it at all, is made clearly evident in the writings of that remarkable man Descartes.

Descartes wrote in the seventeenth century. The long sleep of the Middle Ages was past, and the several sciences had sprung into a vigorous and independent life. It was not enough for Descartes to describe the relation of mind and body in the loose terms that had prevailed up to his time. He had made a careful study of anatomy, and he realized that the brain is a central organ to which messages are carried by the nerves from all parts of the body. He knew that an injury to the nerve might prevent the receipt of a message, *i.e.* he knew that a conscious sensation did not come into being until something happened in the brain.

Nor was he content merely to refer the mind to the brain in a general way. He found the "little pineal gland" in the midst of the brain to be in what he regarded as an admirable position to serve as the seat of the soul. To this convenient little central office he relegated it; and he describes in a way that may to-day well provoke a smile the movements that the soul imparts to the pineal gland, making it incline itself in this direction and in that, and making it push the "animal spirits," the fluid contained in the cavities of the brain, towards various "pores."

Thus he writes:[1] "Let us, then, conceive of the soul as having her chief seat in the little gland that is in the middle of the brain, whence she radiates to all the rest of the body by means of the spirits, the nerves, and even the blood, which, participating in the impressions of the spirits, can carry them through the arteries to all the members." And again: "Thus, when the soul wills to call anything to remembrance, this volition brings it about that the gland, inclining itself successively in different directions, pushes the spirits towards divers parts of the brain, until they find the part which has the traces that the object which one wishes to recollect has left there."

We must admit that Descartes' scientific studies led him to make this mind that sits in the little pineal gland something very material. It is spoken of as though it pushed the gland about; it is affected by the motions of the gland, as though it were a bit of matter. It seems to be a less inconsistent thing than the "all in the whole body" soul of Plotinus; but it appears to have purchased its comprehensibility at the expense of its immateriality.

Shall we say that Descartes frankly repudiated the doctrine that had obtained for so many centuries? We cannot say that; he still held to it. But how could he? The reader has perhaps remarked above that he speaks of the soul as having her *chief* seat in the pineal gland. It seems odd that he should do so, but he still held, even after he had come to his definite conclusions as to the soul's seat, to the ancient doctrine that the soul is united to all the parts of the body "conjointly." He could not wholly repudiate a venerable tradition.

We have seen, thus, that men first conceived of the mind as material and later came to rebel against such a conception. But we have seen, also, that the attempt to conceive it as immaterial was not wholly successful. It resulted in a something that we may describe as inconsistently material rather than as not material at all.

32. MODERN COMMON SENSE NOTIONS OF THE MIND.—Under this heading I mean to sum up the opinions as to the nature of the mind usually held by the intelligent persons about us to-day who make no claim to be regarded as philosophers. Is it not true that a great many of them believe:—

39

(1) That the mind is in the body?
(2) That it acts and reacts with matter?
(3) That it is a substance with attributes?
(4) That it is nonextended and immaterial?

I must remark at the outset that this collection of opinions is by no means something gathered by the plain man from his own experience. These opinions are the echoes of old philosophies. They are a heritage from the past, and have become the common property of all intelligent persons who are even moderately well-educated. Their sources have been indicated in the preceding sections; but most persons who cherish them have no idea of their origin.

Men are apt to suppose that these opinions seem reasonable to them merely for the reason that they find in their own experience evidence of their truth. But this is not so.

Have we not seen above how long it took men to discover that they must not think of the mind as being a breath, or a flame, or a collection of material atoms? The men who erred in this way were abler than most of us can pretend to be, and they gave much thought to the matter. And when at last it came to be realized that mind must not thus be conceived as material, those who endeavored to conceive it as something else gave, after their best efforts, a very queer account of it indeed.

Is it in the face of such facts reasonable to suppose that our friends and acquaintances, who strike us as having reflective powers in nowise remarkable, have independently arrived at the conception that the mind is a nonextended and immaterial substance? Surely they have not thought all this out for themselves. They have taken up and appropriated unconsciously notions which were in the air, so to speak. They have inherited their doctrines, not created them. It is well to remember this, for it may make us the more willing to take up and examine impartially what we have uncritically turned into articles of belief.

The first two articles, namely, that the mind is in the body and that it acts upon, and is acted upon by, material things, I shall discuss at length in the next chapter. Here I pause only to point out that the plain man does not put the mind into the body quite unequivocally. I think it would surprise him to be told that a line might be drawn through two heads in such a way as to transfix two minds. And I remark, further, that he has no clear idea of what it means for mind to act upon body or body to act upon mind. How does an immaterial thing set a material thing in motion? Can it touch it? Can it push it? Then what does it do?

But let us pass on to the last two articles of faith mentioned above.

We all draw the distinction between *substance* and its *attributes* or *qualities*. The distinction was remarked and discussed many centuries ago, and much has been written upon it. I take up the ruler on my desk; it is recognized at once as a bit of wood. How? It has such and such qualities. My paper-knife is of silver. How do I know it? It has certain other qualities. I speak of my mind. How do I know that I have a mind? I have sensations and ideas. If I experienced no mental phenomena of any sort, evidence of the existence of a mind would be lacking.

Now, whether I am concerned with the ruler, with the paper-knife, or with the mind, have I direct evidence of the existence of anything more than the whole group of qualities? Do I ever perceive the substance?

In the older philosophy, the substance (*substantia*) was conceived to be a something not directly perceived, but only inferred to exist—a something underlying the qualities of things and, as it were, holding them together. It was believed in by philosophers who were quite ready to admit that they could not tell anything about it. For example, John Locke (1632-1704), the English philosopher, holds to it stoutly, and yet describes it as a mere "we know not what," whose function it is to hold together the bundles of qualities that constitute the things we know.

In the modern philosophy men still distinguish between substance and qualities. It is a useful distinction, and we could scarcely get on without it. But an increasing number of thoughtful persons repudiate the old notion of substance altogether.

We may, they say, understand by the word "substance" the whole group of qualities *as a group*—not merely the qualities that are revealed at a given time, but all those that we have reason to believe a fuller knowledge would reveal. In short, we may understand by it just what is left when the "we know not what" of the Lockian has been discarded.

This notion of substance we may call the more modern one; yet we can hardly say that it is the notion of the plain man. He does not make very clear to himself just what is in his thought, but I think we do him no injustice in maintaining that he is something of a Lockian, even if he has never heard of Locke. The Lockian substance is, as the reader has seen, a sort of "unknowable."

And now for the doctrine that the mind is nonextended and immaterial. With these affirmations we may heartily agree; but we must admit that the plain man enunciates them without having a very definite idea of what the mind is.

He regards as in his mind all his sensations and ideas, all his perceptions and mental images of things. Now, suppose I close my eyes and picture to myself a barber's pole. Where is the image? We say, in the mind. Is it extended? We feel impelled to answer, No. But it certainly *seems* to be extended; the white and the red upon it appear undeniably side by side. May I assert that this mental image has no extension whatever? Must I deny to it *parts*, or assert that its parts are not side by side?

It seems odd to maintain that a something as devoid of parts as is a mathematical point should yet appear to have parts and to be extended. On the other hand, if we allow the image to be extended, how can we refer it to a nonextended mind?

To such questions as these, I do not think that the plain man has an answer. That they can be answered, I shall try to show in the last section of this chapter. But one cannot answer them until one has attained to rather a clear conception of what is meant by the mind.

And until one has attained to such a conception, the statement that the mind is immaterial must remain rather vague and indefinite. As we saw above, even the Plotinic soul was inconsistently material rather than immaterial. It was not excluded from space; it was referred to space in an absurd way. The mind as common sense conceives it, is the successor of this Plotinic soul, and seems to keep a flavor of what is material after all. This will come out in the next chapter, where we shall discuss mind and body.

33. THE PSYCHOLOGIST AND THE MIND.—When we ask how the psychologist conceives of the mind, we must not forget that psychologists are many and that they differ more or less from each other in their opinions. When we say "the psychologist" believes this or that, we mean usually no more than that the opinion referred to is prevalent among men of that class, or that it is the opinion of those whom we regard as its more enlightened members.

Taking the words in this somewhat loose sense, I shall ask what the psychologist's opinion is touching the four points set forth in the preceding section. How far does he agree with the plain man?

(1) There can be no doubt that he refers the mind to the body in some way, although he may shake his head over the use of the word "in."

(2) As to whether the mind acts and reacts with matter, in any sense of the words analogous to that in which they are commonly used, there is a division in the camp. Some affirm such interaction; some deny it. The matter will be discussed in the next chapter.

(3) The psychologist—the more modern one—inclines to repudiate any substance or substratum of the sort accepted in the Middle Ages and believed in by many men now. To him the mind is the whole complex of mental phenomena in their interrelations. In other words, the mind is not an unknown and indescribable something that is merely inferred; it is something revealed in consciousness and open to observation.

(4) The psychologist is certainly not inclined to regard the mind or any idea belonging to it as material or as extended. But he does recognize implicitly, if not explicitly, that ideas are composite. To him, as to the plain man, the image held in the memory or imagination *seems* to be extended, and he can distinguish its parts. He does not do much towards clearing away the difficulty alluded to at the close of the last section. It remains for the metaphysician to do what he can with it, and to him we must turn if we wish light upon this obscure subject.

34. THE METAPHYSICIAN AND THE MIND.—I have reserved for the next chapter the first two points mentioned as belonging to the plain man's doctrine of the mind. In what sense the mind may be said to be in the body, and how it may be conceived to be related to the body, are topics that deserve to be treated by themselves in a chapter on "Mind and Body." Here I shall consider what the metaphysician has to say about the mind as substance, and about the mind as nonextended and immaterial.

It has been said that the Lockian substance is really an "unknowable." No one pretends to have experience of it; it is revealed to no sense; it is, indeed, a name for a mere nothing, for when we abstract from a thing, in thought, every single quality, we find that there is left to us nothing whatever.

We cannot say that the substance, in this sense of the word, is the *reality* of which the qualities are *appearances*. In Chapter V we saw just what we may legitimately mean by realities and appearances, and it was made clear that an unknowable of any sort cannot possibly be the reality to which this or that appearance is referred. Appearances and realities are experiences which are observed to be related in certain ways. That which is not open to observation at all, that of which we have, and can have, no experience, we have no reason to call the reality of anything. We have, in truth, no reason to talk about it at all, for we know nothing whatever about it; and when we do talk about it, it is because we are laboring under a delusion.

This is equally true whether we are concerned with the substance of material things or with the substance of minds. An "unknowable" is an "unknowable" in any case, and we may simply discard it. We lose nothing by so doing, for one cannot lose what one has never had, and what, by hypothesis, one can never have. The loss of a mere word should occasion us no regret.

Now, we have seen that we do not lose the world of real material things in rejecting the "Unknowable" (Chapter V). The things are complexes of qualities, of physical phenomena; and the more we know about these, the more do we know about real things.

But we have also seen (Chapter IV) that physical phenomena are not the only phenomena of which we have experience. We are conscious of mental phenomena as well, of the phenomena of the subjective order, of sensations and ideas. Why not admit that these *constitute* the mind, as physical phenomena constitute the things which belong to the external world?

He who says this says no more than that the mind is known and is knowable. It is what it is perceived to be; and the more we know of mental phenomena, the more do we know of the mind. Shall we call the mind as thus known a *substance*? That depends on the significance which we give to this word. It is better, perhaps, to avoid it, for it is fatally easy to slip into the old use of the word, and then to say, as men have said, that we do not know the mind as it is, but only as it appears to us to be—that we do not know the reality, but only its appearances.

And if we keep clearly before us the view of the mind which I am advocating, we shall find an easy way out of the difficulties that seem to confront us when we consider it as nonextended and immaterial.

Certain complexes of mental phenomena—for example, the barber's pole above alluded to—certainly appear to be extended. Are they really extended? If I imagine a tree a hundred feet high, is it really a hundred feet high? Has it any real size at all?

Our problem melts away when we realize what we mean by this "real size." In Chapter V, I have distinguished between apparent space and real space. Real space is, as was pointed out, the "plan" of the real physical world. To occupy any portion of real space, a thing must be a real external thing; that is, the experiences constituting it must belong to the objective order, they must not be of the class called mental. We all recognize this, in a way. We know that a real material foot rule cannot be applied to an imaginary tree. We say, How big did the tree seen in a dream *seem*; we do not say, How big was it *really*? If we did ask such a question, we should be puzzled to know where to look for an answer.

And this for a very good reason. He who asks: How big was that imaginary tree really? asks, in effect: How much real space did the unreal tree fill? The question is a foolish one. It assumes that phenomena not in the objective order are in the objective order. As well ask how a color smells or how a sound tastes. When we are dealing with the material we are not dealing with the mental, and we must never forget this.

The tree imagined or seen in a dream seems extended. Its extension is *apparent*extension, and this apparent extension has no place in the external world whatever. But we must not confound this apparent extension with a real mathematical point, and call the tree nonextended in this sense. If we do this we are still in the old error—we have not gotten away from real space, but have substituted position in that space for extension in that space. Nothing mental can have even a position in real space. To do that it would have to be a real thing in the sense indicated.

Let us, then, agree with the plain man in affirming that the mind is nonextended, but let us avoid misconception. The mind is constituted of experiences of the subjective order. None of these are in space—real space. But some of them have apparent extension, and we must not overlook all that this implies.

Now for the mind as immaterial. We need not delay long over this point. If we mean by the mind the phenomena of the subjective order, and by what is material the phenomena of the objective order, surely we may and must say that the mind is immaterial. The two classes of phenomena separate themselves out at once.

[1] "The Passions," Articles 34 and 42.

CHAPTER IX
MIND AND BODY

35. IS THE MIND IN THE BODY?—There was a time, as we have seen in the last chapter (section 30), when it did not seem at all out of the way to think of the mind as in the body, and very literally in the body. He who believes the mind to be a breath, or a something composed of material atoms, can conceive it as being in the body as unequivocally as chairs can be in a room. Breath can be inhaled and exhaled; atoms can be in the head, or in the chest, or the heart, or anywhere else in the animal economy. There is nothing dubious about this sense of the preposition "in."

But we have also seen (section 31) that, as soon as men began to realize that the mind is not material, the question of its presence in the body became a serious problem. If I say that a chair is in a room, I say what is comprehensible to every one. It is assumed that it is in a particular place in the room and is not in some other place. If, however, I say that the chair is, as a whole, in every part of the room at once, I seem to talk nonsense. This is what Plotinus and those who came after him said about the mind. Are their statements any the less nonsensical because they are talking about minds? When one speaks about things mental, one must not take leave of good sense and utter unmeaning phrases.

If minds are enough like material things to be in anything, they must be in things in some intelligible sense of the word. It will not do to say: I use the word "in," but I do not really mean *in*. If the meaning has disappeared, why continue to use the word? It can only lead to mystification.

Descartes seemed to come back to something like an intelligible meaning when he put the mind in the pineal gland in the brain. Yet, as we have seen, he clung to the old conception. He could not go back to the frank materialization of mind.

And the plain man to-day labors under the same difficulty. He puts the mind in the body, in the brain, but he does not put it there frankly and unequivocally. It is in the brain and yet not exactly in the brain. Let us see if this is not the case.

If we ask him: Does the man who wags his head move his mind about? does he who mounts a step raise his mind some inches? does he who sits down on a chair lower his mind? I think we shall find that he hesitates in his answers. And if we go on to say: Could a line be so drawn as to pass through your image of me and my image of you, and to measure their distance from one another? I think he will say, No. He does not regard minds and their ideas as existing in space in this fashion.

Furthermore, it would not strike the plain man as absurd if we said to him: Were our senses far more acute than they are, it is conceivable that we should be able to perceive every atom in a given human body, and all its motions. But would he be willing to admit that an increase in the sharpness of sense would reveal to us directly the mind connected with such a body? It is not, then, in the body as the atoms are. It cannot be seen or touched under any conceivable circumstances. What can it mean, hence, to say that it is*there*? Evidently, the word is used in a peculiar sense, and the plain man cannot help us to a clear understanding of it.

His position becomes intelligible to us when we realize that he has inherited the doctrine that the mind is immaterial, and that he struggles, at the same time, with the tendency so natural to man to conceive it after the analogy of things material. He thinks of it as in the body, and, nevertheless, tries to dematerialize this "in." His thought is sufficiently vague, and is inconsistent, as might be expected.

If we will bear in mind what was said in the closing section of the last chapter, we can help him over his difficulty. That mind and body are related there can be no doubt. But should we use the word "in" to express this relation?

The body is a certain group of phenomena in the objective order; that is, it is a part of the external world. The mind consists of experiences in the subjective order. We have seen that no mental phenomenon can occupy space—real space, the space of the external world—and that it cannot even have a position in space (section 34). As mental, it is excluded from the objective order altogether. The mind is not, then, strictly speaking, *in*the body, although it is related to it. It remains, of course, to ask ourselves how we ought to conceive the relation. This we shall do later in the present chapter.

But, it may be said, it would sound odd to deny that the mind is in the body. Does not every one use the expression? What can we substitute for it? I answer: If it is convenient to use the expression let us continue to do so. Men must talk so as to be understood. But let us not perpetuate error, and, as occasion demands it, let us make clear to ourselves and to others what we have a right to understand by this *in* when we use it.

36. THE DOCTRINE OF THE INTERACTIONIST.—There is no man who does not know that his mind is related to his body as it is not to other material things. We open our eyes, and we see things; we stretch out our hand, and we feel them; our body receives a blow, and we feel pain; we wish to move, and the muscles are set in motion.

These things are matters of common experience. We all perceive, in other words, that there is an interaction, in some sense of the term, between mind and body.

But it is important to realize that one may be quite well aware of all such facts, and yet may have very vague notions of what one means by body and by mind, and may have no definite theory at all of the sort of relation that obtains between them. The philosopher tries to attain to a clearer conception of these things. His task, be it remembered, is to analyze and explain, not to deny, the experiences which are the common property of mankind.

In the present day the two theories of the relation of mind and body that divide the field between them and stand opposed to each other are *interactionism* and *parallelism*. I have used the word "interaction" a little above in a loose sense to indicate our common experience of the fact that we become conscious of certain changes brought about in our body, and that our purposes realize themselves in action. But every one who accepts this fact is not necessarily an interactionist. The latter is a man who holds a certain more or less definite theory as to what is implied by the fact. Let us take a look at his doctrine.

Physical things interact. A billiard ball in motion strikes one which has been at rest; the former loses its motion, the latter begins to roll away. We explain the occurrence by a reference to the laws of mechanics; that is to say, we point out that it is merely an instance of the uniform behavior of matter in motion under such and such circumstances. We distinguish between the state of things at one instant and the state of things at the next, and we call the former *cause* and the latter *effect*.

It should be observed that both cause and effect here belong to the one order, the objective order. They have their place in the external world. Both the balls are material things; their motion, and the space in which they move, are aspects of the external world.

If the balls did not exist in the same space, if the motion of the one could not be towards or away from the other, if contact were impossible, we would manifestly have no interaction *in the sense of the word employed above*. As it is, the interaction of physical things is something that we can describe with a good deal of definiteness. Things interact in that they stand in certain physical relations, and undergo changes of relations according to certain laws.

Now, to one who conceives the mind in a grossly material way, the relation of mind and body can scarcely seem to be a peculiar problem, different from the problem of the relation of one physical thing to another. If my mind consists of atoms disseminated through my body, its presence in the body appears as unequivocal as the presence of a dinner in a man who has just risen from the table. Nor can the interaction of mind and matter present any unusual difficulties, for mind is matter. Atoms may be conceived to approach each other, to clash, to rearrange themselves. Interaction of mind and body is nothing else than an interaction of bodies. One is not forced to give a new meaning to the word.

When, however, one begins to think of the mind as immaterial, the case is very different. How shall we conceive an immaterial thing to be related to a material one?

Descartes placed the mind in the pineal gland, and in so far he seemed to make its relation to the gland similar to that between two material things. When he tells us that the soul brings it about that the gland bends in different directions, we incline to view the occurrence as very natural—is not the soul in the gland?

But, on the other hand, Descartes also taught that the essence of mind is *thought* and the essence of body is *extension*. He made the two natures so different from each other that men began to ask themselves how the two things could interact at all. The mind wills, said one philosopher, but that volition does not set matter in motion; when the mind wills, God brings about the appropriate change in material things. The mind perceives things, said another, but that is not because they affect it directly; it sees things in God. Ideas and things, said a third, constitute two independent series; no idea can cause a change in things, and no thing can cause a change in ideas.

The interactionist is a man who refuses to take any such turn as these philosophers. His doctrine is much nearer to that of Descartes than it is to any of theirs. He uses the one word "interaction" to describe the relation between material things and also the relation between mind and body, nor does he dwell upon the difference between the two. He insists that mind and matter stand in the one causal nexus; that a change in the outside world may be the *cause* of a perception coming into being in a mind, and that a volition may be the *cause* of changes in matter.

What shall we call the plain man? I think we may call him an interactionist in embryo. The stick in his hand knocks an apple off of the tree; his hand seems to him to be set in motion because he wills it. The relation between his volition and the motion of his hand appears to him to be of much the same sort as that between the motion of the stick and the fall of the apple. In each case he thinks he has to do with the relation of cause and effect.

The opponent of the interactionist insists, however, that the plain man is satisfied with this view of the matter only because he has not completely stripped off the tendency to conceive the mind as a material thing. And he accuses the interactionist of having fallen a prey to the same weakness.

Certainly, it is not difficult to show that the interactionists write as though the mind were material, and could be somewhere in space. The late Dr. McCosh fairly represents the thought of many, and he was capable of expressing himself as follows;[1] "It may be difficult to ascertain the exact point or surface at which the mind and body come together and influence each other, in particular, how far into the body (Descartes without proof thought it to be in the pineal gland), but it is certain, that when they do meet mind knows body as having its essential properties of extension and resisting energy."

44

How can an immaterial thing be located at some point or surface within the body? How can a material thing and an immaterial thing "come together" at a point or surface? And if they cannot come together, what have we in mind when we say they interact?

The parallelist, for it is he who opposes interactionism, insists that we must not forget that mental phenomena do not belong to the same order as physical phenomena. He points out that, when we make the word "interaction" cover the relations of mental phenomena to physical phenomena as well as the relations of the latter to each other, we are assimilating heedlessly facts of two different kinds and are obliterating an important distinction. He makes the same objection to calling the relations between mental phenomena and physical phenomena *causal*. If the relation of a volition to the movement of the arm is not the same as that of a physical cause to its physical effect, why, he argues, do you disguise the difference by calling them by the same name?

37. THE DOCTRINE OF THE PARALLELIST.—Thus, the parallelist is a man who is so impressed by the gulf between physical facts and mental facts that he refuses to regard them as parts of the one order of causes and effects. You cannot, he claims, make a single chain out of links so diverse.

Some part of a human body receives a blow; a message is carried along a sensory nerve and reaches the brain; from the brain a message is sent out along a motor nerve to a group of muscles; the muscles contract, and a limb is set in motion. The immediate effects of the blow, the ingoing message, the changes in the brain, the outgoing message, the contraction of the muscles—all these are physical facts. One and all may be described as motions in matter.

But the man who received the blow becomes conscious that he was struck, and both interactionist and parallelist regard him as becoming conscious of it when the incoming message reaches some part of the brain. What shall be done with this consciousness? The interactionist insists that it must be regarded as a link in the physical chain of causes and effects—he breaks the chain to insert it. The parallelist maintains that it is inconceivable that such an insertion should be made. He regards the physical series as complete in itself, and he places the consciousness, as it were, on a *parallel* line.

It must not be supposed that he takes this figure literally. It is his effort to avoid materializing the mind that forces him to hold the position which he does. To put the mind in the brain is to make of it a material thing; to make it parallel to the brain, in the literal sense of the word, would be just as bad. All that we may understand him to mean is that mental phenomena and physical, although they are related, cannot be built into the one series of causes and effects. He is apt to speak of them as *concomitant*.

We must not forget that neither parallelist nor interactionist ever dreams of repudiating our common experiences of the relations of mental phenomena and physical. Neither one will, if he is a man of sense, abandon the usual ways of describing such experiences. Whatever his theory, he will still say: I am suffering because I struck my hand against that table; I sat down because I chose to do so. His doctrine is not supposed to deny the truth contained in such statements; it is supposed only to give a fuller understanding of it. Hence, we cannot condemn either doctrine simply by an uncritical appeal to such statements and to the experiences they represent. We must look much deeper.

Now, what can the parallelist mean by *referring* sensations and ideas to the brain and yet denying that they are *in* the brain? What is this reference?

Let us come back to the experiences of the physical and the mental as they present themselves to the plain man. They have been discussed at length in Chapter IV. It was there pointed out that every one distinguishes without difficulty between sensations and things, and that every one recognizes explicitly or implicitly that a sensation is an experience referred in a certain way to the body.

When the eyes are open, we *see*; when the ears are open, we *hear*; when the hand is laid on things, we *feel*. How do we know that we are experiencing sensations? The setting tells us that. The experience in question is given together with an experience of the body. This is *concomitance of the mental and the physical* as it appears in the experience of us all; and from such experiences as these the philosopher who speaks of the concomitance of physical and mental phenomena must draw the whole meaning of the word.

Let us here sharpen a little the distinction between sensations and things. Standing at some distance from the tree, I see an apple fall to the ground. Were I only half as far away, my experience would not be exactly the same—I should have somewhat different sensations. As we have seen (section 17), the apparent sizes of things vary as we move, and this means that the quantity of sensation, when I observe the apple from a nearer point, is greater. The man of science tells me that the image which the object looked at projects upon the retina of the eye grows larger as we approach objects. The thing, then, may remain unchanged; our sensations will vary according to the impression which is made upon our body.

Again. When I have learned something of physics, I am ready to admit that, although light travels with almost inconceivable rapidity, still, its journey through space does take time. Hence the impression made upon my eye by the falling apple is not simultaneous with the fall itself; and if I stand far away it is made a little later than when I am near. In the case in point the difference is so slight as to pass unnoticed, but there are cases in which it seems apparent even to the unlearned that sensations arise later than the occurrences of which we take them to be the report.

Thus, I stand on a hill and watch a laborer striking with his sledge upon the distant railway. I hear the sound of the blow while I see his tool raised above his head. I account for this by saying that it has taken some time for the sound-waves to reach my ear, and I regard my sensation as arising only when this has been accomplished.

But this conclusion is not judged sufficiently accurate by the man of science. The investigations of the physiologist and the psychologist have revealed that the brain holds a peculiar place in the economy of the body. If the nerve which connects the sense organ with the brain be severed, the sensation does not arise. Injuries to the brain affect the mental life as injuries to other parts of the body do not. Hence, it is concluded that, to get the real time of the emergence of a sensation, we must not inquire merely when an impression was made upon the organ of sense, but must determine when the message sent along the nerve has reached some part of the brain. The resulting brain change is regarded as the true concomitant of the sensation. If there is a brain change of a certain kind, there is the corresponding sensation. It need hardly be said that no one knows as yet much about the brain motions which are supposed to be concomitants of sensations, although a good deal is said about them.

It is very important to remark that in all this no new meaning has been given to the word "concomitance." The plain man remarks that sensations and their changes must be referred to the body. With the body disposed in a certain way, he has sensations of a certain kind; with changes in the body, the sensations change. He does not perceive the sensations to be in the body. As I recede from a house I have a whole series of visual experiences differing from each other and ending in a faint speck which bears little resemblance to the experience with which I started. I have had, as we say, a series of sensations, or groups of such. Did any single group, did the experience which I had at any single moment, seem to me to be *in my body*? Surely not. Its relation to my body is other than that.

And when the man of science, instead of referring sensations vaguely to the body, refers them to the brain, the reference is of precisely the same nature. From our common experience of the relation of the physical and the mental he starts out. He has no other ground on which to stand. He can only mark the reference with greater exactitude.

I have been speaking of the relation of sensations to the brain. It is scarcely necessary for me to show that all other mental phenomena must be referred to the brain as well, and that the reference must be of the same nature. The considerations which lead us to refer ideas to the brain are set forth in our physiologies and psychologies. The effects of cerebral disease, injuries to the brain, etc., are too well known to need mention; and it is palpably as absurd to put ideas in the brain as it is to put sensations there.

Now, the parallelist, if he be a wise man, will not attempt to *explain* the reference of mental phenomena to the brain—to *explain* the relation between mind and matter. The relation appears to be unique. Certainly it is not identical with the relation between two material things. We explain things, in the common acceptation of the word, when we show that a case under consideration is an exemplification of some general law—when we show, in other words, that it does not stand alone. But this does stand alone, and is admitted to stand alone. We admit as much when we say that the mind is immaterial, and yet hold that it is related to the body. We cannot, then, ask for an *explanation* of the relation.

But this does not mean that the reference of mental phenomena to the body is a meaningless expression. We can point to those experiences of concomitance that we all have, distinguish them carefully from relations of another kind, and say: This is what the word means, whether it be used by the plain man or by the man of science.

I have said above: "If there is a brain change of a certain kind, there is the corresponding sensation." Perhaps the reader will feel inclined to say here: If you can say as much as this, why can you not go a little farther and call the brain change the *cause* of the sensation?

But he who speaks thus, forgets what has been said above about the uniqueness of the relation. In the objective order of our experiences, in the external world, we can distinguish between antecedents and consequents, between causes and their effects. The causes and their effects belong to the one order, they stand in the same series. The relation of the physical to the mental is, as we have seen, a different relation. Hence, the parallelist seems justified in objecting to the assimilation of the two. He prefers the word "concomitance," just because it marks the

46

difference. He does not mean to indicate that the relation is any the less uniform or dependable when he denies that it is causal.

38. IN WHAT SENSE MENTAL PHENOMENA HAVE A TIME AND PLACE.—We have seen in Chapters VI and VII what space and time—real space and time—are. They are the plan of the real external world and its changes; they are aspects of the objective order of experience.

To this order no mental phenomenon can belong. It cannot, as we have seen (section 35), occupy any portion of space or even have a location in space. It is equally true that no series of mental changes can occupy any portion of time, real time, or even fill a single moment in the stream of time. There are many persons to whom this latter statement will seem difficult of acceptance; but the relation of mental phenomena to space and to time is of the same sort, and we can consider the two together.

Psychologists speak unhesitatingly of the localization of sensations in the brain, and they talk as readily of the moment at which a sensation arises and of the duration of the sensation. What can they mean by such expressions?

We have seen that sensations are not in the brain, and their localization means only the determination of their concomitant physical phenomena, of the corresponding brain-change. And it ought to be clear even from what has been said above that, in determining the moment at which a sensation arises, we are determining only the time of the concomitant brain process. Why do we say that a sensation arises later than the moment at which an impression is made upon the organ of sense and earlier than the resulting movement of some group of muscles? Because the change in the brain, to which we refer the sensation, occurs later than the one and earlier than the other. This has a place in real time, it belongs to that series of world changes whose succession constitutes real time. If we ask *when* anything happened, we always refer to this series of changes. We try to determine its place in the world order.

Thus, we ask: When was Julius Caesar born? We are given a year and a day. How is the time which has elapsed since measured? By changes in the physical world, by revolutions of the earth about the sun. We ask: When did he conceive the plan of writing his Commentaries? If we get an answer at all, it must be an answer of the same kind—some point in the series of physical changes which occur in real time must be indicated. Where else should we look for an answer? In point of fact, we never do look elsewhere.

Again. We have distinguished between apparent space and real space (section 34). We have seen that, when we deny that a mental image can occupy any portion of space, we need not think of it as losing its parts and shrivelling to a point. We may still attribute to it apparent space; may affirm that it seems extended. Let us mark the same distinction when we consider time. The psychologist speaks of the duration of a sensation. Has it real duration? It is not in time at all, and, of course, it cannot, strictly speaking, occupy a portion of time. But we can try to measure the duration of the physical concomitant, and call this the real duration of the sensation.

We all distinguish between the real time of mental phenomena, in the sense indicated just above, and the apparent time. We know very well that the one may give us no true measure of the other. A sermon *seems* long; was it *really* long? There is only one way of measuring its real length. We must refer to the clock, to the sun, to some change in the physical world. We *seem* to live years in a dream; was the dream *really* a long one? The real length can only be determined, if at all, by a physical reference. Those apparent years of the dream have no place in the real time which is measured by the clock. We do not have to cut it and insert them somewhere. They belong to a different order, and cannot be inserted any more than the thought of a patch can be inserted in a rent in a real coat.

We see, thus, when we reflect upon the matter, that mental phenomena cannot, strictly speaking, be said to have a time and place. He who attributes these to them materializes them. But their physical concomitants have a time and place, and mental phenomena can be ordered by a reference to these. They can be assigned a time and place of existing in a special sense of the words not to be confounded with the sense in which we use them when we speak of the time and place of material things. This makes it possible to relate every mental phenomenon to the world system in a definite way, and to distinguish it clearly from every other, however similar.

We need not, when we come to understand this, change our usual modes of speech. We may still say: The pain I had two years ago is like the pain I have to-day; my sensation came into being at such a moment; my regret lasted two days. We speak that we may be understood; and such phrases express a truth, even if they are rather loose and inaccurate. But we must not be deceived by such phrases, and assume that they mean what they have no right to mean.

39. OBJECTIONS TO PARALLELISM.—What objections can be brought against parallelism? It is sometimes objected by the interactionist that it abandons the plain man's notion of the mind as a substance with its attributes, and makes of it a mere collection of mental

phenomena. It must be admitted that the parallelist usually holds a view which differs rather widely from that of the unlearned.

But even supposing this objection well taken, it can no longer be regarded as an objection specifically to the doctrine of parallelism, for the view of the mind in question is becoming increasingly popular, and it is now held by influential interactionists as well as by parallelists. One may believe that the mind consists of ideas, and may still hold that ideas can cause motions in matter.

There is, however, another objection that predisposes many thoughtful persons to reject parallelism uncompromisingly. It is this. If we admit that the chain of physical causes and effects, from a blow given to the body to the resulting muscular movements made in self-defense, is an unbroken one, what part can we assign to the mind in the whole transaction? Has it *done* anything? Is it not reduced to the position of a passive spectator? Must we not regard man as "a physical automaton with parallel psychical states"?

Such an account of man cannot fail to strike one as repugnant; and yet it is the parallelist himself whom we must thank for introducing us to it. The account is not a caricature from the pen of an opponent. "An automaton," writes Professor Clifford,[2] "is a thing that goes by itself when it is wound up, and we go by ourselves when we have had food. Excepting the fact that other men are conscious, there is no reason why we should not regard the human body as merely an exceedingly complicated machine which is wound up by putting food into the mouth. But it is not *merely* a machine, because consciousness goes with it. The mind, then, is to be regarded as a stream of feelings which runs parallel to, and simultaneous with, a certain part of the action of the body, that is to say, that particular part of the action of the brain in which the cerebrum and the sensory tracts are excited."

The saving statement that the body is not *merely* a machine, because consciousness goes with it, does not impress one as being sufficient to redeem the illustration. Who wants to be an automaton with an accompanying consciousness? Who cares to regard his mind as an "epiphenomenon"—a thing that exists, but whose existence or nonexistence makes no difference to the course of affairs?

The plain man's objection to such an account of himself seems to be abundantly justified. As I have said earlier in this chapter, neither interactionist nor parallelist has the intention of repudiating the experience of world and mind common to us all. We surely have evidence enough to prove that minds count for something. No house was ever built, no book was ever written, by a creature without a mind; and the better the house or book, the better the mind. *That* there is a fixed and absolutely dependable relation between the planning mind and the thing accomplished, no man of any school has the right to deny. The only legitimate question is: *What is the nature* of the relation? Is it *causal*, or should it be conceived to be *something else*?

The whole matter will be more fully discussed in Chapter XI. This chapter I shall close with a brief summary of the points which the reader will do well to bear in mind when he occupies himself with parallelism.

(1) Parallelism is a protest against the interactionist's tendency to materialize the mind.

(2) The name is a figurative expression, and must not be taken literally. The true relation between mental phenomena and physical is given in certain common experiences that have been indicated, and it is a unique relation.

(3) It is a fixed and absolutely dependable relation. It is impossible that there should be a particular mental fact without its corresponding physical fact; and it is impossible that this physical fact should occur without its corresponding mental fact.

(4) The parallelist objects to calling this relation *causal*, because this obscures the distinction between it and the relation between facts both of which are physical. He prefers the word "concomitance."

(5) Such objections to parallelism as that cited above assume that the concomitance of which the parallelist speaks is analogous to physical concomitance. The chemist puts together a volume of hydrogen gas and a volume of chlorine gas, and the result is two volumes of hydrochloric acid gas. We regard it as essential to the result that there should be the two gases and that they should be brought together. But the fact that the chemist has red hair we rightly look upon as a concomitant phenomenon of no importance. The result would be the same if he had black hair or were bald. But this is not the concomitance that interests the parallelist. The two sorts of concomitance are alike only in the one point. Some phenomenon is regarded as excluded from the series of causes and effects under discussion. On the other hand, the difference between the two is all-important; in the one case, the concomitant phenomenon is an accidental circumstance that might just as well be absent; in the other, it is nothing of the sort; it *cannot* be absent—the mental fact *must* exist if the brain-change in question exists.

It is quite possible that, on reading this list of points, one may be inclined to make two protests.

First: Is a parallelism so carefully guarded as this properly called *parallelism* at all? To this I answer: The name matters little. I have used it because I have no better term. Certainly, it is not the parallelism which is sometimes brought forward, and which peeps out from the citation from Clifford. It is nothing more than an insistence upon the truth that we should not treat the mind as though it were a material thing. If any one wishes to take the doctrine and discard the name, I have no objection. As so guarded, the doctrine is, I think, true.

Second: If it is desirable to avoid the word "cause," in speaking of the relation of the mental and the physical, on the ground that otherwise we give the word a double sense, why is it not desirable to avoid the word "concomitance"? Have we not seen that the word is ambiguous? I admit the inconsistency and plead in excuse only that I have chosen the lesser of two evils. It is fatally easy to slip into the error of thinking of the mind as though it were material and had a place in the physical world. In using the word "concomitance" I enter a protest against this. But I have, of course, no right to use it without showing just what kind of concomitance I mean.

[1] "First and Fundamental Truths," Book I, Part II, Chapter II. New York, 1889.

[2] "Lectures and Essays," Vol. II, p. 57. London, 1879.

CHAPTER X

HOW WE KNOW THERE ARE OTHER MINDS

40. IS IT CERTAIN THAT WE KNOW IT?—I suppose there is no man in his sober senses who seriously believes that no other mind than his own exists. There is, to be sure, an imaginary being more or less discussed by those interested in philosophy, a creature called the Solipsist, who is credited with this doctrine. But men do not become solipsists, though they certainly say things now and then that other men think logically lead to some such unnatural view of things; and more rarely they say things that sound as if the speaker, in some moods, at least, might actually harbor such a view.

Thus the philosopher Fichte (1762-1814) talks in certain of his writings as though he believed himself to be the universe, and his words cause Jean Paul Richter, the inimitable, to break out in his characteristic way: "The very worst of it all is the lazy, aimless, aristocratic, insular life that a god must lead; he has no one to go with. If I am not to sit still for all time and eternity, if I let myself down as well as I can and make myself finite, that I may have something in the way of society, still I have, like petty princes, only my own creatures to echo my words. . . . Every being, even the highest Being, wishes something to love and to honor. But the Fichtean doctrine that I am my own body-maker leaves me with nothing whatever—with not so much as the beggar's dog or the prisoner's spider. . . . Truly I wish that there were men, and that I were one of them. . . . If there exists, as I very much fear, no one but myself, unlucky dog that I am, then there is no one at such a pass as I."

Just how much Fichte's words meant to the man who wrote them may be a matter for dispute. Certainly no one has shown a greater moral earnestness or a greater regard for his fellowmen than this philosopher, and we must not hastily accuse any one of being a solipsist. But that to certain men, and, indeed, to many men, there have come thoughts that have seemed to point in this direction—that not a few have had doubts as to their ability to *prove* the existence of other minds—this we must admit.

It appears somewhat easier for a man to have doubts upon this subject when he has fallen into the idealistic error of regarding the material world, which seems to be revealed to him, as nothing else than his "ideas" or "sensations" or "impressions." If we will draw the whole "telephone exchange" into the clerk, there seems little reason for not including all the subscribers as well. If other men's bodies are my sensations, may not other men's minds be my imaginings? But doubts may be felt also by those who are willing to admit a real external world. How do we know that our inference to the existence of other minds is a justifiable inference? Can there be such a thing as *verification* in this field?

For we must remember that no man is directly conscious of any mind except his own. Men cannot exhibit their minds to their neighbors as they exhibit their wigs. However close may seem to us to be our intercourse with those about us, do we ever attain to anything more than our ideas of the contents of their minds? We do not experience these contents; we picture them, we represent them by certain proxies. To be sure, we believe that the originals exist, but can we be quite sure of it? Can there be a *proof* of this right to make the leap from one consciousness to another? We seem to assume that we can make it, and then we make it again and again; but suppose, after all, that there were nothing there. Could we ever find out our error? And in a field where it is impossible to prove error, must it not be equally impossible to prove truth?

The doubt has seemed by no means a gratuitous one to certain very sensible practical men. "It is wholly impossible," writes Professor Huxley,[1] "absolutely to prove the presence or absence of consciousness in anything but one's own brain, though by analogy, we are justified in assuming its existence in other men." "The existence of my conception of you in my consciousness," says Clifford,[2] "carries with it a belief in the existence of you outside of my consciousness. . . . How this inference is justified, how consciousness can testify to the existence of anything outside of itself, I do not pretend to say: I need not untie a knot which the world has cut for me long ago. It may very well be that I myself am the only existence, but it is simply ridiculous to suppose that anybody else is. The position of absolute idealism may, therefore, be left out of count, although each individual may be unable to justify his dissent from it."

These are writers belonging to our own modern age, and they are men of science. Both of them deny that the existence of other minds is a thing that can be *proved*; but the one tells us that we are "justified in assuming" their existence, and the other informs us that, although "it may very well be" that no other mind exists, we may leave that possibility out of count.

Neither position seems a sensible one. Are we justified in assuming what cannot be proved? or is the argument "from analogy" really a proof of some sort? Is it right to close our eyes to what "may very well be," just because we choose to do so? The fact is that both of these writers had the conviction, shared by us all, that there are other minds, and that we know something about them; and yet neither of them could see that the conviction rested upon an unshakable foundation.

Now, I have no desire to awake in the mind of any one a doubt of the existence of other minds. But I think we must all admit that the man who recognizes that such minds are not directly perceived, and who harbors doubts as to the nature of the inference which leads to their assumption, may, perhaps, be able to say that *he feels certain* that there are other minds; but must we not at the same time admit that he is scarcely in a position to say: *it is certain* that there are other minds? The question will keep coming back again: May there not, after all, be a legitimate doubt on the subject?

To set this question at rest there seems to be only one way, and that is this: to ascertain the nature of the inference which is made, and to see clearly what can be meant by *proof* when one is concerned with such matters as these. If it turns out that we have proof, in the only sense of the word in which it is reasonable to ask for proof, our doubt falls away of itself.

41. THE ARGUMENT FOR OTHER MINDS.—I have said early in this volume (section 7) that the plain man perceives that other men act very much as he does, and that he attributes to them minds more or less like his own. He reasons from like to like—other bodies present phenomena which, in the case of his own body, he perceives to be indicative of mind, and he accepts them as indicative of mind there also. The psychologist makes constant use of this inference; indeed, he could not develop his science without it.

John Stuart Mill (1806-1873), whom it is always a pleasure to read because he is so clear and straightforward, presents this argument in the following form:[3]—

"By what evidence do I know, or by what considerations am I led to believe, that there exist other sentient creatures; that the walking and speaking figures which I see and hear, have sensations and thoughts, or, in other words, possess Minds? The most strenuous Intuitionist does not include this among the things that I know by direct intuition. I conclude it from certain things, which my experience of my own states of feeling proves to me to be marks of it. These marks are of two kinds, antecedent and subsequent; the previous conditions requisite for feeling, and the effects or consequences of it. I conclude that other human beings have feelings like me, because, first, they have bodies like me, which I know, in my own case, to be the antecedent condition of feelings; and because, secondly, they exhibit the acts, and other outward signs, which in my own case I know by experience to be caused by feelings. I am conscious in myself of a series of facts connected by a uniform sequence, of which the beginning is modifications of my body, the middle is feelings, the end is outward demeanor. In the case of other human beings I have the evidence of my senses for the first and last links of the series, but not for the intermediate link. I find, however, that the sequence between the first and last is as regular and constant in those other cases as it is in mine. In my own case I know that the first link produces the last through the intermediate link, and could not produce it without. Experience, therefore, obliges me to conclude that there must be an intermediate link; which must either be the same in others as in myself, or a different one. I must either believe them to be alive, or to be automatons; and by believing them to be alive, that is, by supposing the link to be of the same nature as in the case of which I have experience, and which is in all respects similar, I bring other human beings, as phenomena, under the same generalizations which I know by experience to be the true theory of my own existence. And in doing so I conform to the legitimate rules of experimental inquiry. The process is exactly parallel to that by which Newton proved that the force which keeps the planets in their orbits is identical with that by which an apple falls to the ground. It was not incumbent on Newton to prove the impossibility of its being any other force;

he was thought to have made out his point when he had simply shown that no other force need be supposed. We know the existence of other beings by generalization from the knowledge of our own; the generalization merely postulates that what experience shows to be a mark of the existence of something within the sphere of our consciousness, may be concluded to be a mark of the same thing beyond that sphere."

Now, the plain man accepts the argument from analogy, here insisted upon, every day of his life. He is continually forming an opinion as to the contents of other minds on a basis of the bodily manifestations presented to his view. The process of inference is so natural and instinctive that we are tempted to say that it hardly deserves to be called an inference. Certainly the man is not conscious of distinct steps in the process; he perceives certain phenomena, and they are at once illuminated by their interpretation. He reads other men as we read a book—the signs on the paper are scarcely attended to, our whole thought is absorbed in that for which they stand. As I have said above, the psychologist accepts the argument, and founds his conclusions upon it.

Upon what ground can one urge that this inference to other minds is a doubtful one? It is made universally. We have seen that even those who have theoretic objections against it, do not hesitate to draw it, as a matter of fact. It appears unnatural in the extreme to reject it. What can induce men to regard it with suspicion?

I think the answer to this question is rather clearly suggested in the sentence already quoted from Professor Huxley: "It is wholly impossible absolutely to prove the presence or absence of consciousness in anything but one's own brain, though, by analogy, we are justified in assuming its existence in other men."

Here Professor Huxley admits that we have something like a proof, for he regards the inference as *justified*. But he does not think that we have *absolute proof*—the best that we can attain to appears to be a degree of probability falling short of the certainty which we should like to have.

Now, it should be remarked that the discredit cast upon the argument for other minds has its source in the fact that it does not satisfy a certain assumed standard. What is that standard? It is the standard of proof which we may look for and do look for where we are concerned to establish the existence of material things with the highest degree of certainty.

There are all sorts of indirect ways of proving the existence of material things. We may read about them in a newspaper, and regard them as highly doubtful; we may have the word of a man whom, on the whole, we regard as veracious; we may infer their existence, because we perceive that certain other things exist, and are to be accounted for. Under certain circumstances, however, we may have proof of a different kind: we may see and touch the things themselves. Material things are open to direct inspection. Such a direct inspection constitutes *absolute proof*, so far as material things are concerned.

But we have no right to set this up as our standard of absolute proof, when we are talking about other minds. In this field it is not proof at all. Anything that can be directly inspected is not another mind. We cannot cast a doubt upon the existence of colors by pointing to the fact that we cannot smell them. If they could be smelt, they would not be colors. We must in each case seek a proof of the appropriate kind.

What have we a right to regard as absolute proof of the existence of another mind? Only this: the analogy upon which we depend in making our inference must be a very close one. As we shall see in the next section, the analogy is sometimes very remote, and we draw the inference with much hesitation, or, perhaps, refuse to draw it at all. It is not, however, the *kind of inference* that makes the trouble; it is the lack of detailed information that may serve as a basis for inference. Our inference to other minds is unsatisfactory only in so far as we are ignorant of our own minds and bodies and of other bodies. Were our knowledge in these fields complete, we should know without fail the signs of mind, and should know whether an inference were or were not justified.

And *justified* here means proved—proved in the only sense in which we have a right to ask for proof. No single fact is known that can discredit such a proof. Our doubt is, then, gratuitous and can be dismissed. We may claim that we have *verification* of the existence of other minds. Such verification, however, must consist in showing that, in any given instance, the signs of mind really are present. It cannot consist in presenting minds for inspection as though they were material things.

One more matter remains to be touched upon in this section. It has doubtless been observed that Mill, in the extract given above, seems to place "feelings," in other words, mental phenomena, between one set of bodily motions and another. He makes them the middle link in a chain whose first and third links are material. The parallelist cannot treat mind in this way. He claims that to make mental phenomena effects or causes of bodily motions is to make them material.

51

Must, then, the parallelist abandon the argument for other minds? Not at all. The force of the argument lies in interpreting the phenomena presented by other bodies as one knows by experience the phenomena of one's own body must be interpreted. He who concludes that the relation between his own mind and his own body can best be described as a "parallelism," must judge that other men's minds are related to their bodies in the same way. He must treat his neighbor as he treats himself. The argument from analogy remains the same.

42. WHAT OTHER MINDS ARE THERE?—That other men have minds nobody really doubts, as we have seen above. They resemble us so closely, their actions are so analogous to our own, that, although we sometimes give ourselves a good deal of trouble to ascertain what sort of minds they have, we never think of asking ourselves whether they have minds.

Nor does it ever occur to the man who owns a dog, or who drives a horse, to ask himself whether the creature has a mind. He may complain that it has not much of a mind, or he may marvel at its intelligence—his attitude will depend upon the expectations which he has been led to form. But regard the animal as he would regard a bicycle or an automobile, he will not. The brute is not precisely like us, but its actions bear an unmistakable analogy to our own; pleasure and pain, hope and fear, desire and aversion, are so plainly to be read into them that we feel that a man must be "high gravel blind" not to see their significance.

Nevertheless, it has been possible for man, under the prepossession of a mistaken philosophical theory, to assume the whole brute creation to be without consciousness. When Descartes had learned something of the mechanism of the human body, and had placed the human soul—*hospes comesque corporis*—in the little pineal gland in the midst of the brain, the conception in his mind was not unlike that which we have when we picture to ourselves a locomotive engine with an engineer in its cab. The man gives intelligent direction; but, under some circumstances, the machine can do a good deal in the absence of the man; if it is started, it can run of itself, and to do this, it must go through a series of complicated motions.

Descartes knew that many of the actions performed by the human body are not the result of conscious choice, and that some of them are in direct contravention of the will's commands. The eye protects itself by dropping its lid, when the hand is brought suddenly before it; the foot jerks away from the heated object which it has accidentally touched. The body was seen to be a mechanism relatively independent of the mind, and one rather complete in itself. Joined with a soul, the circle of its functions was conceived to be widened; but even without the assistance of the soul, it was thought that it could keep itself busy, and could do many things that the unreflective might be inclined to attribute to the efficiency of the mind.

The bodies of the brutes Descartes regarded as mechanisms of the same general nature as the human body. He was unwilling to allow a soul to any creature below man, so nothing seemed left to him save to maintain that the brutes are machines without consciousness, and that their apparently purposive actions are to be classed with such human movements as the sudden closing of the eye when it is threatened with the hand. The melancholy results of this doctrine made themselves evident among his followers. Even the mild and pious Malebranche could be brutal to a dog which fawned upon him, under the mistaken notion that it did not really hurt a dog to kick it.

All this reasoning men have long ago set aside. For one thing, it has come to be recognized that there may be consciousness, perhaps rather dim, blind, and fugitive, but still consciousness, which does not get itself recognized as do our clearly conscious purposes and volitions. Many of the actions of man which Descartes was inclined to regard as unaccompanied by consciousness may not, in fact, be really unconscious. And, in the second place, it has come to be realized that we have no right to class all the actions of the brutes with those reflex actions in man which we are accustomed to regard as automatic.

The belief in animal automatism has passed away, it is to be hoped, never to return. That lower animals have minds we must believe. But what sort of minds have they?

It is hard enough to gain an accurate notion of what is going on in a human mind. Men resemble each other more or less closely, but no two are precisely alike, and no two have had exactly the same training. I may misunderstand even the man who lives in the same house with me and is nearly related to me. Does he really suffer and enjoy as acutely as he seems to? or must his words and actions be accepted with a discount? The greater the difference between us, the more danger that I shall misjudge him. It is to be expected that men should misunderstand women; that men and women should misunderstand children; that those who differ in social station, in education, in traditions and habits of life, should be in danger of reading each other as one reads a book in a tongue imperfectly mastered. When these differences are very great, the task is an extremely difficult one. What are the emotions, if he has any, of the Chinaman in the laundry near by? His face seems as difficult of interpretation as are the hieroglyphics that he has pasted up on his window.

When we come to the brutes, the case is distinctly worse. We think that we can attain to some notion of the minds to be attributed to such animals as the ape, the dog, the cat, the horse, and it is not nonsense to speak of an animal psychology. But who will undertake to tell us anything definite of the mind of a fly, a grasshopper, a snail, or a cuttlefish? That they have minds, or something like minds, we must believe; what their minds are like, a prudent man scarcely even attempts to say. In our distribution of minds may we stop short of even the very lowest animal organisms? It seems arbitrary to do so.

More than that; some thoughtful men have been led by the analogy between plant life and animal life to believe that something more or less remotely like the consciousness which we attribute to animals must be attributed also to plants. Upon this belief I shall not dwell, for here we are evidently at the limit of our knowledge, and are making the vaguest of guesses. No one pretends that we have even the beginnings of a plant psychology. At the same time, we must admit that organisms of all sorts do bear some analogy to each other, even if it be a remote one; and we must admit also that we cannot*prove* plants to be wholly devoid of a rudimentary consciousness of some sort.

As we begin with man and descend the scale of beings, we seem, in the upper part of the series, to be in no doubt that minds exist. Our only question is as to the precise contents of those minds. Further down we begin to ask ourselves whether anything like mind is revealed at all. That this should be so is to be expected. Our argument for other minds is the argument from analogy, and as we move down the scale our analogy grows more and more remote until it seems to fade out altogether. He who harbors doubts as to whether the plants enjoy some sort of psychic life, may well find those doubts intensified when he turns to study the crystal; and when he contemplates inorganic matter he should admit that the thread of his argument has become so attenuated that he cannot find it at all.

43. THE DOCTRINE OF MIND-STUFF.—Nevertheless, there have been those who have attributed something like consciousness even to inorganic matter. If the doctrine of evolution be true, argues Professor Clifford,[4] "we shall have along the line of the human pedigree a series of imperceptible steps connecting inorganic matter with ourselves. To the later members of that series we must undoubtedly ascribe consciousness, although it must, of course, have been simpler than our own. But where are we to stop? In the case of organisms of a certain complexity, consciousness is inferred. As we go back along the line, the complexity of the organism and of its nerve-action insensibly diminishes; and for the first part of our course we see reason to think that the complexity of consciousness insensibly diminishes also. But if we make a jump, say to the tunicate mollusks, we see no reason there to infer the existence of consciousness at all. Yet not only is it impossible to point out a place where any sudden break takes place, but it is contrary to all the natural training of our minds to suppose a breach of continuity so great."

We must not, says Clifford, admit any breach of continuity. We must assume that consciousness is a complex of elementary feelings, "or rather of those remoter elements which cannot even be felt, but of which the simplest feeling is built up." We must assume that such elementary facts go along with the action of every organism, however simple; but we must assume also that it is only when the organism has reached a certain complexity of nervous structure that the complex of psychic facts reaches the degree of complication that we call Consciousness.

So much for the assumption of something like mind in the mollusk, where Clifford cannot find direct evidence of mind. But the argument does not stop here: "As the line of ascent is unbroken, and must end at last in inorganic matter, we have no choice but to admit that every motion of matter is simultaneous with some . . . fact or event which might be part of a consciousness."

Of the universal distribution of the elementary constituents of mind Clifford writes as follows: "That element of which, as we have seen, even the simplest feeling is a complex, I shall call *Mind-stuff*. A moving molecule of inorganic matter does not possess mind or consciousness; but it possesses a small piece of mind-stuff. When molecules are so combined together as to form the film on the under side of a jellyfish, the elements of mind-stuff which go along with them are so combined as to form the faint beginnings of Sentience. When the molecules are so combined as to form the brain and nervous system of a vertebrate, the corresponding elements of mind-stuff are so combined as to form some kind of consciousness; that is to say, changes in the complex which take place at the same time get so linked together that the repetition of one implies the repetition of the other. When matter takes the complex form of a living human brain, the corresponding mind-stuff takes the form of a human consciousness, having intelligence and volition."

This is the famous mind-stuff doctrine. It is not a scientific doctrine, for it rests on wholly unproved assumptions. It is a play of the speculative fancy, and has its source in the author's strong desire to fit mental phenomena into some general evolutionary scheme. As he is a parallelist, and cannot make of physical phenomena and of mental one single series of causes and effects, he must attain his end by making the mental series complete and independent in itself. To do this, he is forced to make several very startling assumptions:—

(1) We have seen that there is evidence that there is consciousness somewhere—it is revealed by certain bodies. Clifford assumes consciousness, or rather its raw material,*mind-stuff*, to be everywhere. For this assumption we have not a whit of evidence.

(2) To make of the stuff thus attained a satisfactory evolutionary series, he is compelled to assume that mental phenomena are related to each other much as physical phenomena are related to each other. This notion he had from Spinoza, who held that, just as all that takes place in the physical world must be accounted for by a reference to physical causes, so all happenings in the world of ideas must be accounted for by a reference to mental causes, *i.e.* to ideas. For this assumption there is no more evidence than for the former.

(3) Finally, to bring the mental phenomena we are familiar with, sensations of color, sound, touch, taste, etc., into this evolutionary scheme, he is forced to assume that all such mental phenomena are made up of elements which do not belong to these classes at all, of something that "cannot even be felt." For this assumption there is as little evidence as there is for the other two.

The fact is that the *mind-stuff* doctrine is a castle in the air. It is too fanciful and arbitrary to take seriously. It is much better to come back to a more sober view of things, and to hold that there is evidence that other minds exist, but no evidence that every material thing is animated. If we cannot fit this into our evolutionary scheme, perhaps it is well to reexamine our evolutionary scheme, and to see whether some misconception may not attach to that.

[1] "Collected Essays," Vol. I, p. 219, New York, 1902.
[2] "On the Nature of Things-in-Themselves," in "Lectures and Essays," Vol. II.
[3] "Examination of Sir William Hamilton's Philosophy," Chapter XII.
[4] "On the Nature of Things-in-Themselves."

CHAPTER XI

OTHER PROBLEMS OF WORLD AND MIND

44. IS THE MATERIAL WORLD A MECHANISM?—So far we have concerned ourselves with certain leading problems touching the external world and the mind,—problems which seem to present themselves unavoidably to those who enter upon the path of reflection. And we have seen, I hope, that there is much truth, as well as some misconception, contained in the rather vague opinions of the plain man.

But the problems that we have taken up by no means exhaust the series of those that present themselves to one who thinks with patience and persistency. When we have decided that men are not mistaken in believing that an external world is presented in their experience; when we have corrected our first crude notions of what this world is, and have cleared away some confusions from our conceptions of space and time; when we have attained to a reasonably clear view of the nature of the mind, and of the nature of its connection with the body; when we have escaped from a tumble into the absurd doctrine that no mind exists save our own, and have turned our backs upon the rash speculations of the adherents of "mind-stuff"; there still remain many points upon which we should like to have definite information.

In the present chapter I shall take up and turn over a few of these, but it must not be supposed that one can get more than a glimpse of them within such narrow limits. First of all we will raise the question whether it is permissible to regard the material world, which we accept, as through and through a mechanism.

There can be little doubt that there is a tendency on the part of men of science at the present day so to regard it. It should, of course, be frankly admitted that no one is in a position to prove that, from the cosmic mist, in which we grope for the beginnings of our universe, to the organized whole in which vegetable and animal bodies have their place, there is an unbroken series of changes all of which are explicable by a reference to mechanical laws. Chemistry, physics, and biology are still separate and distinct realms, and it is at present impossible to find for them a common basis in mechanics. The belief of the man of science must, hence, be regarded as a faith; the doctrine of the mechanism of nature is a working hypothesis, and it is unscientific to assume that it is anything more.

There can be no objection to a frank admission that we are not here walking in the light of established knowledge. But it does seem to savor of dogmatism for a man to insist that no increase in our knowledge can ever reveal that the physical world is an orderly system throughout, and that all the changes in material things are explicable in terms of the one unified science. Earnest objections have, however, been made to the tendency to regard nature as a mechanism. To one of the most curious of them we have been treated lately by Dr. Ward in his book on "Naturalism and Agnosticism."

It is there ingeniously argued that, when we examine with care the fundamental concepts of the science of mechanics, we find them to be self-contradictory and absurd. It follows that we are not justified in turning to them for an explanation of the order of nature.

The defense of the concepts of mechanics we may safely leave to the man of science; remembering, of course, that, when a science is in the making, it is to be expected that the concepts of which it makes use should undergo revision from time to time. But there is one general consideration that it is not well to leave out of view when we are contemplating such an assault upon the notion of the world as mechanism as is made by Dr. Ward. It is this.

Such attacks upon the conception of mechanism are not purely destructive in their aim. The man who makes them wishes to destroy one view of the system of things in order that he may set up another. If the changes in the system of material things cannot be accounted for mechanically, it is argued, we are compelled to turn for our explanation to the action and interaction of minds. This seems to give mind a very important place in the universe, and is believed to make for a view of things that guarantees the satisfaction of the highest hopes and aspirations of man.

That a recognition of the mechanical order of nature is incompatible with such a view of things as is just above indicated, I should be the last to admit. The notion that it is so is, I believe, a dangerous error. It is an error that tends to put a man out of sympathy with the efforts of science to discover that the world is an orderly whole, and tempts him to rejoice in the contemplation of human ignorance.

But the error is rather a common one; and see to what injustice it may lead one. It is concluded that the conception of *matter* is an obscure one; that we do not know clearly what we mean when we speak of the *mass* of a body; that there are disputes as to proper significance to be given to the words *cause* and *effect*; that the *laws of motion*, as they are at present formulated, do not seem to account satisfactorily for the behavior of all material particles. From this it is inferred that we must give up the attempt to explain mechanically the order of physical things.

Now, suppose that it were considered a dangerous and heterodox doctrine, that the changes in the system of things are due to the activities of minds. Would not those who now love to point out the shortcomings of the science of mechanics discover a fine field for their destructive criticism? Are there no disputes as to the ultimate nature of mind? Are men agreed touching the relations of mind and matter? What science even attempts to tell us how a mind, by an act of volition, sets material particles in motion or changes the direction of their motion? How does one mind act upon another, and what does it mean for one mind to act upon another?

If the science of mechanics is not in all respects as complete a science as it is desirable that it should be, surely we must admit that when we turn to the field of mind we are not dealing with what is clear and free from difficulties. Only a strong emotional bias can lead a man to dwell with emphasis upon the difficulties to be met with in the one field, and to pass lightly over those with which one meets in the other.

One may, however, refuse to admit that the order of nature is throughout mechanical, without taking any such unreasonable position as this. One may hold that many of the changes in material things do not *appear* to be mechanical, and that it is too much of an assumption to maintain that they are such, even as an article of faith. Thus, when we pass from the world of the inorganic to that of organic life, we seem to make an immense step. No one has even begun to show us that the changes that take place in vegetable and animal organisms are all mechanical changes. How can we dare to assume that they are?

With one who reasons thus we may certainly feel a sympathy. The most ardent advocate of mechanism must admit that his doctrine is a working hypothesis, and not *proved* to be true. Its acceptance would, however, be a genuine convenience from the point of view of science, for it does introduce, at least provisionally, a certain order into a vast number of facts, and gives a direction to investigation. Perhaps the wisest thing to do is, not to combat the doctrine, but to accept it tentatively and to examine carefully what conclusions it may seem to carry with it—how it may affect our outlook upon the world as a whole.

45. THE PLACE OF MIND IN NATURE.—One of the very first questions which we think of asking when we contemplate the possibility that the physical world is throughout a mechanical system is this: How can we conceive minds to be related to such a system? That minds, and many minds, do exist, it is not reasonable to doubt. What shall we do with them?

One must not misunderstand the mechanical view of things. When we use the word "machine," we call before our minds certain gross and relatively simple mechanisms constructed by man. Between such and a flower, a butterfly, and a human body, the difference is enormous. He who elects to bring the latter under the title of mechanism cannot mean that he discerns no difference between them and a steam engine or a printing press. He can only mean that he believes he might, could he attain to a glimpse into their infinite complexity, find an explanation of the physical changes which take place in them, by a reference to certain general laws which describe the behavior of material particles everywhere.

And the man who, having extended his notion of mechanism, is inclined to overlook the fact that animals and men have minds, that thought and feeling, plan and purpose, have their place in the world, may justly be accused of a headlong and heedless enthusiasm. Whatever may be our opinion on the subject of the mechanism of nature, we have no right to minimize the significance of thought and feeling and will. Between that which has no mind and that which has a mind there is a difference which cannot be obliterated by bringing both under the concept of mechanism. It is a difference which furnishes the material for the sciences of psychology and ethics, and gives rise to a whole world of distinctions which find no place in the realm of the merely physical.

There are, then, minds as well as bodies; what place shall we assign to these minds in the system of nature?

Several centuries ago it occurred to the man of science that the material world should be regarded as a system in which there is constant transformation, but in which nothing is created. This way of looking at things expressed itself formerly in the statement that, through all the changes that take place in the world, the quantity of matter and motion remains the same. To-day the same idea is better expressed in the doctrine of the eternity of mass and the conservation of energy. In plain language, this doctrine teaches that every change in every part of the physical world, every motion in matter, must be preceded by physical conditions which may be regarded as the equivalent of the change in question.

But this makes the physical world a closed system, a something complete in itself. Where is there room in such a system for minds?

It does indeed seem hard to find in such a system a place for minds, if one conceives of minds as does the interactionist. We have seen (section 36) that the interactionist makes the mind act upon matter very much as one particle of matter is supposed to act upon another. Between the physical and the mental he assumes that there are *causal* relations; *i.e.* physical changes must be referred to mental causes sometimes, and mental changes to physical. This means that he finds a place for mental facts by inserting them as links in the one chain of causes and effects with physical facts. If he is not allowed to break the chain and insert them, he does not know what to do with them.

The parallelist has not the same difficulty to face. He who holds that mental phenomena must not be built into the one series of causes and effects with physical phenomena may freely admit that physical phenomena form a closed series, an orderly system of their own, and he may yet find a place in the world for minds. He refuses to regard them as a part of the world-mechanism, but he *relates* them to physical things, conceiving them as *parallel to* the physical in the sense described (sections 37-39). He insists that, even if we hold that there are gaps in the physical order of causes and effects, we cannot conceive these gaps to be filled by mental phenomena, simply because they are mental phenomena. They belong to an order of their own. Hence, the assumption that the physical series is unbroken does not seem to him to crowd mental phenomena out of their place in the world at all. They must, in any case, occupy the place that is appropriate to them (section 38).

It will be noticed that this doctrine that the chain of physical causes and effects is nowhere broken, and that mental phenomena are related to it as the parallelist conceives them to be, makes the world-system a very orderly one. Every phenomenon has its place in it, and can be accounted for, whether it be physical or mental. To some, the thought that the world is such an orderly thing is in the highest degree repugnant. They object that, in such a world, there is no room for *free-will*; and they object, further, that there is no room for the *activity of minds*. Both of these objections I shall consider in this chapter.

But first, I must say a few words about a type of doctrine lately insisted upon,[1] which bears some resemblance to interactionism as we usually meet with it, and, nevertheless, tries to hold on to the doctrine of the conservation of energy. It is this:—

The concept of energy is stretched in such a way as to make it cover mental phenomena as well as physical. It is claimed that mental phenomena and physical phenomena are alike "manifestations of energy," and that the coming into being of a consciousness is a mere "transformation," a something to be accounted for by the disappearance from the physical world of a certain equivalent—perhaps of some motion. It will be noticed that this is one rather subtle way of obliterating the distinction between mental phenomena and physical. In so far it resembles the interactionist's doctrine.

56

In criticism of it we may say that he who accepts it has wandered away from a rather widely recognized scientific hypothesis, and has substituted for it a very doubtful speculation for which there seems to be no whit of evidence. It is, moreover, a speculation repugnant to the scientific mind, when its significance is grasped. Shall we assume without evidence that, when a man wakes in the morning and enjoys a mental life suspended or diminished during the night, his thoughts and feelings have come into being at the expense of his body? Shall we assume that the mass of his body has been slightly diminished, or that motions have disappeared in a way that cannot be accounted for by a reference to the laws of matter in motion? This seems an extraordinary assumption, and one little in harmony with the doctrine of the eternity of mass and the conservation of energy as commonly understood. We need not take it seriously so long as it is quite unsupported by evidence.

46. THE ORDER OF NATURE AND "FREE-WILL."—In a world as orderly as, in the previous section, this world is conceived to be, is there any room for freedom? What if the man of science is right in suspecting that the series of physical causes and effects is nowhere broken? Must we then conclude that we are never free?

To many persons it has seemed that we are forced to draw this conclusion, and it is not surprising that they view the doctrine with dismay. They argue: Mental phenomena are made parallel with physical, and the order of physical phenomena seems to be determined throughout, for nothing can happen in the world of matter unless there is some adequate cause of its happening. If, then, I choose to raise my finger, that movement must be admitted to have physical causes, and those causes other causes, and so on without end. If such a movement must always have its place in a causal series of this kind, how can it be regarded as a free movement? It is determined, and not free.

Now, it is far from a pleasant thing to watch the man of science busily at work trying to prove that the physical world is an orderly system, and all the while to feel in one's heart that the success of his efforts condemns one to slavery. It can hardly fail to make one's attitude towards science that of alarm and antagonism. From this I shall try to free the reader by showing that our freedom is not in the least danger, and that we may look on unconcerned.

When we approach that venerable dispute touching the freedom of the will, which has inspired men to such endless discussions, and upon which they have written with such warmth and even acrimony, the very first thing to do is to discover what we have a right to mean when we call a man *free*. As long as the meaning of the word is in doubt, the very subject of the dispute is in doubt. When may we, then, properly call a man free? What is the normal application of the term?

I raise my finger. Every man of sense must admit that, under normal conditions, I can raise my finger or keep it down, *as I please*. There is no ground for a difference of opinion so far. But there is a further point upon which men differ. One holds that my "pleasing" and the brain-change that corresponds to it have their place in the world-order; that is, he maintains that every volition can be *accounted for*. Another holds that, under precisely the same circumstances, one may "please" or not "please"; which means that the "pleasing" cannot be wholly accounted for by anything that has preceded. The first man is a *determinist*, and the second a "*free-willist*." I beg the reader to observe that the word "free-willist" is in quotation marks, and not to suppose that it means simply a believer in the freedom of the will.

When in common life we speak of a man as free, what do we understand by the word? Usually we mean that he is free from external compulsion. If my finger is held by another, I am not free to raise it. But I may be free in this sense, and yet one may demur to the statement that I am a free man. If a pistol be held to my head with the remark, "Hands up!" my finger will mount very quickly, and the bystanders will maintain that I had no choice.

We speak in somewhat the same way of men under the influence of intoxicants, of men crazed by some passion and unable to take into consideration the consequences of their acts, and of men bound by the spell of hypnotic suggestion. Indeed, whenever a man is in such a condition that he is glaringly incapable of leading a normal human life and of being influenced by the motives that commonly move men, we are inclined to say that he is not free.

But does it ever occur to us to maintain that, in general, the possession of a character and the capacity of being influenced by considerations make it impossible for a man to be free? Surely not. If I am a prudent man, I will invest my money in good securities. Is it sensible to say that I cannot have been free in refusing a twenty per cent investment, *because I am by nature prudent?* Am I a slave *because I eat when I am hungry*, and can I partake of a meal freely, only when there is no reason why I should eat at all?

He who calls me free only when my acts do violence to my nature or cannot be justified by a reference to anything whatever has strange notions of freedom. Patriots, poets, moralists, have had much to say of freedom; men have lived for it, and have died for it; men love it as they

57

love their own souls. Is the object of all this adoration the metaphysical absurdity indicated above?

To insist that a man is free only in so far as his actions are unaccountable is to do violence to the meaning of a word in very common use, and to mislead men by perverting it to strange and unwholesome uses. Yet this is done by the "free-willist." He keeps insisting that man is free, and then goes on to maintain that he cannot be free unless he is "free." He does not, unfortunately, supply the quotation marks, and he profits by the natural mistake in identity. As he defines freedom it becomes "freedom," which is a very different thing.

What is this "freedom"? It is not freedom from external constraint. It is not freedom from overpowering passion. It is freedom from all the motives, good as well as bad, that we can conceive of as influencing man, and freedom also from oneself.

It is well to get this quite clear. The "free-willist" maintains that, *in so far as a man is "free,"* his actions cannot be accounted for by a reference to the order of causes at all—not by a reference to his character, hereditary or acquired; not by a reference to his surroundings. "Free" actions, in so far as they are "free," have, so to speak, sprung into being out of the void. What follows from such a doctrine? Listen:—

(1) It follows that, in so far as I am "free," I am not the author of what appear to be my acts; who can be the cause of causeless actions?

(2) It follows that no amount of effort on my part can prevent the appearance of "free" acts of the most deplorable kind. If one can condition their appearance or non-appearance, they are not "free" acts.

(3) It follows that there is no reason to believe that there will be any congruity between my character and my "free" acts. I may be a saint by nature, and "freely" act like a scoundrel.

(4) It follows that I can deserve no credit for "free" acts. I am not their author.

(5) It follows that, in so far as I am "free," it is useless to praise me, to blame me, to punish me, to endeavor to persuade me. I must be given over to unaccountable sainthood or to a reprobate mind, as it happens to happen. I am quite beyond the pale of society, for my neighbor cannot influence my "free" acts any more than I can.

(6) It follows that, in so far as I am "free," I am in something very like a state of slavery; and yet, curiously enough, it is a slavery without a master. In the old stories of Fate, men were represented as puppets in the hand of a power outside themselves. Here I am a puppet in no hand; but I am a puppet just the same, for I am the passive spectator of what appear to be my acts. I do not do the things I seem to do. They are done for me or in me—or, rather, they are not done, but just happen.

Such "freedom" is a wretched thing to offer to a man who longs for freedom; for the freedom to act out his own impulses, to guide his life according to his own ideals. It is a mere travesty on freedom, a fiction of the philosophers, which inspires respect only so long as one has not pierced the disguise of its respectable name. True freedom is not a thing to be sought in a disorderly and chaotic world, in a world in which actions are inexplicable and character does not count. Let us rinse our minds free of misleading verbal associations, and let us realize that a "free-will" neighbor would certainly not be to us an object of respect. He would be as offensive an object to have in our vicinity as a "free-will" gun or a "free-will" pocketknife. He would not be a rational creature.

Our only concern need be for freedom, and this is in no danger in an orderly world. We all recognize this truth, in a way. We hold that a man of good character freely chooses the good, and a man of evil character freely chooses evil. Is not this a recognition of the fact that the choice is a thing to be accounted for, and is, nevertheless, a free choice?

I have been considering above the world as it is conceived to be by the parallelist, but, to the reader who may not incline towards parallelism, I wish to point out that these reasonings touching the freedom of the will concern the interactionist just as closely. They have no necessary connection with parallelism. The interactionist, as well as the parallelist, may be a determinist, a believer in freedom, or he may be a "free-willist."

He regards mental phenomena and physical phenomena as links in the one chain of causes and effects. Shall he hold that certain mental links are "free-will" links, that they are wholly unaccountable? If he does, all that has been said above about the "free-willist" applies to him. He believes in a disorderly world, and he should accept the consequences of his doctrine.

47. THE PHYSICAL WORLD AND THE MORAL WORLD.—I have said a little way back that, when we think of bodies as having minds, we are introduced to a world of distinctions which have no place in the realm of the merely physical. One of the objections made to the orderly world of the parallelist was that in it there is no room for the activity of minds. Before we pass judgment on this matter, we should try to get some clear notion of what we may mean by

the word "activity." The science of ethics must go by the board, if we cannot think of men as *doing* anything, as acting rightly or acting wrongly.

Let us conceive a billiard ball in motion to come into collision with one at rest. We commonly speak of the first ball as active, and of the second as the passive subject upon which it exercises its activity. Are we justified in thus speaking?

In one sense, of course, we are. As I have several times had occasion to remark, we are, in common life, justified in using words rather loosely, provided that it is convenient to do so, and that it does not give rise to misunderstandings.

But, in a stricter sense, we are not justified in thus speaking, for in doing so we are carrying over into the sphere of the merely physical a distinction which does not properly belong there, but has its place in another realm. The student of mechanics tells us that the second ball has affected the first quite as much as the first has affected the second. We cannot simply regard the first as cause and the second as effect, nor may we regard the motion of the first as cause and the subsequent motion of the second as its effect alone. *The whole situation at the one instant*—both balls, their relative positions and their motion and rest—must be taken as the cause of *the whole situation at the next instant*, and in this whole situation the condition of the second ball has its place as well as that of the first.

If, then, we insist that to have causal efficiency is the same thing as to be active, we should also admit that the second ball was active, and quite as active as the first. It has certainly had as much to do with the total result. But it offends us to speak of it in this way. We prefer to say that the first was active and the second was acted upon. What is the source of this distinction?

Its original source is to be found in the judgments we pass upon conscious beings, bodies with minds; and it could never have been drawn if men had not taken into consideration the relations of minds to the changes in the physical world. As carried over to inanimate things it is a transferred distinction; and its transference to this field is not strictly justifiable, as has been indicated above.

I must make this clear by an illustration. I hurry along a street towards the university, because the hour for my lecture is approaching. I am struck down by a falling tile. In my advance up the street I am regarded as active; in my fall to the ground I am regarded as passive.

Now, looking at both occurrences from the purely physical point of view, we have nothing before us but a series of changes in the space relations of certain masses of matter; and in all those changes both my body and its environment are concerned. As I advance, my body cannot be regarded as the sole cause of the changes which are taking place. My progress would be impossible without the aid of the ground upon which I tread. Nor can I accuse the tile of being the sole cause of my demolition. Had I not been what I was and where I was, the tile would have fallen in vain. I must be regarded as a concurrent cause of my own disaster, and my unhappy state is attributable to me as truly as it is to the tile.

Why, then, am I in the one case regarded as active and in the other as passive? In each case I am a cause of the result. How does it happen that, in the first instance, I seem to most men to be *the* cause, and in the second to be not a cause at all? The rapidity of my motion in the first instance cannot account for this judgment. He who rides in the police van and he who is thrown from the car of a balloon may move with great rapidity and yet be regarded as passive.

Men speak as they do because they are not content to point out the physical antecedents of this and that occurrence and stop with that. They recognize that, between my advance up the street and my fall to the ground there is one very important difference. In the first case what is happening *may be referred to an idea in my mind*. Were the idea not there, I should not do what I am doing. In the second case, what has happened *cannot be referred to an idea in my mind*.

Here we have come to the recognition that there are such things as *purposes* and *ends*; that an idea and some change in the external world may be related as *plan* and *accomplishment*. In other words, we have been brought face to face with what has been given the somewhat misleading name of *final cause*. In so far as that in the bringing about of which I have had a share is my *end*, I am *active*; in so far as it is not my end, but comes upon me as something not planned, I am *passive*. The enormous importance of the distinction may readily be seen; it is only in so far as I am a creature who can have purposes, that *desire* and *will, foresight* and *prudence, right* and *wrong*, can have a significance for me.

I have dwelt upon the meaning of the words "activity" and "passivity," and have been at pains to distinguish them from cause and effect, because the two pairs of terms have often been confounded with each other, and this confusion has given rise to a peculiarly unfortunate error. It is this error that lies at the foundation of the objection referred to at the beginning of this section.

We have seen that certain men of science are inclined to look upon the physical world as a great system, all the changes in which may be accounted for by an appeal to physical causes. And we have seen that the parallelist regards ideas, not as links in this chain, but as parallel with physical changes.

It is argued by some that, if this is a true view of things, we must embrace the conclusion that *the mind cannot be active at all,* that it can *accomplish nothing.* We must look upon the mind as an "epiphenomenon," a useless decoration; and must regard man as "a physical automaton with parallel psychical states."

Such abuse of one's fellow-man seems unchristian, and it is wholly uncalled for on any hypothesis. Our first answer to it is that it seems to be sufficiently refuted by the experiences of common life. We have abundant evidence that men's minds do count for something. I conclude that I want a coat, and I order one of my tailor; he believes that I will pay for it, he wants the money, and he makes the coat; his man desires to earn his wages and he delivers it. If I had not wanted the coat, if the tailor had not wanted my money, if the man had not wanted to earn his wages, the end would not have been attained. No philosopher has the right to deny these facts.

Ah! but, it may be answered, these three "wants" are not supposed to be the *causes* of the motions in matter which result in my appearing well-dressed on Sunday. They are only *concomitant phenomena.*

To this I reply: What of that? We must not forget what is meant by such concomitance (section 39). We are dealing with a fixed and necessary relation, not with an accidental one. If these "wants" had been lacking, there would have been no coat. So my second answer to the objector is, that, on the hypothesis of the parallelist, the relations between mental phenomena and physical phenomena are just as dependable as that relation between physical phenomena which we call that of cause and effect. Moreover, since activity and causality are not the same thing, there is no ground for asserting that the mind cannot be active, merely because it is not material and, hence, cannot be, strictly speaking, a cause of motions in matter.

The plain man is entirely in the right in thinking that minds are active. The truth is that *nothing can be active except as it has a mind.* The relation of purpose and end is the one we have in view when we speak of the activity of minds.

It is, thus, highly unjust to a man to tell him that he is "a physical automaton with parallel psychical states," and that he is wound up by putting food into his mouth. He who hears this may be excused if he feels it his duty to emit steam, walk with a jerk, and repudiate all responsibility for his actions. Creatures that think, form plans, and *act,* are not what we call automata. It is an abuse of language to call them such, and it misleads us into looking upon them as we have no right to look upon them. If men really were automata in the proper sense of the word, we could not look upon them as wise or unwise, good or bad; in short, the whole world of moral distinctions would vanish.

Perhaps, in spite of all that has been said in this and in the preceding section, some will feel a certain repugnance to being assigned a place in a world as orderly as our world is in this chapter conceived to be—a world in which every phenomenon, whether physical or mental, has its definite place, and all are subject to law. But I suppose our content or discontent will not be independent of our conception of what sort of a world we conceive ourselves to be inhabiting.

If we conclude that we are in a world in which God is revealed, if the orderliness of it is but another name for Divine Providence, we can scarcely feel the same as we would if we discovered in the world nothing of the Divine. I have in the last few pages been discussing the doctrine of purposes and ends, teleology, but I have said nothing of the significance of that doctrine for Theism. The reader can easily see that it lies at the very foundation of our belief in God. The only arguments for theism that have had much weight with mankind have been those which have maintained there are revealed in the world generally evidences of a plan and purpose at least analogous to what we discover when we scrutinize the actions of our fellow-man. Such arguments are not at the mercy of either interactionist or parallelist. On either hypothesis they stand unshaken.

With this brief survey of some of the most interesting problems that confront the philosopher, I must content myself here. Now let us turn and see how some of the fundamental problems treated in previous chapters have been approached by men belonging to certain well-recognized schools of thought.

And since it is peculiarly true in philosophy that, to understand the present, one must know something of the past, we shall begin by taking a look at the historical background of the types of philosophical doctrine to which reference is constantly made in the books and journals of the day.

[1] Ostwald, "Vorlesungen über Naturphilosophie," s. 396. Leipzig, 1902.

IV. SOME TYPES OF PHILOSOPHICAL THEORY
CHAPTER XII

48. THE DOCTRINE OF REPRESENTATIVE PERCEPTION.—We have seen in Chapter II that it seems to the plain man abundantly evident that he really is surrounded by material things and that he directly perceives such things. This has always been the opinion of the plain man and it seems probable that it always will be. It is only when he begins to reflect upon things and upon his knowledge of them that it occurs to him to call it in question.

Very early in the history of speculative thought it occurred to men, however, to ask how it is that we know things, and whether we are sure we do know them. The problems of reflection started into life, and various solutions were suggested. To tell over the whole list would take us far afield, and we need not, for the purpose we have in view, go back farther than Descartes, with whom philosophy took a relatively new start, and may be said to have become, in spirit and method, at least, modern.

I have said (section 31) that Descartes (1596-1650) was fairly well acquainted with the functioning of the nervous system, and has much to say of the messages which pass along the nerves to the brain. The same sort of reasoning that leads the modern psychologist to maintain that we know only so much of the external world as is reflected in our sensations led him to maintain that the mind is directly aware of the ideas through which an external world is represented, but can know the world itself only indirectly and through these ideas.

Descartes was put to sore straits to prove the existence of an external world, when he had once thus placed it at one remove from us. If we accept his doctrine, we seem to be shut up within the circle of our ideas, and can find no door that will lead us to a world outside. The question will keep coming back: How do we *know* that, corresponding to our ideas, there are material things, if we have never perceived, in any single instance, a material thing? And the doubt here suggested may be reinforced by the reflection that the very expression "a material thing" ought to be meaningless to a man who, having never had experience of one, is compelled to represent it by the aid of something so different from it as ideas are supposed to be. Can material things really be to such a creature anything more than some complex of ideas?

The difficulties presented by any philosophical doctrine are not always evident at once. Descartes made no scruple of accepting the existence of an external world, and his example has been followed by a very large number of those who agree with his initial assumption that the mind knows immediately only its own ideas.

Preëminent among such we must regard John Locke, the English philosopher (1632-1704), whose classic work, "An Essay concerning Human Understanding," should not be wholly unknown to any one who pretends to an interest in the English literature.

Admirably does Locke represent the position of what very many have regarded as the prudent and sensible man,—the man who recognizes that ideas are not external things, and that things must be known through ideas, and yet holds on to the existence of a material world which we assuredly know.

He recognizes, it is true, that some one may find a possible opening for the expression of a doubt, but he regards the doubt as gratuitous; "I think nobody can, in earnest, be so skeptical as to be uncertain of the existence of those things which he sees and feels." As we have seen (section 12), he meets the doubt with a jest.

Nevertheless, those who read with attention Locke's admirably clear pages must notice that he does not succeed in really setting to rest the doubt that has suggested itself. It becomes clear that Locke felt so sure of the existence of the external world because he now and then slipped into the inconsistent doctrine that he perceived it immediately, and not merely through his ideas. Are those things "which he sees and feels" *external* things? Does he see and feel them directly, or must he infer from his ideas that he sees and feels them? If the latter, why may one not still doubt? Evidently the appeal is to a direct experience of material things, and Locke has forgotten that he must be a Lockian.

"I have often remarked, in many instances," writes Descartes, "that there is a great difference between an object and its idea." How could the man possibly have remarked this, when he had never in his life perceived the object corresponding to any idea, but had been altogether shut up to ideas? "Thus I see, whilst I write this," says Locke,[1] "I can change the appearance of the paper, and by designing the letters tell beforehand what new idea it shall exhibit the very next moment, by barely drawing my pen over it, which will neither appear (let me fancy as much as I will), if my hand stands still, or though I move my pen, if my eyes be shut; nor, when those characters are once made on the paper, can I choose afterward but see them as they are; that is, have the ideas of such letters as I have made. Whence it is manifest, that they are not barely the sport and play of my own imagination, when I find that the characters that were made at the pleasure of my own thought do not obey them; nor yet cease to be, whenever I shall fancy it; but continue to affect the senses constantly and regularly, according to the figures I made them."

Locke is as bad as Descartes. Evidently he regards himself as able to turn to the external world and perceive the relation that things hold to ideas. Such an inconsistency may escape the writer who has been guilty of it, but it is not likely to escape the notice of all those who come after him. Some one is sure to draw the consequences of a doctrine more rigorously, and to come to conclusions, it may be, very unpalatable to the man who propounded the doctrine in the first instance.

The type of doctrine represented by Descartes and Locke is that of *Representative Perception*. It holds that we know real external things only through their mental representatives. It has also been called *Hypothetical Realism*, because it accepts the existence of a real world, but bases our knowledge of it upon an inference from our sensations or ideas.

49. THE STEP TO IDEALISM.—The admirable clearness with which Locke writes makes it the easier for his reader to detect the untenability of his position. He uses simple language, and he never takes refuge in vague and ambiguous phrases. When he tells us that the mind is wholly shut up to its ideas, and then later assumes that it is not shut up to its ideas, but can perceive external things, we see plainly that there must be a blunder somewhere.

George Berkeley (1684-1753), Bishop of Cloyne, followed out more rigorously the consequences to be deduced from the assumption that all our direct knowledge is of ideas; and in a youthful work of the highest genius entitled "The Principles of Human Knowledge," he maintained that there is no material world at all.

When we examine with care the objects of sense, the "things" which present themselves to us, he argues, we find that they resolve themselves into sensations, or "ideas of sense." What can we mean by the word "apple," if we do not mean the group of experiences in which alone an apple is presented to us? The word is nothing else than a name for this group as a group. Take away the color, the hardness, the odor, the taste; what have we left? And color, hardness, odor, taste, and anything else that may be referred to any object as a quality, can exist, he claims, only in a perceiving mind; for such things are nothing else than sensations, and how can there be an unperceived sensation?

The things which we perceive, then, he calls complexes of ideas. Have we any reason to believe that these ideas, which exist in the mind, are to be accepted as representatives of things of a different kind, which are not mental at all? Not a shadow of a reason, says Berkeley; there is simply no basis for inference at all, and we cannot even make clear what it is that we are setting out to infer under the name of matter. We need not, therefore, grieve over the loss of the material world, for we have suffered no loss; one cannot lose what one has never had.

Thus, the objects of human knowledge, the only things of which it means anything to speak, are: (1) Ideas of Sense; (2) Ideas of Memory and Imagination; (3) The Passions and Operations of the Mind; and (4) The Self that perceives all These.

From Locke's position to that of Berkeley was a bold step, and it was much criticised, as well it might be. It was felt then, as it has been felt by many down to our own time, that, when we discard an external world distinct from our ideas, and admit only the world revealed in our ideas, we really do lose.

It is legitimate to criticise Berkeley, but it is not legitimate to misunderstand him; and yet the history of his doctrine may almost be called a chronicle of misconceptions. It has been assumed that he drew no distinction between real things and imaginary things, that he made the world no better than a dream, etc. Arbuthnot, Swift, and a host of the greater and lesser lights in literature, from his time to ours, have made merry over the supposed unrealities in the midst of which the Berkeleian must live.

But it should be remembered that Berkeley tried hard to do full justice to the world of things in which we actually find ourselves; not a hypothetical, inferred, unperceived world, but the world of the things we actually perceive. He distinguished carefully between what is real and what is merely imaginary, though he called both "ideas"; and he recognized something like a system of nature. And, by the argument from analogy which we have already examined (section 41), he inferred the existence of other finite minds and of a Divine Mind.

But just as John Locke had not completely thought out the consequences which might be deduced from his own doctrines, so Berkeley left, in his turn, an opening for a successor. It was possible for that acutest of analysts, David Hume (1711-1776), to treat him somewhat as he had treated Locke.

Among the objects of human knowledge Berkeley had included the *self* that perceives things. He never succeeded in making at all clear what he meant by this object; but he regarded it as a substance, and believed it to be a cause of changes in ideas, and quite different in its nature from all the ideas attributed to it. But Hume maintained that when he tried to get a good look at this self, to catch it, so to speak, and to hold it up to inspection, he could not find anything whatever save perceptions, memories, and other things of that kind. The self is, he said, "but a bundle or collection of different perceptions which succeed each other with inconceivable rapidity, and are in a perpetual flux and movement."

As for the objects of sense, our own bodies, the chairs upon which we sit, the tables at which we write, and all the rest—these, argues Hume, we are impelled by nature to think of as existing continuously, but we have no evidence whatever to prove that they do thus exist. Are not the objects of sense, after all, only sensations or impressions? Do we not experience these sensations or impressions interruptedly? Who sees or feels a table continuously day after day? If the table is but a name for the experiences in question, if we have no right to infer material things behind and distinct from such experiences, are we not forced to conclude that the existence of the things that we see and feel is an interrupted one?

Hume certainly succeeded in raising more questions than he succeeded in answering. We are compelled to admire the wonderful clearness and simplicity of his style, and the acuteness of his intellect, in every chapter. But we cannot help feeling that he does injustice to the world in which we live, even when we cannot quite see what is wrong. Does it not seem certain to science and to common sense that there is an order of nature in some sense independent of our perceptions, so that objects may be assumed to exist whether we do or do not perceive them?

When we read Hume we have a sense that we are robbed of our real external world; and his account of the mind makes us feel as a badly tied sheaf of wheat may be conceived to feel—in danger of falling apart at any moment. Berkeley we unhesitatingly call an *Idealist*, but whether we shall apply the name to Hume depends upon the extension we are willing to give to it. His world is a world of what we may broadly call *ideas*; but the tendencies of his philosophy have led some to call it a *Skepticism*.

50. THE REVOLT OF "COMMON SENSE."—Hume's reasonings were too important to be ignored, and his conclusions too unpalatable to satisfy those who came after him. It seemed necessary to seek a way of escape out of this world of mere ideas, which appeared to be so unsatisfactory a world. One of the most famous of such attempts was that made by the Scotchman Thomas Reid (1710-1796).

At one time Reid regarded himself as the disciple of Berkeley, but the consequences which Hume deduced from the principles laid down by the former led Reid to feel that he must build upon some wholly different foundation. He came to the conclusion that the line of philosophers from Descartes to Hume had made one capital error in assuming "that nothing is perceived but what is in the mind that perceives it."

Once admit, says Reid, that the mind perceives nothing save ideas, and we must also admit that it is impossible to prove the existence either of an external world or of a mind different from "a bundle of perceptions." Hence, Reid maintains that we perceive—not infer, but perceive—*things* external to the mind. He writes:[2]—

"Let a man press his hand against the table—*he feels it hard.* But what is the meaning of this? The meaning undoubtedly is, that he hath a certain feeling of touch, from which he concludes, without any reasoning, or comparing ideas, that there is something external really existing, whose parts stick so firmly together that they cannot be displaced without considerable force.

"There is here a feeling, and a conclusion drawn from it, or some way suggested by it. In order to compare these, we must view them separately, and then consider by what tie they are connected, and wherein they resemble one another. The hardness of the table is the conclusion, the feeling is the medium by which we are led to that conclusion. Let a man attend distinctly to this medium, and to the conclusion, and he will perceive them to be as unlike as any two things in nature. The one is a sensation of the mind, which can have no existence but in a sentient being; nor can it exist one moment longer than it is felt; the other is in the table, and we conclude, without any difficulty, that it was in the table before it was felt, and continues after the feeling is over. The one implies no kind of extension, nor parts, nor cohesion; the other implies all these. Both, indeed, admit of degrees, and the feeling, beyond a certain degree, is a species of pain; but adamantine hardness does not imply the least pain.

"And as the feeling hath no similitude to hardness, so neither can our reason perceive the least tie or connection between them; nor will the logician ever be able to show a reason why we should conclude hardness from this feeling, rather than softness, or any other quality whatsoever. But, in reality, all mankind are led by their constitution to conclude hardness from this feeling."

It is well worth while to read this extract several times, and to ask oneself what Reid meant to say, and what he actually said. He is objecting, be it remembered, to the doctrine that the mind perceives immediately only its own ideas or sensations and must infer all else. His contention is that we *perceive* external things.

Does he say this? He says that we have feelings of touch *from which we conclude* that there is something external; that there is a feeling, "*and a conclusion drawn from it, or some way suggested by it*;" that "the hardness of the table is the *conclusion*, and the feeling is the *medium* by which we are *led to the conclusion*."

Could Descartes or Locke have more plainly supported the doctrine of representative perception? How could Reid imagine he was combatting that doctrine when he wrote thus? The point in which he differs from them is this: he maintains that we draw the conclusion in question without any reasoning, and, indeed, in the absence of any conceivable reason why we should draw it. We do it instinctively; we are led by the constitution of our nature.

In effect Reid says to us: When you lay your hand on the table, you have a sensation, it is true, but you also know the table is hard. How do you know it? I cannot tell you; you simply know it, and cannot help knowing it; and that is the end of the matter.

Reid's doctrine was not without its effect upon other philosophers. Among them we must place Sir William Hamilton (1788-1856), whose writings had no little influence upon British philosophy in the last half of the last century.

Hamilton complained that Reid did not succeed in being a very good *Natural Realist*, and that he slipped unconsciously into the position he was concerned to condemn. Sir William tried to eliminate this error, but the careful reader of his works will find to his amusement that this learned author gets his feet upon the same slippery descent. And much the same thing may be said of the doctrine of Herbert Spencer (1820-1903), who claims that, when we have a sensation, we know directly that there is an external thing, and then manages to sublimate that external thing into an Unknowable, which we not only do not know directly, but even do not know at all.

All of these men were anxious to avoid what they regarded as the perils of Idealism, and yet they seem quite unable to retain a foothold upon the position which they consider the safer one.

Reid called his doctrine the philosophy of "Common Sense," and he thought he was coming back from the subtleties of the metaphysicians to the standpoint of the plain man. That he should fall into difficulties and inconsistencies is by no means surprising. As we have seen (section 12), the thought of the plain man is far from clear. He certainly believes that we perceive an external world of things, and the inconsistent way in which Descartes and Locke appeal from ideas to the things themselves does not strike him as unnatural. Why should not a man test his ideas by turning to things and comparing the former with the latter? On the other hand, he knows that to perceive things we must have sense organs and sensations, and he cannot quarrel with the psychologists for saying that we know things only in so far as they are revealed to us through our sensations. How does he reconcile these two positions? He does not reconcile them. He accepts them as they stand.

Reid and various other philosophers have tried to come back to "Common Sense" and to stay there. Now, it is a good position to come back to for the purpose of starting out again. The experience of the plain man, the truths which he recognizes as truths, these are not things to be despised. Many a man whose mind has been, as Berkeley expresses it, "debauched by learning," has gotten away from them to his detriment, and has said very unreasonable things. But "Common Sense" cannot be the ultimate refuge of the philosopher; it can only serve him as material for investigation. The scholar whose thought is as vague and inconsistent as that of the plain man has little profit in the fact that the apparatus of his learning has made it possible for him to be ponderously and unintelligibly vague and inconsistent.

Hence, we may have the utmost sympathy with Reid's protest against the doctrine of representative perception, and we may, nevertheless, complain that he has done little to explain how it is that we directly know external things and yet cannot be said to know things except in so far as we have sensations or ideas.

51. THE CRITICAL PHILOSOPHY.—The German philosopher, Immanuel Kant (1724-1804), was moved, by the skeptical conclusions to which Hume's philosophy seemed to lead, to seek a way of escape, somewhat as Reid was. But he did not take refuge in "Common Sense"; he developed an ingenious doctrine which has had an enormous influence in the philosophical world, and has given rise to a Kantian literature of such proportions that no man can hope to read all of it, even if he devotes his life to it. In Germany and out of it, it has for a hundred years and more simply rained books, pamphlets, and articles on Kant and his philosophy, some of them good, many of them far from clear and far from original. Hundreds of German university students have taken Kant as the subject of the dissertation by which they hoped to win the degree of Doctor of Philosophy;—I was lately offered two hundred and seventy-four such dissertations in one bunch;—and no student is supposed to have even a

moderate knowledge of philosophy who has not an acquaintance with that famous work, the "Critique of Pure Reason."

It is to be expected from the outset that, where so many have found so much to say, there should reign abundant differences of opinion. There are differences of opinion touching the interpretation of Kant, and touching the criticisms which may be made upon, and the development which should be given to, his doctrine. It is, of course, impossible to go into all these things here; and I shall do no more than indicate, in untechnical language and in briefest outline, what he offers us in place of the philosophy of Hume.

Kant did not try to refute, as did Reid, the doctrine, urged by Descartes and by his successors, that all those things which the mind directly perceives are to be regarded as complexes of ideas. On the contrary, he accepted it, and he has made the words "phenomenon" and "noumenon" household words in philosophy.

The world which seems to be spread out before us in space and time is, he tells us, a world of things *as they are revealed to our senses and our intelligence*; it is a world of manifestations, of phenomena. What things-in-themselves are like we have no means of knowing; we know only things as they appear to us. We may, to be sure, talk of a something distinct from phenomena, a something not revealed to the senses, but thought of, a *noumenon*; but we should not forget that this is a negative conception; there is nothing in our experience that can give it a filling, for our experience is only of phenomena. The reader will find an unmistakable echo of this doctrine in Herbert Spencer's doctrine of the "Unknowable" and its "manifestations."

Now, Berkeley had called all the things we immediately perceive *ideas*. As we have seen, he distinguished between "ideas of sense" and "ideas of memory and imagination." Hume preferred to give to these two classes different names—he called the first *impressions* and the second *ideas*.

The associations of the word "impression" are not to be mistaken. Locke had taught that between ideas in the memory and genuine sensations there is the difference that the latter are due to the "brisk acting" of objects without us. Objects impress us, and we have sensations or impressions. To be sure, Hume, after employing the word "impression," goes on to argue that we have no evidence that there are external objects, which cause impressions. But he retains the word "impression," nevertheless, and his use of it perceptibly colors his thought.

In Kant's distinction between phenomena and noumena we have the lineal descendant of the old distinction between the circle of our ideas and the something outside of them that causes them and of which they are supposed to give information. Hume said we have no reason to believe such a thing exists, but are impelled by our nature to believe in it. Kant is not so much concerned to prove the nonexistence of noumena, things-in-themselves, as he is to prove that the very conception is an empty one. His reasonings seem to result in the conclusion that we can make no intelligible statement about things so cut off from our experience as noumena are supposed to be; and one would imagine that he would have felt impelled to go on to the frank declaration that we have no reason to believe in noumena at all, and had better throw away altogether so meaningless and useless a notion. But he was a conservative creature, and he did not go quite so far.

So far there is little choice between Kant and Hume. Certainly the former does not appear to have rehabilitated the external world which had suffered from the assaults of his predecessors. What important difference is there between his doctrine and that of the man whose skeptical tendencies he wished to combat?

The difference is this: Descartes and Locke had accounted for our knowledge of things by maintaining that things act upon us, and make an impression or sensation—that their action, so to speak, begets ideas. This is a very ancient doctrine as well as a very modern one; it is the doctrine that most men find reasonable even before they devote themselves to the study of philosophy. The totality of such impressions received from the external world, they are accustomed to regard as our *experience* of external things; and they are inclined to think that any knowledge of external things not founded upon experience can hardly deserve the name of knowledge.

Now, Hume, when he cast doubt upon the existence of external things, did not, as I have said above, divest himself of the suggestions of the word "impression." He insists strenuously that all our knowledge is founded upon experience; and he holds that no experience can give us knowledge that is necessary and universal. We know things as they are revealed to us in our experience; but who can guarantee that we may not have new experiences of a quite different kind, and which flatly contradict the notions which we have so far attained of what is possible and impossible, true and untrue.

It is here that Kant takes issue with Hume. A survey of our knowledge makes clear, he thinks, that we are in the possession of a great deal of information that is not of the unsatisfactory kind that, according to Hume, all our knowledge of things must be. There, for example, are all the truths of mathematics. When we enunciate a truth regarding the relations of the lines and angles of a triangle, we are not merely unfolding in the predicate of our proposition what was implicitly contained in the subject. There are propositions that do no more than this; they are *analytical, i.e.* they merely analyze the subject. Thus, when we say: Man is a rational animal, we may merely be defining the word "man"—unpacking it, so to speak. But a *synthetic* judgment is one in which the predicate is not contained in the subject; it adds to one's information. The mathematical truths are of this character. So also is the truth that everything that happens must have a cause.

Do we connect things with one another in this way merely because we have had*experience* that they are thus connected? Is it because they are *given* to us connected in this way? That cannot be the case, Kant argues, for what is taken up as mere experienced act cannot be known as universally and necessarily true. We perceive that these things *must* be so connected. How shall we explain this necessity?

We can only explain it, said Kant, in this way: We must assume that what is given us from without is merely the raw material of sensation, the *matter* of our experience; and that the ordering of this matter, the arranging it into a world of phenomena, the furnishing of *form*, is the work of the mind. Thus, we must think of space, time, causality, and of all other relations which obtain between the elements of our experience, as due to the nature of the mind. It perceives the world of phenomena that it does, because it *constructs* that world. Its knowledge of things is stable and dependable because it cannot know any phenomenon which does not conform to its laws. The water poured into a cup must take the shape of the cup; and the raw materials poured into a mind must take the form of an orderly world, spread out in space and time.

Kant thought that with this turn he had placed human knowledge upon a satisfactory basis, and had, at the same time, indicated the limitations of human knowledge. If the world we perceive is a world which we make; if the forms of thought furnished by the mind have no other function than the ordering of the materials furnished by sense; then what can we say of that which may be beyond phenomena? What of *noumena*?

It seems clear that, on Kant's principles, we ought not to be able to say anything whatever of *noumena*. To say that such may exist appears absurd. All conceivable connection between them and existing things as we know them is cut off. We cannot think of a noumenon as a *substance*, for the notions of substance and quality have been declared to be only a scheme for the ordering of phenomena. Nor can we think of one as a cause of the sensations that unite into a world, for just the same reason. We are shut up logically to the world of phenomena, and that world of phenomena is, after all, the successor of the world of ideas advocated by Berkeley.

This is not the place to discuss at length the value of Kant's contribution to philosophy.[3] There is something terrifying in the prodigious length at which it seems possible for men to discuss it. Kant called his doctrine "Criticism," because it undertook to establish the nature and limits of our knowledge. By some he has been hailed as a great enlightener, and by others he has been accused of being as dogmatic in his assumptions as those whom he disapproved.

But one thing he certainly has accomplished. He has made the words "phenomena" and "noumena" familiar to us all, and he has induced a vast number of men to accept it as established fact that it is not worth while to try to extend our knowledge beyond phenomena. One sees his influence in the writings of men who differ most widely from one another.

[1] "Essay," Book IV, Chapter XI, section 7.

[2] "An Inquiry into the Human Mind," Chapter V, section 5.

[3] The reader will find a criticism of the Critical Philosophy in Chapter XV.

CHAPTER XIII

REALISM AND IDEALISM

52. REALISM.—The plain man is a realist. That is to say, he believes in a world which is not to be identified with his own ideas or those of any other mind. At the same time, as we have seen (section 12), the distinction between the mind and the world is by no means clear to him. It is not difficult, by judicious questioning, to set his feet upon the slippery descent that shoots a man into idealism.

The vague realism of the plain man may be called *Naïve* or *Unreflective Realism*. It has been called by some *Natural Realism*, but the latter term is an unfortunate one. It is, of course, natural for the unreflective man to be unreflective, but, on the other hand, it is also natural for the reflective man to be reflective. Besides, in dubbing any doctrine "natural," we are apt to assume that doctrines contrasted with it may properly be called "unnatural" or "artificial." It is an ancient rhetorical device, to obtain sympathy for a cause in which one may happen to be interested by giving it a taking name; but it is a device frowned upon by logic and by good sense.

One kind of realism is, then, naïve realism. It is the position from which we all set out, when we begin to reflect upon the system of things. It is the position to which some try to come back, when their reflections appear to be leading them into strange or unwelcome paths.

We have seen how Thomas Reid (section 50) recoiled from the conclusions to which the reasonings of the philosophers had brought him, and tried to return to the position of the plain man. The attempt was a failure, and was necessarily a failure, for Reid tried to come back to the position of the plain man *and still be a philosopher.* He tried to live in a cloud and, nevertheless, to see clearly—a task not easy to accomplish.

It should be remarked, however, that he tried, at least, to insist that we know the external world *directly.* We may divide realists into two broad classes, those who hold to this view, and those who maintain that we know it only indirectly and through our ideas.

The plain man belongs, of course, to the first class, if it is just to speak of a man who says inconsistent things as being wholly in any one class. Certainly he is willing to assert that the ground upon which he stands and the staff in his hand are perceived by him directly.

But we are compelled to recognize that there are subdivisions in this first class of realists. Reid tried to place himself beside the plain man and failed to do so. Hamilton (section 50) tried also, and he is not to be classed precisely either with the plain man or with Reid. He informs us that the object as it appears to us is a composite something to the building up of which the knowing mind contributes its share, the medium through which the object is perceived its share, and the object in itself its share. He suggests, by way of illustration, that the external object may contribute one third. This seems to make, at least, *something* external directly known. But, on the other hand, he maintains that the mind knows immediately only what is in immediate contact with the bodily organ—with the eyes, with the hands, etc.; and he believes it knows this immediately because it is actually present in all parts of the body. And, further, in distinguishing as he does between existence "as it is in itself" and existence "as it is revealed to us," and in shutting us up to the latter, he seems to rob us even of the modicum of externality that he has granted us.

I have already mentioned Herbert Spencer (section 50) as a man not without sympathy for the attempt to rehabilitate the external world. He is very severe with the "insanities" of idealism. He is not willing even to take the first step toward it.

He writes:[1] "The postulate with which metaphysical reasoning sets out is that we are primarily conscious only of our sensations—that we certainly know we have these, and that if there be anything beyond these serving as cause for them, it can be known only by inference from them.

"I shall give much surprise to the metaphysical reader if I call in question this postulate; and the surprise will rise into astonishment if I distinctly deny it. Yet I must do this. Limiting the proposition to those epiperipheral feelings produced in us by external objects (for these are alone in question), I see no alternative but to affirm that the thing primarily known is not that a sensation has been experienced, but that there exists an outer object."

According to this, the outer object is not known through an inference; it is known directly. But do not be in haste to class Spencer with the plain man, or with Reid. Listen to a citation once before made (section 22), but worth repeating in this connection: "When we are taught that a piece of matter, regarded by us as existing externally, cannot be really known, but that we can know only certain impressions produced on us, we are yet, by the relativity of thought, compelled to think of these in relation to a cause—the notion of a real existence which generated these impressions becomes nascent. If it be proved that every notion of a real existence which we can frame is inconsistent with itself,—that matter, however conceived by us, cannot be matter as it actually is,—our conception, though transfigured, is not destroyed: there remains the sense of reality, dissociated as far as possible from those special forms under which it was before represented in thought."

It is interesting to place the two extracts side by side. In the one, we are told that we do not know external objects by an inference from our sensations; in the other we are taught that the piece of matter which we regard as existing externally cannot be really known; that we can know only certain impressions produced on us, and must refer them to a cause; that this cause cannot be what we think it. It is difficult for the man who reads such statements not to forget that Spencer regarded himself as a realist who held to a direct knowledge of something external.

There are, as it is evident, many sorts of realists that may be gathered into the first class mentioned above—men who, however inconsistent they may be, try, at least, to maintain that our knowledge of the external world is a direct one. And it is equally true that there are various sorts of realists that may be put into the second class.

These men have been called *Hypothetical Realists*. In the last chapter it was pointed out that Descartes and Locke belong to this class. Both of these men believed in an external world, but believed that its existence is a thing to be inferred.

Now, when a man has persuaded himself that the mind can know directly only its own ideas, and must infer the world which they are supposed to represent, he may conceive of that external world in three different ways.

(1) He may believe that what corresponds to his idea of a material object, for example, an apple, is in very many respects like the idea in his mind. Thus, he may believe that the odor, taste, color, hardness, etc., that he perceives directly, or as ideas, have corresponding to them real external odor, taste, color, hardness, etc. It is not easy for a man to hold to this position, for a very little reflection seems to make it untenable; but it is theoretically possible for one to take it, and probably many persons have inclined to the view when they have first been tempted to believe that the mind perceives directly only its ideas.

(2) He may believe that such things as colors, tastes, and odors cannot be qualities of external bodies at all, but are only effects, produced upon our minds by something very different in kind. We seem to perceive bodies, he may argue, to be colored, to have taste, and to be odorous; but what we thus perceive is not the external thing; the external thing that produces these appearances cannot be regarded as having anything more than "solidity, extension, figure, motion or rest, and number." Thus did Locke reason. To him the external world as it really exists, is, so to speak, a paler copy of the external world as we seem to perceive it. It is a world with fewer qualities, but, still, a world with qualities of some kind.

(3) But one may go farther than this. One may say: How can I know that even the extension, number, and motion of the things which I directly perceive have corresponding to them extension, number, and motion, in an outer world? If what is not colored can cause me to perceive color, why may not that which is not extended cause me to perceive extension? And, moved by such reflections, one may maintain that there exists outside of us that which we can only characterize as an Unknown Cause, a Reality which we cannot more nearly define.

This last position resembles very closely one side of Spencer's doctrine—that represented in the last of the two citations, as the reader can easily see. It is the position of the follower of Immanuel Kant who has not yet repudiated the noumenon or thing-in-itself discussed in the last chapter (section 51).

I am not concerned to defend any one of the varieties of Direct or of Hypothetical Realism portrayed above. But I wish to point out that they all have some sort of claim to the title *Realism*, and to remind the reader that, when we call a man a realist, we do not do very much in the way of defining his position. I may add that the account of the external world contained in Chapter IV is a sort of realism also.

If this last variety, which I advocate, *must* be classified, let it be placed in the first broad class, for it teaches that we know the external world directly. But I sincerely hope that it will not be judged wholly by the company it keeps, and that no one will assign to it either virtues or defects to which it can lay no just claim.

Before leaving the subject of realism it is right that I should utter a note of warning touching one very common source of error. It is fatally easy for men to be misled by the names which are applied to things. Sir William Hamilton invented for a certain type of metaphysical doctrine the offensive epithet "nihilism." It is a type which appeals to many inoffensive and pious men at the present day, some of whom prefer to call themselves idealists. Many have been induced to become "free-willists" because the name has suggested to them a proper regard for that freedom which is justly dear to all men. We can scarcely approach with an open mind an account of ideas and sensations which we hear described as "sensationalism," or worse yet, as "sensualism." When a given type of philosophy is set down as "dogmatism," we involuntarily feel a prejudice against it.

He who reads as reflectively as he should will soon find out that philosophers "call names" much as other men do, and that one should always be on one's guard. "Every form of phenomenalism," asseverated a learned and energetic old gentleman, who for many years occupied a chair in one of our leading institutions of learning, "necessarily leads to atheism." He inspired a considerable number of students with such a horror for "phenomenalism" that they never took pains to find out what it was.

I mention these things in this connection, because I suspect that not a few in our own day are unduly influenced by the associations which cling to the words "realism" and "idealism." Realism in literature, as many persons understand it, means the degradation of literature to the portrayal of what is coarse and degrading, in a coarse and offensive way. Realism in painting often means the laborious representation upon canvas of things from which we would gladly avert our eyes if we met them in real life. With the word "idealism," on the other hand, we are apt to connect the possession of ideals, a regard for what is best and noblest in life and literature.

The reader must have seen that realism in the philosophic sense of the word has nothing whatever to do with realism in the senses just mentioned. The word is given a special meaning, and it is a weakness to allow associations drawn from other senses of the word to color our judgment when we use it.

And it should be carefully held in view that the word "idealism" is given a special sense when it is used to indicate a type of doctrine contrasted with the doctrine of the realist. Some forms of philosophical idealism have undoubtedly been inspiring; but some have been, and are, far from inspiring. They should not be allowed to posture as saints merely because they are cloaked with an ambiguous name.

53. IDEALISM.—Idealism we may broadly define as the doctrine that all existence is mental existence. So far from regarding the external world as beyond and independent of mind, it maintains that it can have its being only in consciousness.

We have seen (section 49) how men were led to take the step to idealism. It is not a step which the plain man is impelled to take without preparation. To say that the real world of things in which we perceive ourselves to live and move is a something that exists only in the mind strikes him as little better than insane. He who becomes an idealist usually does so, I think, after weighing the arguments presented by the hypothetical realist, and finding that they seem to carry one farther than the latter appears to recognize.

The type of idealism represented by Berkeley has been called *Subjective Idealism*. Ordinarily our use of the words "subjective" and "objective" is to call attention to the distinction between what belongs to the mind and what belongs to the external order of things. My sensations are subjective, they are referred to my mind, and it is assumed that they can have no existence except in my mind; the qualities of things are regarded as objective, that is, it is commonly believed that they exist independently of my perception of them.

Of course, when a man becomes an idealist, he cannot keep just this distinction. The question may, then, fairly be raised: How can he be a *subjective idealist?* Has not the word "subjective" lost its significance?

To this one has to answer: It has, and it has not. The man who, with strict consistency, makes the desk at which he sits as much his "idea" as is the pain in his finger or his memory of yesterday, cannot keep hold of the distinction of subjective and objective. But men are not always as consistent as this. Remember the illustration of the "telephone exchange" (section 14). The mind is represented as situated at the brain terminals of the sensory nerves; and then brain, nerves, and all else are turned into ideas in this mind, which are merely "projected outwards."

Now, in placing the mind at a definite location in the world, and contrasting it with the world, we retain the distinction between subjective and objective—what is in the mind can be distinguished from what is beyond it. On the other hand, in making the whole system of external things a complex of ideas in the mind, we become idealists, and repudiate realism. The position is an inconsistent one, of course, but it is possible for men to take it, for men have taken it often enough.

The idealism of Professor Pearson (section 14) is more palpably subjective than that of Berkeley, for the latter never puts the mind in a "telephone exchange." Nevertheless, he names the objects of sense, which other men call material things, "ideas," and he evidently assimilates them to what we commonly call ideas and contrast with things. Moreover, he holds them in some of the contempt which men reserve for "mere ideas," for he believes that idolaters might be induced to give over worshiping the heavenly bodies could they be persuaded that these are nothing more than their own ideas.

With the various forms of subjective idealism it is usual to contrast the doctrine of *Objective Idealism*. This does not maintain that the world which I perceive is my "idea"; it maintains that the world is "idea."

It is rather a nice question, and one which no man should decide without a careful examination of the whole matter, whether we have any right to retain the word "idea" when we have rubbed out the distinction which is usually drawn between ideas and external things. If we maintain that all men are always necessarily selfish, we stretch the meaning of the word quite beyond what is customary, and selfishness becomes a thing we have no reason to disapprove, since it characterizes saint and sinner alike. Similarly, if we decide to name "idea," not only what the plain man and the realist admit to have a right to that name, but also the great system which these men call an external material world, it seems right to ask; Why use the word "idea" at all? What does it serve to indicate? Not a distinction, surely, for the word seems to be applicable to all things without distinction.

Such considerations as these lead me to object to the expression "objective idealism": if the doctrine is really *objective, i.e.* if it recognizes a system of things different and distinct from what men commonly call ideas, it scarcely seems to have a right to the title*idealism*; and if it is really *idealism*, and does not rob the word idea of all significance, it can scarcely be *objective* in any proper sense of the word.

Manifestly, there is need of a very careful analysis of the meaning of the word "idea," and of the proper significance of the terms "subjective" and "objective," if error is to be avoided and language used soberly and accurately. Those who are not in sympathy with the doctrine of the objective idealists think that in such careful analysis and accurate statement they are rather conspicuously lacking.

We think of Hegel (1770-1831) as the typical objective idealist. It is not easy to give an accurate account of his doctrine, for he is far from a clear writer, and he has made it possible for his many admirers to understand him in many ways. But he seems to have accepted the system of things that most men call the real external world, and to have regarded it as the Divine Reason in its self-development. And most of those whom we would to-day be inclined to gather together under the title of objective idealists appear to have been much influenced, directly or indirectly, by his philosophy. There are, however, great differences of opinion among them, and no man should be made responsible for the opinions of the class as a class.

I have said a few pages back that some forms of idealism are inspiring, and that some are not.

Bishop Berkeley called the objects of sense ideas. He regarded all ideas as inactive, and thought that all changes in ideas—and this includes all the changes that take place in nature—must be referred to the activity of minds. Some of those changes he could refer to finite minds, his own and others. Most of them he could not, and he felt impelled to refer them to a Divine Mind. Hence, the world became to him a constant revelation of God; and he uses the word "God" in no equivocal sense. It does not signify to him the system of things as a whole, or an Unknowable, or anything of the sort. It signifies a spirit akin to his own, but without its limitations. He writes:[2]—

"A human spirit or person is not perceived by sense, as not being an idea; when, therefore, we see the color, size, figure, and motions of a man, we perceive only certain sensations or ideas excited in our own minds; and these being exhibited to our view in sundry distinct collections serve to mark out unto us the existence of finite and created spirits like ourselves. Hence, it is plain we do not see a man,—if by *man* is meant that which lives, moves, perceives, and thinks as we do,—but only such a certain collection of ideas as directs us to think there is a distinct principle of thought and motion, like to ourselves, accompanying and represented by it. And after the same manner we see God; all the difference is that, whereas some one finite and narrow assemblage of ideas denotes a particular human mind, whithersoever we direct our view, we do at all times and in all places perceive manifest tokens of the Divinity—everything we see, hear, feel, or any wise perceive by sense, being a sign or effect of the power of God; as is our perception of those very motions which are produced by men."

With Berkeley's view of the world as a constant revelation of God, many men will sympathize who have little liking for his idealism as idealism. They may criticise in detail his arguments to prove the nonexistence of a genuinely external world, but they will be ready to admit that his doctrine is an inspiring one in the view that it takes of the world and of man.

With this I wish to contrast the doctrine of another idealist, Mr. Bradley, whose work, "Appearance and Reality," has been much discussed in the last few years, in order that the reader may see how widely different forms of idealism may differ from each other, and how absurd it is to praise or blame a man's philosophy merely on the ground that it is idealistic.

Mr. Bradley holds that those aspects of our experience which we are accustomed to regard as real—qualities of things, the relations between things, the things themselves, space, time, motion, causation, activity, the self—turn out when carefully examined to be self-contradictory and absurd. They are not real; they are unrealities, mere appearances.

But these appearances exist, and, hence, must belong to reality. This reality must be sentient, for "there is no being or fact outside of that which is commonly called psychical existence."

Now, what is this reality with which appearances—the whole world of things which seem to be given in our experience—are contrasted? Mr. Bradley calls it the Absolute, and indicates that it is what other men recognize as the Deity. How shall we conceive it?

We are told that we are to conceive it as consisting of the contents of finite minds, or "centers of experience," subjected to "an all-pervasive transfusion with a reblending of all material." In the Absolute, finite things are "transmuted" and lose "their individual natures."

What does this mean in plain language? It means that there are many finite minds of a higher and of a lower order, "centers of experience," and that the contents of these are unreal appearances. There is not a God or Absolute outside of and distinct from these, but rather one that in some sense *is their reality*. This mass of unrealities transfused and transmuted so that no one of them retains its individual nature is the Absolute. That is to say, time must become indistinguishable from space, space from motion, motion from the self, the self from the qualities of things, etc., before they are fit to become constituents of the Absolute and to be regarded as real.

As the reader has seen, this Absolute has nothing in common with the God in which Berkeley believed, and in which the plain man usually believes. It is the night in which all cats are gray, and there appears to be no reason why any one should harbor toward it the least sentiment of awe or veneration.

Whether such reasonings as Mr. Bradley's should be accepted as valid or should not, must be decided after a careful examination into the foundations upon which they rest and the consistency with which inferences are drawn from premises. I do not wish to prejudge the matter. But it is worth while to set forth the conclusions at which he arrives, that it may be clearly realized that the associations which often hang about the word "idealism" should be carefully stripped away when we are forming our estimate of this or that philosophical doctrine.

[1] "Principles of Psychology," Part VII, Chapter VI, section 404.

[2] "Principles," section 148.

CHAPTER XIV

MONISM AND DUALISM

54. THE MEANING OF THE WORDS.—In common life men distinguish between minds and material things, thus dividing the things, which taken together make up the world as we know it, into two broad classes. They think of minds as being very different from material objects, and of the latter as being very different from minds. It does not occur to them to find in the one class room for the other, nor does it occur to them to think of both classes as "manifestations" or "aspects" of some one "underlying reality." In other words, the plain man to-day is a *Dualist*.

In the last chapter (section 52) I have called him a Naïve Realist; and here I shall call him a *Naïve Dualist*, for a man may regard mind and matter as quite distinct kinds of things, without trying to elevate his opinion, through reflection, into a philosophical doctrine. The reflective man may stand by the opinion of the plain man, merely trying to make less vague and indefinite the notions of matter and of mind. He then becomes a *Philosophical Dualist*. There are several varieties of this doctrine, and I shall consider them a little later (section 58).

But it is possible for one to be less profoundly impressed by the differences which characterize matter and mind. One may feel inclined to refer mental phenomena to matter, and to deny them the prominence accorded them by the dualist. On the other hand, one may be led by one's reflections to resolve material objects into mere ideas, and to claim that they can have no existence except in a mind. Finally, it is possible to hold that both minds and material things, as we know them, are only manifestations, phenomena, and that they must be referred to an ulterior "reality" or "substance." One may claim that they are "aspects" of the one reality, which is neither matter nor mind.

These doctrines are different forms of *Monism*. In whatever else they differ from one another, they agree in maintaining that the universe does not contain two kinds of things fundamentally different. Out of the duality of things as it seems to be revealed to the plain man they try to make some kind of a unity.

35. MATERIALISM.—The first of the forms of monism above mentioned is *Materialism*. It is not a doctrine to which the first impulse of the plain man leads him at the present time. Even those who have done no reading in philosophy have inherited many of their ways of looking at things from the thinkers who lived in the ages past, and whose opinions have become the common property of civilized men. For more than two thousand years the world and the mind have been discussed, and it is impossible for any of us to escape from the influence of those discussions and to look at things with the primitive simplicity of the wholly untutored.

But it was not always so. There was a time when men who were not savages, but possessed great intellectual vigor and much cultivation, found it easy and natural to be materialists. This I have spoken of before (section 30), but it will repay us to take up again a little more at length the clearest of the ancient forms of materialism, that of the Atomists, and to see what may be said for and against it.

Democritus of Abdera taught that nothing exists except atoms and empty space. The atoms, he maintained, differ from one another in size, shape, and position. In other respects they are alike. They have always been in motion. Perhaps he conceived of that motion as originally a fall through space, but there seems to be uncertainty upon this point. However, the atoms in motion collide with one another, and these collisions result in mechanical combinations from which spring into being world-systems.

According to this doctrine, nothing comes from nothing, and nothing can become nonexistent. All the changes which have ever taken place in the world are only changes in the position of material particles—they are regroupings of atoms. We cannot directly perceive them to be such, for our senses are too dull to make such fine observations, but our reason tells us that such is the case.

Where, in such a world as this, is there room for mind, and what can we mean by mind? Democritus finds a place for mind by conceiving it to consist of fine, smooth, round atoms, which are the same as the atoms which constitute fire. These are distributed through the whole body, and lie among the other atoms which compose it. They are inhaled with and exhaled into the outer air. While they are in the body their functions are different according as they are located in this organ or in that. In the brain they give rise to thought, in the heart to anger, and in the liver to desire.

I suppose no one would care, at the present time, to become a Democritean. The "Reason," which tells us that the mind consists of fine, round atoms, appears to have nothing but its bare word to offer us. But, apart from this, a peculiar difficulty seems to face us; even supposing there are atoms of fire in the brain, the heart, and the liver, what are the *thought, anger,* and *desire,* of which mention is made?

Shall we conceive of these last as atoms, as void space, or as the motion of atoms? There really seems to be no place in the world for them, and *these are the mind so far as the mind appears to be revealed*—they are *mental phenomena*. It does not seem that they are to be identified with anything that the Atomistic doctrine admits as existing. They are simply overlooked.

Is the modern materialism more satisfactory? About half a century ago there was in the scientific world something like a revival of materialistic thinking. It did not occur to any one to maintain that the mind consists of fine atoms disseminated through the body, but statements almost as crude were made. It was said, for example, that the brain secretes thought as the liver secretes bile.

It seems a gratuitous labor to criticise such statements as these in detail. There are no glands the secretions of which are not as unequivocally material as are the glands themselves. This means that such secretions can be captured and analyzed; the chemical elements of which they are composed can be enumerated. They are open to inspection in precisely the same way as are the glands which secrete them.

Does it seem reasonable to maintain that thoughts and feelings are related to brains in this way? Does the chemist ever dream of collecting them in a test tube, and of drawing up for us a list of their constituent elements? When the brain is active, there are, to be sure, certain material products which pass into the blood and are finally eliminated from the body; but among these products no one would be more surprised than the materialist to discover pains and pleasures, memories and anticipations, desires and volitions. This talk of thought as a "secretion" we can afford to set aside.

Nor need we take much more seriously the seemingly more sober statement that thought is a "function" of the brain. There is, of course, a sense in which we all admit the statement; minds are not disembodied, and we have reason to believe that mind and brain are most intimately related. But the word "function" is used in a very broad and loose sense when it serves to indicate this relation; and one may employ it in this way without being a materialist at all. In a stricter sense of the word, the brain has no functions that may not be conceived as mechanical changes,—as the motion of atoms in space,—and to identify mental phenomena with these is inexcusable. It is not theoretically inconceivable that, with finer senses, we might directly perceive the motions of the atoms in another man's brain; it is inconceivable that we should thus directly perceive his melancholy or his joy; they belong to another world.

56. SPIRITUALISM.—The name *Spiritualism* is sometimes given to the doctrine that there is no existence which we may not properly call mind or spirit. It errs in the one direction as materialism errs in the other.

One must not confound with this doctrine that very different one, Spiritism, which teaches that a certain favored class of persons called mediums may bring back the spirits of the departed and enable us to hold communication with them. Such beliefs have always existed among the common people, but they have rarely interested philosophers. I shall have nothing to say of them in this book.

There have been various kinds of spiritualists. The name may be applied to the idealists, from Berkeley down to those of our day; at some of the varieties of their doctrine we have taken a glance (sections 49, 53). To these we need not recur; but there is one type of spiritualistic

72

doctrine which is much discussed at the present day and which appears to appeal strongly to a number of scientific men. We must consider it for a moment.

We have examined Professor Clifford's doctrine of Mind-stuff (section 43). Clifford maintained that all the material things we perceive are our perceptions—they are in our consciousness, and are not properly external at all. But, believing, as he did, that all nature is animated, he held that every material thing, every perception, may be taken as a revelation of something not in our consciousness, of a mind or, at least, of a certain amount of mind-stuff. How shall we conceive the relation between what is in our mind and the something corresponding to it not in our mind?

We must, says Clifford, regard the latter as the *reality* of which the former is the *appearance* or *manifestation*. "What I perceive as your brain is really in itself your consciousness, is You; but then that which I call your brain, the material fact, is merely my perception."

This doctrine is *Panpsychism*, in the form in which it is usually brought to our attention. It holds that the only real existences are minds, and that physical phenomena must be regarded as the manifestations under which these real existences make us aware of their presence. The term panpsychism may, it is true, be used in a somewhat different sense. It may be employed merely to indicate the doctrine that all nature is animated, and without implying a theory as to the relation between bodies perceived and the minds supposed to accompany them.

What shall we say to panpsychism of the type represented by Clifford? It is, I think, sufficiently answered in the earlier chapters of this volume:—

(1) If I call material facts my perceptions, I do an injustice to the distinction between the physical and the mental (Chapter IV).

(2) If I say that all nature is animated, I extend illegitimately the argument for other minds (Chapter X).

(3) If I say that mind is the reality of which the brain is the appearance, I misconceive what is meant by the distinction between appearance and reality (Chapter V).

57. THE DOCTRINE OF THE ONE SUBSTANCE.—In the seventeenth century Descartes maintained that, although mind and matter may justly be regarded as two substances, yet it should be recognized that they are not really independent substances in the strictest sense of the word, but that there is only one substance, in this sense, and mind and matter are, as it were, its attributes.

His thought was that by attribute we mean that which is not independent, but must be referred to something else; by substance, we mean that which exists independently and is not referred to any other thing. It seemed to follow that there could be only one substance.

Spinoza modified Descartes' doctrine in that he refused to regard mind and matter as substances at all. He made them unequivocally attributes of the one and only substance, which he called God.

The thought which influenced Spinoza had impressed many minds before his time, and it has influenced many since. One need not follow him in naming the unitary something to which mind and matter are referred substance. One may call it Being, or Reality, or the Unknowable, or Energy, or the Absolute, or, perhaps, still something else. The doctrine has taken many forms, but he who reads with discrimination will see that the various forms have much in common.

They agree in maintaining that matter and mind, as they are revealed in our experience, are not to be regarded as, in the last analysis, two distinct kinds of thing. They are, rather, modes or manifestations of one and the same thing, and this is not to be confounded with either.

Those who incline to this doctrine take issue with the materialist, who assimilates mental phenomena to physical; and they oppose the idealist, who assimilates physical phenomena to mental, and calls material things "ideas." We have no right, they argue, to call that of which ideas and things are manifestations either mind or matter. It is to be distinguished from both.

To this doctrine the title of *Monism* is often appropriated. In this chapter I have used the term in a broader sense, for both the materialist and the spiritualist maintain that there is in the universe but one kind of thing. Nevertheless, when we hear a man called a monist without qualification, we may, perhaps, be justified in assuming, in the absence of further information, that he holds to some one of the forms of doctrine indicated above. There may be no logical justification for thus narrowing the use of the term, but logical justification goes for little in such matters.

Various considerations have moved men to become monists in this sense of the word. Some have been influenced by the assumption—one which men felt impelled to make early in the history of speculative thought—that the whole universe must be the expression of some unitary principle. A rather different argument is well illustrated in the writings of Professor Höffding, a learned and acute writer of our own time. It has influenced so many that it is worth while to delay upon it.

Professor Höffding holds that mental phenomena and physical phenomena must be regarded as parallel (see Chapter IX), and that we must not conceive of ideas and material things as interacting. He writes:[1]—

"If it is contrary to the doctrine of the persistence of physical energy to suppose a transition from the one province to the other, and if, nevertheless, the two provinces exist in our experience as distinct, then the two sets of phenomena must be unfolded simultaneously, each according to its laws, so that for every phenomenon in the world of consciousness there is a corresponding phenomenon in the world of matter, and conversely (so far as there is reason to suppose that conscious life is correlated with material phenomena). The parallels already drawn point directly to such a relation; it would be an amazing accident, if, while the characteristic marks repeated themselves in this way, there were not at the foundation an inner connection. Both the *parallelism* and the *proportionality* between the activity of consciousness and cerebral activity point to an *identity* at bottom. The difference which remains in spite of the points of agreement compels us to suppose that one and the same principle has found its expression in a double form. We have no right to take mind and body for two beings or substances in reciprocal interaction. We are, on the contrary, impelled to conceive the material interaction between the elements composing the brain and nervous system *as an outer form of the inner ideal unity of consciousness*. What we in our inner experience become conscious of as thought, feeling, and resolution, is thus represented in the material world by certain material processes of the brain, which as such are subject to the law of the persistence of energy, although this law cannot be applied to the relation between cerebral and conscious processes. It is as though the same thing were said in two languages."

Some monists are in the habit of speaking of the one Being to which they refer phenomena of all sorts as the "Absolute." The word is a vague one, and means very different things in different philosophies. It has been somewhat broadly defined as "the ultimate principle of explanation of the universe." He who turns to one principle of explanation will conceive the Absolute in one way, and he who turns to another will, naturally, understand something else by the word.

Thus, the idealist may conceive of the Absolute as an all-inclusive Mind, of which finite minds are parts. To Spencer, it is the Unknowable, a something behind the veil of phenomena. Sometimes it means to a writer much the same thing that the word God means to other men; sometimes it has a significance at the farthest remove from this (section 53). Indeed, the word is so vague and ambiguous, and has proved itself the mother of so many confusions, that it would seem a desirable thing to drop it out of philosophy altogether, and to substitute for it some less ambiguous expression.

It seems clear from the preceding pages, that, before one either accepts or rejects monism, one should very carefully determine just what one means by the word, and should scrutinize the considerations which may be urged in favor of the particular doctrine in question. There are all sorts of monism, and men embrace them for all sorts of reasons. Let me beg the reader to bear in mind;—

(1) The monist may be a materialist; he may be an idealist; he may be neither. In the last case, he may, with Spinoza, call the one Substance God; that is, he may be a Pantheist. On the other hand, he may, with Spencer, call it the Unknowable, and be an Agnostic. Other shades of opinion are open to him, if he cares to choose them.

(2) It does not seem wise to assent hastily to such statements as; "The universe is the manifestation of one unitary Being"; or: "Mind and matter are the expression of one and the same principle." We find revealed in our experience mental phenomena and physical phenomena. In what sense they are one, or whether they are one in any sense,—this is something to be determined by an examination of the phenomena and of the relations in which we find them. It may turn out that the universe is one only in the sense that all phenomena belong to the one orderly system. If we find that this is the case, we may still, if we choose, call our doctrine monism, but we should carefully distinguish such a monism from those represented by Höffding and Spencer and many others. There seems little reason to use the word, when the doctrine has been so far modified.

58. DUALISM.—The plain man finds himself in a world of physical things and of minds, and it seems to him that his experience directly testifies to the existence of both. This means that the things of which he has experience appear to belong to two distinct classes.

It does not mean, of course, that he has only two kinds of experiences. The phenomena which are revealed to us are indefinitely varied; all physical phenomena are not just alike, and all mental phenomena are not just alike.

Nevertheless, amid all the bewildering variety that forces itself upon our attention, there stands out one broad distinction, that of the physical and the mental. It is a distinction that the man who has done no reading in the philosophers is scarcely tempted to obliterate; to him the world consists of two kinds of things widely different from each other; minds are not material things and material things are not minds. We are justified in regarding this as the opinion of the plain man even when we recognize that, in his endeavor to make clear to himself what he means by minds, he sometimes speaks as though he were talking about something material or semi-material.

Now, the materialist allows these two classes to run together; so does the idealist. The one says that everything is matter; the other, that everything is mind. It would be foolish to maintain that nothing can be said for either doctrine, for men of ability have embraced each. But one may at least say that both seem to be refuted by our common experience of the world, an experience which, so far as it is permitted to testify at all, lifts up its voice in favor of *Dualism*.

Dualism is sometimes defined as the doctrine that there are in the world two kinds of substances, matter and mind, which are different in kind and should be kept distinct. There are dualists who prefer to avoid the use of the word substance, and to say that the world of our experiences consists of physical phenomena and of mental phenomena, and that these two classes of facts should be kept separate.

The dualist may maintain that we have a direct knowledge of matter and of mind, and he may content himself with such a statement, doing little to make clear what we mean by matter and by mind. In this case, his position is little different from that of the plain man who does not attempt to philosophize. Thomas Reid (section 50) belongs to this class.

On the other hand, the dualist may attempt to make clear, through philosophical reflection, what we mean by the matter and mind which experience seems to give us. He may conclude:—

(1) That he must hold, as did Sir William Hamilton, that we perceive directly only physical and mental phenomena, but are justified in inferring that, since the phenomena are different, there must be two kinds of underlying substances to which the phenomena are referred. Thus, he may distinguish between the two substances and their manifestations, as some monists distinguish between the one substance and its manifestations.

(2) Or he may conclude that it is futile to search for substances or realities of any sort*behind* phenomena, arguing that such realities are never revealed in experience, and that no sound reason for their assumption can be adduced. In this case, he may try to make plain what mind and matter are, by simply analyzing our experiences of mind and matter and coming to a clearer comprehension of their nature.

As the reader has probably remarked, the philosophy presented in the earlier chapters of this book (Chapters III to XI) is *dualistic* as well as *realistic*. That is to say, it refuses to rub out the distinction between physical phenomena and mental phenomena, either by dissolving the material world into ideas; by calling ideas secretions or functions of the brain; or by declaring them one in a fictitious entity behind the veil and not supposed to be exactly identical with either. And as it teaches that the only reality that it means anything to talk about must be found in experience, it is a dualism of the type described in the paragraph which immediately precedes.

Such a philosophy does not seem to do violence to the common experience of minds and of physical things shared by us all, whether we are philosophers or are not. It only tries to make clear what we all know dimly and vaguely. This is, I think, a point in its favor. However, men of great ability and of much learning have inclined to doctrines very different; and we have no right to make up our minds on such a subject as this without trying to give them an attentive and an impartial hearing.

59. SINGULARISM AND PLURALISM.—There are those who apply to the various forms of monism the title *Singularism*, and who contrast with this *Pluralism*, a word which is meant to cover the various doctrines which maintain that there is more than one ultimate principle or being in the universe.

It is argued that we should have some word under which we may bring such a doctrine, for example, as that of the Greek philosopher Empedocles (born about 490 B.C.). This thinker made earth, water, fire, and air the four material principles or "roots" of things. He was not a monist, and we can certainly not call him a dualist.

Again. The term pluralism has been used to indicate the doctrine that individual finite minds are not parts or manifestations of one all-embracing Mind,—of God or the Absolute,—but are relatively independent beings. This doctrine has been urged in our own time, with eloquence and feeling, by Professor Howison.[2] Here we have a pluralism which is idealistic, for it admits in the universe but one *kind* of thing, minds; and yet refuses to call itself monistic. It will readily be seen that in this paragraph and in the one preceding the word is used in different senses.

I have added the above sentences to this chapter that the reader may have an explanation of the meaning of a word sometimes met with. But the title of the chapter is "Monism and Dualism," and it is of this contrast that it is especially important to grasp the significance.

[1] "Outlines of Psychology," pp. 64-65, English translation, 1891.

[2] "The Limits of Evolution, and Other Essays," revised edition. New York, 1905.

CHAPTER XV

RATIONALISM, EMPIRICISM, CRITICISM, AND CRITICAL EMPIRICISM

60. RATIONALISM.—As the content of a philosophical doctrine must be determined by the *initial assumptions* which a philosopher makes and by the *method* which he adopts in his reasonings, it is well to examine with some care certain broad differences in this respect which characterize different philosophers, and which help to explain how it is that the results of their reflections are so startlingly different.

I shall first speak of *Rationalism,* which I may somewhat loosely define as the doctrine that the reason can attain truths independently of observation—can go beyond experienced fact and the deductions which experience seems to justify us in making from experienced fact. The definition cannot mean much to us until it is interpreted by a concrete example, and I shall turn to such. It must, however, be borne in mind that the word "rationalism" is meant to cover a great variety of opinions, and we have said comparatively little about him when we have called a man a rationalist in philosophy. Men may agree in believing that the reason can go beyond experienced fact, and yet may differ regarding the particular truths which may be thus attained.

Now, when Descartes found himself discontented with the philosophy that he and others had inherited from the Middle Ages, and undertook a reconstruction, he found it necessary to throw over a vast amount of what had passed as truth, if only with a view to building up again upon a firmer foundation. It appeared to him that much was uncritically accepted as true in philosophy and in the sciences which a little reflection revealed to be either false or highly doubtful. Accordingly, he decided to clear the ground by a sweeping doubt, and to begin his task quite independently.

In accordance with this principle, he rejected the testimony of the senses touching the existence of a world of external things. Do not the senses sometimes deceive us? And, since men seem to be liable to error in their reasonings, even in a field so secure as that of mathematical demonstration, he resolved further to repudiate all the reasonings he had heretofore accepted. He would not even assume himself to be in his right mind and awake; might he not be the victim of a diseased fancy, or a man deluded by dreams?

Could anything whatever escape this all-devouring doubt? One truth seemed unshakable: his own existence, at least, emerged from this sea of uncertainties. I may be deceived in thinking that there is an external world, and that I am awake and really perceive things; but I surely cannot be deceived unless I exist. *Cogito, ergo sum*—I think, hence I exist; this truth Descartes accepted as the first principle of the new and sounder philosophy which he sought.

As we read farther in Descartes we discover that he takes back again a great many of those things that he had at the outset rejected as uncertain. Thus, he accepts an external world of material things. How does he establish its existence? He cannot do it as the empiricist does it, by a reference to experienced fact, for he does not believe that the external world is directly given in our experience. He thinks we are directly conscious only of our *ideas* of it, and must somehow prove that it exists over against our ideas.

By his principles, Descartes is compelled to fall back upon a curious roundabout argument to prove that there is a world. He must first prove that God exists, and then argue that God would not deceive us into thinking that it exists when it does not.

Now, when we come to examine Descartes' reasonings in detail we find what appear to us some very uncritical assumptions. Thus, he proves the existence of God by the following argument:—

I exist, and I find in me the idea of God; of this idea I cannot be the author, for it represents something much greater than I, and its cause must be as great as the reality it represents. In other words, nothing less than God can be the cause of the idea of God which I find in me, and, hence, I may infer that God exists.

Where did Descartes get this notion that every idea must have a cause which contains as much external reality as the idea does represented reality? How does he prove his assumption? He simply appeals to what he calls "the natural light," which is for him a source of all sorts of information which cannot be derived from experience. This "natural light" furnishes him with a vast number of "eternal truths", these he has not brought under the sickle of his sweeping doubt, and these help him to build up again the world he has overthrown, beginning with the one indubitable fact discussed above.

To the men of a later time many of Descartes' eternal truths are simply inherited philosophical prejudices, the results of the reflections of earlier thinkers, and in sad need of revision. I shall not criticise them in detail. The important point for us to notice is that we have here a type of philosophy which depends upon truths revealed by the reason, independently of experience, to carry one beyond the sphere of experience.

I again remind the reader that there are all sorts of rationalists, in the philosophical sense of the word. Some trust the power of the unaided reason without reserve. Thus Spinoza, the pantheist, made the magnificent but misguided attempt to deduce the whole system of things physical and things mental from what he called the attributes of God, Extension and Thought.

On the other hand, one may be a good deal of an empiricist, and yet something of a rationalist, too. Thus Professor Strong, in his recent brilliant book, "Why the Mind has a Body," maintains that we know intuitively that other minds than our own exist; know it without gathering our information from experience, and without having to establish the fact in any way. This seems, at least, akin to the doctrine of the "natural light," and yet no one can say that Professor Strong does not, in general, believe in a philosophy of observation and experiment.

61. EMPIRICISM.—I suppose every one who has done some reading in the history of philosophy will, if his mother tongue be English, think of the name of John Locke when empiricism is mentioned.

Locke, in his "Essay concerning Human Understanding," undertakes "to inquire into the original, certainty, and extent of human knowledge, together with the grounds and degrees of belief, opinion, and assent." His sober and cautious work, which was first published in 1690, was peculiarly English in character; and the spirit which it exemplifies animates also Locke's famous successors, George Berkeley (1684-1753), David Hume (1711-1776), and John Stuart Mill (1806-1873). Although Locke was a realist, Berkeley an idealist, Hume a skeptic, and Mill what has been called a sensationalist; yet all were empiricists of a sort, and emphasized the necessity of founding our knowledge upon experience.

Now, Locke was familiar with the writings of Descartes, whose work he admired, but whose rationalism offended him. The first book of the "Essay" is devoted to the proof that there are in the mind of man no "innate ideas" and no "innate principles." That is to say, Locke tries to show that one must not seek, in the "natural light" to which Descartes turned, a distinct and independent source of information,

"Let us, then," he continues, "suppose the mind to be, as we say, white paper, void of all characters, without any ideas; how comes it to be furnished? Whence comes it by that vast store which the busy and boundless fancy of man has painted on it, with an almost endless variety? Whence has it all the materials of reason and knowledge? To this I answer in one word, from experience; in that all our knowledge is founded, and from that it ultimately derives itself. Our observation, employed either about external sensible objects, or about the internal operations of our minds, perceived and reflected on by ourselves, is that which supplies our understandings with all the materials of thinking. These two are the fountains of knowledge, from whence all the ideas we have, or can naturally have, do spring." [1]

Thus, all we know and all we ever shall know of the world of matter and of minds must rest ultimately upon observation,—observation of external things and of our own mind. We must clip the erratic wing of a "reason" which seeks to soar beyond such knowledge; which leaves the solid earth, and hangs suspended in the void.

"But hold," exclaims the critical reader; "have we not seen that Locke, as well as Descartes (section 48), claims to know what he cannot prove by direct observation or even by a legitimate inference from what has been directly observed? Does he not maintain that the mind has an immediate knowledge or experience only of its own ideas? How can he prove that there are material extended things outside causing these ideas? And if he cannot prove it by an appeal to experience, to direct observation, is he not, in accepting the existence of the external world at all, just as truly as Descartes, a rationalist?"

The objection is well taken. On his own principles, Locke had no right to believe in an external world. He has stolen his world, so to speak; he has taken it by violence. Nevertheless, as I pointed out in the section above referred to, Locke is not a rationalist of *malice prepense*. He *tries* to be an empiricist. He believes in the external world because he thinks it is directly revealed to the senses—he inconsistently refers to experience as evidence of its existence.

It has often been claimed by those who do not sympathize with empiricism that the empiricists make assumptions much as others do, but have not the grace to admit it. I think we must frankly confess that a man may try hard to be an empiricist and may not be wholly successful. Moreover, reflection forces us to the conclusion that when we have defined empiricism as a doctrine which rests throughout upon an appeal to "experience" we have not said anything very definite.

77

What is *experience*? What may we accept as directly revealed fact? The answer to such questions is far from an easy one to give. It is a harder matter to discuss intelligently than any one can at all realize until he has spent some years in following the efforts of the philosophers to determine what is "revealed fact." We are supposed to have experience of our own minds, of space, of time, of matter. What are these things as revealed in our experience? We have seen in the earlier chapters of this book that one cannot answer such questions off-hand.

62. CRITICISM.—I have in another chapter (section 51) given a brief account of the philosophy of Immanuel Kant. He called his doctrine "Criticism," and he distinguished it from "Dogmatism" and "Empiricism."

Every philosophy that transcends experience, without first critically examining our faculty of knowledge and determining its right to spread its wings in this way, Kant calls "dogmatism." The word seems rather an offensive one, in its usual signification, at least; and it is as well not to use it. As Kant used the word, Descartes was a dogmatist; but let us rather call him a rationalist. He certainly had no intention of proceeding uncritically, as we shall see a little later. If we call him a dogmatist we seem to condemn him in advance, by applying to him an abusive epithet.

Empiricism, according to Kant, confines human knowledge to experience, and thus avoids the errors which beset the dogmatist. But then, as Hume seemed to have shown, empiricism must run out into skepticism. If all our knowledge has its foundations in experience, how can we expect to find in our possession any universal or necessary truths? May not a later experience contradict an earlier? How can we be sure that what has been will be? Can we *know* that there is anything fixed and certain in our world?

Skepticism seemed a forlorn doctrine, and, casting about for a way of escape from it, Kant hit upon the expedient which I have described. So long as we maintain that our knowledge has no other source than the experiences which the world imprints upon us, so to speak, from without, we are without the power of prediction, for new experiences may annihilate any generalizations we have founded upon those already vouchsafed us; but if we assume that the world upon which we gaze, the world of phenomena, is made what it is by the mind that perceives it, are we not in a different position?

Suppose, for example, we take the statement that there must be an adequate cause of all the changes that take place in the world. Can a mere experience of what has been in the past guarantee that this law will hold good in the future? But, when we realize that the world of which we are speaking is nothing more than a world of phenomena, of experiences, and realize further that this whole world is constructed by the mind out of the raw materials furnished by the senses, may we not have a greater confidence in our law? If it is the nature of the mind to connect the phenomena presented to it with one another as cause and effect, may we not maintain that no phenomenon can possibly make its appearance that defies the law in question? How could it appear except under the conditions laid upon all phenomena? If it is our nature to think the world as an orderly one, and if we can know no world save the one we construct ourselves, the orderliness of all the things we can know seems to be guaranteed to us.

It will be noticed that Kant's doctrine has a negative side. He limits our knowledge to phenomena, to experiences, and he is himself, in so far, an empiricist. But in that he finds in experience an order, an arrangement of things, not derived from experience in the usual sense of the word, he is not an empiricist. He has paid his own doctrine the compliment of calling it "criticism," as I have said.

Now, I beg the reader to be here, as elsewhere, on his guard against the associations which attach to words. In calling Kant's doctrine "the critical philosophy," we are in some danger of uncritically assuming and leading others to believe uncritically that it is free from such defects as may be expected to attach to "dogmatism" and to empiricism. Such a position should not be taken until one has made a most careful examination of each of the three types of doctrine, of the assumptions which it makes, and of the rigor with which it draws inferences upon the basis of such assumptions. That we may be the better able to withstand "undue influence," I call attention to the following points:—

(1) We must bear in mind that the attempt to make a critical examination into the foundations of our knowledge, and to determine its scope, is by no means a new thing. Among the Greeks, Plato, Aristotle, the Stoics, the Epicureans, and the Skeptics, all attacked the problem. It did not, of course, present itself to these men in the precise form in which it presented itself to Kant, but each and all were concerned to find an answer to the question: Can we know anything with certainty; and, if so, what? They may have failed to be thoroughly critical, but they certainly made the attempt.

I shall omit mention of the long series of others, who, since that time, have carried on the tradition, and shall speak only of Descartes and Locke, whom I have above brought forward as representatives of the two types of doctrine that Kant contrasts with his own.

To see how strenuously Descartes endeavored to subject his knowledge to a critical scrutiny and to avoid unjustifiable assumptions of any sort, one has only to read that charming little work of genius, the "Discourse on the Method of Rightly Conducting the Reason."

In his youth Descartes was, as he informs us, an eager student; but, when he had finished the whole course of education usually prescribed, he found himself so full of doubts and errors that he did not feel that he had advanced in learning at all. Yet he had been well tutored, and was considered as bright in mind as others. He was led to judge his neighbor by himself, and to conclude that there existed no such certain science as he had been taught to suppose.

Having ripened with years and experience, Descartes set about the task of which I have spoken above, the task of sweeping away the whole body of his opinions and of attempting a general and systematic reconstruction. So important a work should be, he thought, approached with circumspection; hence, he formulated certain Rules of Method.

"The first," he writes, "was never to accept anything for true which I did not clearly know to be such; that is, carefully to avoid haste and prejudice, and to include nothing more in my judgments than what was presented to my mind so clearly and distinctly as to exclude all reason for doubt."

Such was our philosopher's design, and such the spirit in which he set about it. We have seen the result above. It is as if Descartes had decided that a certain room full of people did not appear to be free from suspicious characters, and had cleared out every one, afterwards posting himself at the door to readmit only those who proved themselves worthy. When we examine those who succeeded in passing muster, we discover he has favored all his old friends. He simply *cannot* doubt them; are they not vouched for by the "natural light"? Nevertheless, we must not forget that Descartes sifted his congregation with much travail of spirit. He did try to be critical.

As for John Locke, he reveals in the "Epistle to the Reader," which stands as a preface to the "Essay," the critical spirit in which his work was taken up. "Were it fit to trouble thee," he writes, "with the history of this Essay, I should tell thee, that five or six friends meeting at my chamber, and discoursing on a subject very remote from this, found themselves quickly at a stand, by the difficulties that rose on every side. After we had a while puzzled ourselves, without coming any nearer a resolution of those doubts which perplexed us, it came into my thoughts, that we took a wrong course; and that before we set ourselves upon inquiries of that nature, it was necessary to examine our own abilities, and to see what objects our understandings were, or were not, fitted to deal with."

This problem, proposed by himself to his little circle of friends, Locke attacked with earnestness, and as a result he brought out many years later the work which has since become so famous. The book is literally a critique of the reason, although a very different critique from that worked out by Kant.

"If, by this inquiry into the nature of the understanding," says Locke, "I can discover the powers thereof, how far they reach, to what things they are in any degree proportionate, and where they fail us; I suppose it may be of use to prevail with the busy mind of man to be more cautious in meddling with things exceeding its comprehension; to stop when it is at the utmost extent of its tether; and to sit down in a quiet ignorance of those things which upon examination are found to be beyond the reach of our capacities." [2]

To the difficulties of the task our author is fully alive: "The understanding, like the eye, whilst it makes us see and perceive all other things, takes no notice of itself; and it requires art and pains to set it at a distance, and make it its own object. But whatever be the difficulties that lie in the way of this inquiry, whatever it be that keeps us so much in the dark to ourselves, sure I am that all the light we can let in upon our own minds, all the acquaintance we can make with our own understandings, will not only be very pleasant, but bring us great advantage, in directing our thoughts in the search, of other things." [3]

(2) Thus, many men have attempted to produce a critical philosophy, and in much the same sense as that in which Kant uses the words. Those who have come after them have decided that they were not sufficiently critical, that they have made unjustifiable assumptions. When we come to read Kant, we will, if we have read the history of philosophy with profit, not forget to ask ourselves if he has not sinned in the same way.

For example, we will ask;—

(a) Was Kant right in maintaining that we find in experience synthetic judgments (section 51) that are not founded upon experience, but yield such information as is beyond the reach of the empiricist? There are those who think that the judgments to which he alludes in evidence of his contention—the mathematical, for instance—are not of this character.

(b) Was he justified in assuming that all the ordering of our world is due to the activity of mind, and that merely the raw material is "given" us through the senses? There are many who demur against such a statement, and hold that it is, if not in all senses untrue, at least highly misleading, since it seems to argue that there is no really external world at all. Moreover, they claim that the doctrine is neither self-evident nor susceptible of proper proof.

(c) Was Kant justified in assuming that, even if we attribute the "form" or arrangement of the world we know to the native activity of the mind, the necessity and universality of our knowledge is assured? Let us grant that the proposition, whatever happens must have an adequate cause, is a "form of thought." What guarantee have we that the "forms of thought" must ever remain changeless? If it is an assumption for the empiricist to declare that what has been true in the past will be true in the future, that earlier experiences of the world will not be contradicted by later; what is it for the Kantian to maintain that the order which he finds in his experience will necessarily and always be the order of all future experiences? Transferring an assumption to the field of mind does not make it less of an assumption.

Thus, it does not seem unreasonable to charge Kant with being a good deal of a rationalist. He tried to confine our knowledge to the field of experience, it is true; but he made a number of assumptions as to the nature of experience which certainly do not shine by their own light, and which many thoughtful persons regard as incapable of justification.

Kant's famous successors in the German philosophy, Fichte (1762-1814), Schelling (1775-1854), Hegel (1770-1831), and Schopenhauer (1788-1860), all received their impulse from the "critical philosophy," and yet each developed his doctrine in a relatively independent way.

I cannot here take the space to characterize the systems of these men; I may merely remark that all of them contrast strongly in doctrine and method with the British philosophers mentioned in the last section, Locke, Berkeley, Hume, and Mill. They are *un-empirical*, if one may use such a word; and, to one accustomed to reading the English philosophy, they seem ever ready to spread their wings and hazard the boldest of flights without a proper realization of the thinness of the atmosphere in which they must support themselves.

However, no matter what may be one's opinion of the actual results attained by these German philosophers, one must frankly admit that no one who wishes to understand clearly the development of speculative thought can afford to dispense with a careful reading of them. Much even of the English philosophy of our own day must remain obscure to those who have not looked into their pages. Thus, the thought of Kant and Hegel molded the thought of Thomas Hill Green (1836-1882) and of the brothers Caird; and their influence has made itself widely felt both in England and in America. One cannot criticise intelligently books written from their standpoint, unless one knows how the authors came by their doctrine and out of what it has been developed.

63. CRITICAL EMPIRICISM.—We have seen that the trouble with the rationalists seemed to be that they made an appeal to "eternal truths," which those who followed them could not admit to be eternal truths at all. They proceeded on a basis of assumptions the validity of which was at once called in question.

Locke, the empiricist, repudiated all this, and then also made assumptions which others could not, and cannot, approve. Kant did something of much the same sort; we cannot regard his "criticism" as wholly critical.

How can we avoid such errors? How walk cautiously, and go around the pit into which, as it seems to us, others have fallen? I may as well tell the reader frankly that he sets his hope too high if he expects to avoid all error and to work out for himself a philosophy in all respects unassailable. The difficulties of reflective thought are very great, and we should carry with us a consciousness of that fact and a willingness to revise our most cherished conclusions.

Our initial difficulty seems to be that we must begin by assuming *something*, if only as material upon which to work. We must begin our philosophizing *somewhere*. Where shall we begin? May we not fall into error at the very outset?

The doctrine set forth in the earlier chapters of this volume maintains that we must accept as our material the revelation of the mind and the world which seems to be made in our common experience, and which is extended and systematized in the sciences. But it insists that we must regard such an acceptance as merely provisional, must subject our concepts to a careful criticism, and must always be on our guard against hasty assumptions.

It emphasizes the value of the light which historical study casts upon the real meaning of the concepts which we all use and must use, but which have so often proved to be stones of stumbling in the path of those who have employed them. Its watchword is analysis, always analysis; and a settled distrust of what have so often passed as "self-evident" truths. It regards it as its task to analyze experience, while maintaining that only the satisfactory carrying out of such an analysis can reveal what experience really is, and clear our notions of it from misinterpretations.

No such attempt to give an account of experience can be regarded as fundamentally new in its method. Every philosopher, in his own way, criticises experience, and seeks its interpretation. But one may, warned by the example of one's predecessors, lay emphasis upon the danger of half-analyses and hasty assumptions, and counsel the observance of sobriety and caution.

For convenience, I have called the doctrine *Critical Empiricism*. I warn the reader against the seductive title, and advise him not to allow it to influence him unduly in his judgment of the doctrine.

64. PRAGMATISM.—It seems right that I should, before closing this chapter, say a few words about Pragmatism, which has been so much discussed in the last few years.

In 1878 Mr. Charles S. Peirce wrote an article for the *Popular Science Monthly* in which he proposed as a maxim for the attainment of clearness of apprehension the following: "Consider what effects, which might conceivably have practical bearings, we conceive the object of our conception to have. Then, our conception of these effects is the whole of our conception of the object."

This thought has been taken up by others and given a development which Mr. Peirce regards with some suspicion. He refers[4] especially to the development it has received at the hands of Professor William James, in his two essays, "The Will to Believe" and "Philosophical Conceptions and Practical Results." [5] Professor James is often regarded as foremost among the pragmatists.

I shall not attempt to define pragmatism, for I do not believe that the doctrine has yet attained to that definiteness of formulation which warrants a definition. We seem to have to do not so much with a clear-cut doctrine, the limits and consequences of which have been worked out in detail, as with a tendency which makes itself apparent in the works of various writers under somewhat different forms.

I may roughly describe it as the tendency to take that to be *true* which is *useful* or *serviceable*. It is well illustrated in the two essays to which reference is made above.

Thus, Professor James dwells upon the unsatisfactoriness and uncertainty of philosophical and scientific knowledge: "Objective evidence and certitude are doubtless very fine ideals to play with, but where on this moonlit and dream-visited planet are they found?"

Now, among those things regarding which it appears impossible to attain to intellectual certitude, there are matters of great practical moment, and which affect deeply the conduct of life; for example, the doctrines of religion. Here a merely skeptical attitude seems intolerable.

In such cases, argues Professor James, "we have the right to believe at our own risk any hypothesis that is live enough to tempt our will."

It is important to notice that there is no question here of a logical right. We are concerned with matters regarding which, according to Professor James, we cannot look for intellectual evidence. It is assumed that we believe simply because we choose to believe—we believe arbitrarily.

It is further important to notice that what is a "live" hypothesis to one man need not tempt the will of another man at all. As our author points out, a Turk would naturally will to believe one thing and a Christian would will to believe another. Each would will to believe what struck him as a satisfactory thing to believe.

What shall we say to this doctrine? I think we must say that it is clearly not a philosophical *method of attaining to truth*. Hence, it has not properly a place in this chapter among the attempts which have been made to attain to the truth of things.

It is, in fact, not concerned with truths, but with assumptions, and with assumptions which are supposed to be made on the basis of no evidence. It is concerned with "seemings."

The distinction is a very important one. Our Turk cannot, by willing to believe it, make his hypothesis true; but he can make it *seem* true. Why should he wish to make it seem true whether it is true or not? Why should he strive to attain to a feeling of subjective certainty, not by logically resolving his doubts, but by ignoring them?

The answer is given us by our author. He who lives in the midst of doubts, and refuses to cut his knot with the sword of belief, misses the good of life. This is a practical problem, and one of no small moment. In the last section of this book I have tried to indicate what it is wise for a man to do when he is confronted by doubts which he cannot resolve.

Into the general question whether even a false belief may not, under some circumstances, be more serviceable than no belief at all, I shall not enter. The point I wish to emphasize is that there is all the difference in the world between *producing a belief* and *proving a truth*.

We are compelled to accept it as a fact that men, under the influence of feeling, can believe in the absence of evidence, or, for that matter, can believe in spite of evidence. But a truth cannot be established in the absence of evidence or in the face of adverse evidence. And there is a very wide field in which it is made very clear to us that beliefs adopted in the absence of evidence are in danger of being false beliefs.

The pragmatist would join with the rest of us in condemning the Turk or the Christian who would simply will to believe in the rise or the fall of stocks, and would refuse to consult the state of the market. Some hypotheses are, in the ordinary course of events, put to the test of verification. We are then made painfully aware that beliefs and truths are quite distinct things, and may not be in harmony.

Now, the pragmatist does not apply his principle to this field. He confines it to what may not inaptly be called the field of the unverifiable. The Turk, who wills to believe in the hypothesis that appeals to him as a pious Turk, is in no such danger of a rude awakening as is the man who wills to believe that stocks will go up or down. But mark what this means: it means that *he is not in danger of finding out what the truth really is*. It does not mean that he is in possession of the truth.

So I say, the doctrine which we are discussing is not a method of attaining to truth. What it really attempts to do is to point out to us how it is prudent for us to act when we cannot discover what the truth is.[6]

[1] "An Essay concerning Human Understanding," Book II, Chapter I, section 2.
[2] Book I, Chapter I, section 4.
[3] Book I, Chapter I, section 1.
[4] "Dictionary of Philosophy and Psychology," article "Pragmatism."
[5] Published in 1897 and 1898.
[6] For references to later developments of pragmatism, see the note on page 312.

V. THE PHILOSOPHICAL SCIENCES
CHAPTER XVI
LOGIC

65. INTRODUCTORY: THE PHILOSOPHICAL SCIENCES.—I have said in the first chapter of this book (section 6) that there is quite a group of sciences that are regarded as belonging peculiarly to the province of the teacher of philosophy to-day. Having, in the chapters preceding, given some account of the nature of reflective thought, of the problems touching the world and the mind which present themselves to those who reflect, and of some types of philosophical theory which have their origin in such reflection, I turn to a brief consideration of the philosophical sciences.

Among these I included logic, psychology, ethics, and aesthetics, metaphysics, and the history of philosophy. I did not include epistemology or "the theory of knowledge" as a separate discipline, and my reasons for this will appear in Chapter XIX. I remarked that, to complete the list, we should have to add the philosophy of religion and an investigation into the principles and methods of the sciences generally.

Why, it was asked, should this group of disciplines be regarded as the field of the philosopher, when others are excluded? The answer to this question which finds the explanation of the fact to lie in a mere historical accident was declared unsatisfactory, and it was maintained that the philosophical sciences are those in which we find ourselves carried back to the problems of reflective thought.

With a view to showing the truth of this opinion, I shall take up one by one the philosophical sciences. Of the history of philosophy I shall not speak in this part of the work, but shall treat of it in Chapter XXIII.

66. THE TRADITIONAL LOGIC.—Most of us begin our acquaintance with logic in the study of some such elementary manual as Jevons' "Lessons in Logic."

In such books we are shown how terms represent things and classes of things or their attributes, and how we unite them into propositions or statements. It is indicated at length what statements may be made on a basis of certain other statements and what may not; and emphasis is laid upon the dangers which arise out of a misunderstanding of the language in which we are forced to express our thoughts. Finally, there are described for us the experimental methods by which the workers in the sciences have attained to the general information about the world which has become our heritage.

Such books are useful. It is surely no small profit for a student to gain the habit of scrutinizing the steps by which he has come into the possession of a certain bit of information, and to have a quick eye for loose and inconsistent reasonings.

But it is worthy of remark that one may study such a book as this and yet remain pretty consistently on what may be called the plane of the common understanding. One seems to make the assumptions made in all the special sciences, *e.g.* the assumption that there is a world of real things and that we can know them and reason about them. We are not introduced to such problems as: What *is* truth? and Is *any* knowledge valid? Nor does it seem at once apparent that the man who is studying logic in this way is busying himself with a philosophical discipline.

67. THE "MODERN LOGIC."—It is very puzzling for the student to turn from such a text-book as the one above mentioned to certain others which profess to be occupied with the same science, and which, yet, appear to treat of quite different things.

Thus, in Dr. Bosanquet's little work on "The Essentials of Logic," the reader is at once plunged into such questions as the nature of knowledge, and what is meant by the real world. We seem to be dealing with metaphysics, and not with logic, as we have learned to understand the term. How is it that the logician comes to regard these things as within his province?

A multitude of writers at the present day are treating logic in this way, and in some great prominence is given to problems which the philosopher recognizes as indisputably his own. The term "modern logic" is often employed to denote a logic of this type; one which does not, after the fashion of the natural sciences generally, proceed on the basis of certain assumptions, and leave deeper questions to some other discipline, but tries to get to the bottom of things for itself. The tendency to run into metaphysics is peculiarly marked in those writers who have been influenced by the work of the philosopher Hegel.

I shall not here ask why those who belong to one school are more inclined to be metaphysical than are those who belong to another, but shall approach the broader question why the logicians generally are inclined to be more metaphysical than those who work in certain other special sciences, such as mathematics, for example. Of the general tendency there can be no question. The only problem is: Why does this tendency exist?

68. LOGIC AND PHILOSOPHY.—Let us contrast the science of arithmetic with logic; and let us notice, regarding it, the following points:—

It is, like logic, a *general* science, in that the things treated of in many sciences may be numbered. It considers only a certain aspect of the things.

Now, that things may be counted, added together, subtracted, etc., is guaranteed by the experience of the plain man; and the methods of determining the numerical relations of things are gradually developed before his eyes, beginning with operations of great simplicity. Moreover, verification is possible, and within certain limits verification by direct inspection.

To this we may add, that there has gradually been built up a fine system of unambiguous symbols, and it is possible for a man to know just what he is dealing with.

Thus, a certain beaten path has been attained, and a man may travel this very well without having forced on his attention the problems of reflective thought. The knowledge of numbers with which he starts is sufficient equipment with which to undertake the journey. That one is on the right road is proved by the results one obtains. As a rule, disputes can be settled by well-tried mathematical methods.

There is, then, a common agreement as to initial assumptions and methods of work, and useful results are attained which seem to justify both. Here we have the normal characteristics of a special science.

We must not forget, however, that, even in the mathematical sciences, before a beaten path was attained, disputes as to the significance of numbers and the cogency of proofs were sufficiently common. And we must bear in mind that even to-day, where the beaten path does not seem wholly satisfactory, men seem to be driven to reflect upon the significance of their assumptions and the nature of their method.

Thus, we find it not unnatural that a man should be led to ask; What is a minus quantity really? Can anything be less than nothing? or that he should raise the questions: Can one rightly speak of an infinite number? Can one infinite number be greater than another, and, if so, what can greater mean? What are infinitesimals? and what can be meant by different orders of infinitesimals?

He who has interested himself in such questions as these has betaken himself to philosophical reflection. They are not answered by employing mathematical methods.

Let us now turn to logic. And let us notice, to begin with, that it is broader in its application than the mathematical sciences. It is concerned to discover what constitutes *evidence* in every field of investigation.

There is, it is true, a part of logic that may be developed somewhat after the fashion of mathematics. Thus, we may examine the two statements: All men are mortal, and Caesar is a man; and we may see clearly that, given the truth of these, we must admit that Caesar is mortal. We may make a list of possible inferences of this kind, and point out under what circumstances the truth of two statements implies the truth of a third, and under what circumstances the inference cannot be made. Our results can be set forth in a system of symbols. As in mathematics, we may abstract from the particular things reasoned about, and concern ourselves only with the forms of reasoning. This gives us the theory of the *syllogism*; it is a part of logic in which the mathematician is apt to feel very much at home.

But this is by no means all of logic. Let us consider the following points:—

(1) We are not concerned to know only what statements may be made on the basis of certain other statements. We want to know what is true and what is false. We must ask: Has a man the right to set up these particular statements and to reason from them? That some men accept as true premises which are repudiated by others is an undoubted fact. Thus, it is maintained by certain philosophers that we may assume that any view of the universe which is repellant to our nature cannot be true. Shall we allow this to pass unchallenged? And in ethics, some have held that it is under all circumstances wrong to lie; others have denied this, and have held that in certain cases—for example, to save life or to prevent great and unmerited suffering—lying is permissible. Shall we interest ourselves only in the deductions that each man makes from his assumed premises, and pay no attention to the truth of the premises themselves?

(2) Again. The vast mass of the reasonings that interest men are expressed in the language that we all use and not in special symbols. But language is a very imperfect instrument, and all sorts of misunderstandings are possible to those who express their thoughts in it.

Few men know exactly how much is implied in what they are saying. If I say: All men are mortal, and an angel is not a man; therefore, an angel is not mortal; it is not at once apparent to every one in what respect my argument is defective. He who argues: Feathers are light; light is contrary to darkness; hence, feathers are contrary to darkness; is convicted of error without difficulty. But arguments of the same kind, and quite as bad, are to be found in learned works on matters less familiar to us, and we often fail to detect the fallacy.

Thus, Herbert Spencer argues, in effect, in the fourth and fifth chapters of his "First Principles," as follows:—

We are conscious of the Unknowable,

The Unknowable lies behind the veil of phenomena,

Hence, we are conscious of what lies behind the veil of phenomena.

It is only the critical reader who notices that the Unknowable in the first line is the "raw material of consciousness," and the Unknowable in the second is something not in consciousness at all. The two senses of the word "light" are not more different from one another. Such apparent arguments abound, and it often requires much acuteness to be able to detect their fallacious character.

When we take into consideration the two points indicated above, we see that the logician is at every turn forced to reflect upon our knowledge as men do not ordinarily reflect. He is led to ask: What is truth? He cannot accept uncritically the assumptions which men make; and he must endeavor to become very clearly conscious of the real meaning and the whole meaning of statements expressed in words. Even in the simple logic with which we usually begin our studies, we learn to scrutinize statements in a reflective way; and when we go deeper, we are at once in contact with philosophical problems. It is evidently our task to attain to a clearer insight into the nature of our experience and the meaning of proof than is attainable by the unreflective.

Logic, then, is a reflective science, and it is not surprising that it has held its place as one of the philosophical sciences.

CHAPTER XVII

PSYCHOLOGY

69. PSYCHOLOGY AND PHILOSOPHY.—I think I have said enough in Chapter II (section 10) about what we mean when we speak of psychology as a natural science and as an independent discipline. Certainly there are many psychologists who would not care to be confused with the philosophers, and there are some that regard philosophy with suspicion.

Nevertheless, psychology is commonly regarded as belonging to the philosophical group. That this is the case can scarcely be thought surprising when we see how the psychologist himself speaks of the relation of his science to philosophy.

"I have kept," writes Professor James[1] in that delightful book which has become the common property of us all, "close to the point of view of natural science throughout the book. Every natural science assumes certain data uncritically, and declines to challenge the elements between which its own 'laws' obtain, and from which its own deductions are carried on. Psychology, the science of finite individual minds, assumes as its data (1)*thoughts and feelings*, and (2) *a physical world* in time and space with which they coexist, and which (3) *they know*. Of course, these data themselves are discussable; but the discussion of them (as of other elements) is called metaphysics and falls outside the province of this book."

This is an admirable statement of the scope of psychology as a natural science, and also of the relations of metaphysics to the sciences. But it would not be fair to Professor James to take this sentence alone, and to assume that, in his opinion, it is easy to separate psychology altogether from philosophy. "The reader," he tells us in the next paragraph, "will in vain seek for any closed system in the book. It is mainly a mass of descriptive details, running out into queries which only a metaphysics alive to the weight of her task can hope successfully to deal with." And in the opening sentence of the preface he informs us that some of his chapters are more "metaphysical" than is suitable for students going over the subject for the first time.

That the author is right in maintaining that it is not easy to draw a clear line between philosophy and psychology, and to declare the latter wholly independent, I think we must concede. An independent science should be sure of the things with which it is dealing. Where these are vague and indefinite, and are the subject of constant dispute, it cannot march forward with assurance. One is rather forced to go back and examine the data themselves. The beaten track of the special science has not been satisfactorily constructed.

We are forced to admit that the science of psychology has not yet emerged from the state in which a critical examination of its foundations is necessary, and that the construction of the beaten path is still in progress. This I shall try to make clear by illustrations.

The psychologist studies the mind, and his ultimate appeal must be to introspection, to a direct observation of mental phenomena, and of their relations to external things. Now, if the observation of mental phenomena were a simple and an easy thing; if the mere fact that we are conscious of sensations and ideas implied that we are *clearly* conscious of them and are in a position to describe them with accuracy, psychology would be a much more satisfactory science than it is.

But we are not thus conscious of our mental life. We can and do use our mental states without being able to describe them accurately. In a sense, we are conscious of what is there, but our consciousness is rather dim and vague, and in our attempts to give an account of it we are in no little danger of giving a false account.

Thus, the psychologist assumes that we perceive both physical phenomena and mental— the external world and the mind. He takes it for granted that we perceive mental phenomena to be related to physical. He is hardly in a position to make this assumption, and then to set it aside as a thing he need not further consider. Does he not tell us, as a result of his investigations, that we can know the external world only as it is reflected in our sensations, and thus seem to shut the mind up within the circle of mental phenomena merely, cutting off absolutely a direct knowledge of what is extra-mental? If we can know only mental phenomena, the representatives of things, at first hand, how can we tell that they are representatives? and what becomes of the assumption that we *perceive* that mind is related to an external world?

It may be said, this problem the psychologist may leave to the metaphysician. Certainly, it is one of those problems that the metaphysician discusses; it has been treated in Chapter IV. But my contention is, that he who has given no thought to the matter may easily fall into error as to the very nature of mental phenomena.

For example, when we approach or recede from a physical object we have a series of experiences which are recognized as sensational. When we imagine a tree or a house we are also experiencing a mental phenomenon. All these experiences *seem* plainly to have extension in some sense of the word. We appear to perceive plainly part out of part. In so far, these mental things seem to resemble the physical things which we contrast with what is mental. Shall we say that, because these things are mental and not physical, their apparent extension is a delusion? Shall we say that they really have no parts? Such considerations have impelled psychologists of eminence to maintain, in flat contradiction to what seems to be the unequivocal testimony of direct introspection, that the total content of consciousness at any moment must be looked upon as an indivisible, part-less unit.

We cannot, then, depend merely on direct introspection. It is too uncertain in its deliverances. If we would make clear to ourselves what mental phenomena really are, and how they | differ from physical phenomena, we must fall back upon the reflective analysis of our experience which occupies the metaphysician (section 34). Until we have done this, we are in great danger of error. We are actually uncertain of our materials.

Again. The psychologist speaks of the relation of mind and body. Some psychologists incline to be parallelists, some are warm advocates of interactionism. Now, any theory of the relation of mind to body must depend on observation ultimately. If we had not direct experience of a relation between the physical and the mental somewhere, no hypothesis on the subject would ever have emerged.

But our experiences are not perfectly clear and unequivocal to us. Their significance does not seem to be easily grasped. To comprehend it one is forced to that reflective examination of experience which is characteristic of the philosopher (Chapter IX).

Here it may again be said: Leave the matter to the meta-physician and go on with your psychological work. I answer: The psychologist is not in the same position as the botanist or the zoölogist. He is studying mind in its relation to body. It cannot but be unsatisfactory to him to leave that relation wholly vague; and, as a matter of fact, he usually takes up with one theory or another. We have seen (section 36) that he may easily adopt a theory that leads him to overlook the great difference between physical phenomena and mental phenomena, and to treat them as though they were the same. This one may do in spite of all that introspection has to say about the gulf that separates them.

Psychology is, then, very properly classed among the philosophical sciences. The psychologist is not sufficiently sure of his materials to be able to dispense with reflective thought, in many parts of his field. Some day there may come to be a consensus of opinion touching fundamental facts, and the science may become more independent. A beaten track may be attained; but that has not yet been done.

70. THE DOUBLE AFFILIATION OF PSYCHOLOGY.—In spite of what has been said above, we must not forget that psychology is a *relatively* independent science. One may be a useful psychologist without knowing much about philosophy.

As in logic it is possible to write a text-book not greatly different in spirit and method from text-books concerned with the sciences not classed as philosophical, so it is possible to make a useful study of mental phenomena without entering upon metaphysical analyses. In science, as in common life, we can *use* concepts without subjecting them to careful analysis.

Thus, our common experience reveals that mind and body are connected. We may, for a specific purpose, leave the *nature* of this connection vague, and may pay careful attention to the physiological conditions of mental phenomena, studying in detail the senses and the nervous system. We may, further, endeavor to render our knowledge of mental phenomena more full and accurate by experimentation. In doing this we may be compelled to make use of elaborate apparatus. Of such mechanical aids to investigation our psychological laboratories are full.

It is to such work as this that we owe what is called the "physiological" and the "experimental" psychology. One can carry on such investigations without being a metaphysician. But one can scarcely carry them on without having a good knowledge of certain sciences not commonly supposed to be closely related to psychology at all. Thus, one should be trained in chemistry and physics and physiology, and should have a working knowledge of laboratory methods. Moreover, it is desirable to have a sufficient knowledge of mathematics to enable one to handle experimental data.

The consideration of such facts as these sometimes leads men to raise the question: Should psychology affiliate with philosophy or with the physical sciences? The issue is an illegitimate one. Psychology is one of the philosophical sciences, and cannot dispense with reflection; but that is no reason why it should not acknowledge a close relation to certain physical sciences as well. Parts of the field can be isolated, and one may work as one works in the natural sciences generally; but if one does nothing more, one's concepts remain unanalyzed, and, as we have seen in the previous section, there is some danger of actual misconception.

[1] "Psychology," Preface.

CHAPTER XVIII

ETHICS AND AESTHETICS

71. COMMON SENSE ETHICS.—We may, if we choose, study the actions of men merely with a view to ascertaining what they are and describing them accurately. Something like this is done by the anthropologist, who gives us an account of the manners and customs of the various races of mankind; he tells us *what is*; he may not regard it as within his province at all to inform us regarding *what ought to be*.

But men do not merely act; they judge their actions in the light of some norm or standard, and they distinguish between them as right and wrong. The systematic study of actions as right and wrong yields us the science of ethics.

Like psychology, ethics is a special science. It is concerned with a somewhat limited field of investigation, and is not to be confounded with other sciences. It has a definite aim distinct from theirs. And, also like psychology, ethics is classed as one of the philosophical sciences, and its relation to philosophy is supposed to be closer than that of such sciences as physics and mathematics. It is fair to ask why this is so. Why cannot ethics proceed on the basis of certain assumptions independently, and leave to some other discipline the whole question of an inquiry into the nature and validity of those assumptions?

About half a century ago Dr. William Whewell, one of the most learned of English scholars, wrote a work entitled "The Elements of Morality," in which he attempted to treat the science of ethics as it is generally admitted that one may treat the science of geometry. The book was rather widely read a generation since, but we meet with few references to it in our time.

"Morality and the philosophy of morality," argues the author, "differ in the same manner and in the same degree as geometry and the philosophy of geometry. Of these two subjects, geometry consists of a series of positive and definite propositions, deduced one from another, in succession, by rigorous reasoning, and all resting upon certain definitions and self-evident axioms. The philosophy of geometry is quite a different subject; it includes such inquiries as these: Whence is the cogency of geometrical proof? What is the evidence of the axioms and definitions? What are the faculties by which we become aware of their truth? and the like. The two kinds of speculation have been pursued, for the most part, by two different classes of persons,—the geometers and the metaphysicians; for it has been far more the occupation of metaphysicians than of geometers to discuss such questions as I have stated, the nature of geometrical proofs, geometrical axioms, the geometrical faculty, and the like. And if we construct a complete system of geometry, it will be almost exactly the same, whatever be the views which we take on these metaphysical questions." [1]

Such a system Dr. Whewell wishes to construct in the field of ethics. His aim is to give us a view of morality in which moral propositions are "deduced from axioms, by successive steps of reasoning, so far as to form a connected system of moral truth." Such a "sure and connected knowledge of the duties of man" would, he thinks, be of the greatest importance.

In accordance with this purpose, Dr. Whewell assumes that humanity, justice, truth, purity, order, earnestness, and moral purpose are fundamental principles of human action; and he thinks that all who admit as much as this will be able to go on with him in his development of a system of moral rules to govern the life of man.

It would hardly be worth while for me to speak at length of a way of treating ethics so little likely to be urged upon the attention of the reader who busies himself with the books which are appearing in our own day, were it not that we have here an admirable illustration of the attempt to teach ethics as though it were such a science as geometry. The shortcomings of the method become very evident to one who reads the work attentively.

Thus, we are forced to ask ourselves, have we really a collection of ultimate moral principles which are analogous to the axioms of geometry? For example, to take but a single instance, Dr. Whewell formulates the Principle of Truth as follows: "We must conform to the universal understanding among men which the use of language implies";[2] and he remarks later; "The rules: *Lie not*, Perform your promise, are of universal validity; and the conceptions of *lie* and of *promise* are so simple and distinct that, in general, the rules may be directly and easily applied." [3]

Now, we are struck by the fact that this affirmation of the universal validity of the principle of truth is made in a chapter on "Cases of Conscience," in a chapter concerned with what seem to be conflicts between duties; and this chapter is followed by one which treats of "Cases of Necessity," *i.e.* cases in which a man is to be regarded as justified in violating common rules when there seems to be urgent reason for so doing. We are told that the moralist cannot say: Lie not, except in great emergencies; but must say: Lie not at all. But we are also told that he must grant that there are cases of necessity in which transgressions of moral rules are excusable; and this looks very much as if he said: Go on and do the thing while I close my eyes.

This hardly seems to give us a "sure and connected knowledge of the duties of man" deduced from axiomatic principles. On what authority shall we suspend for the time being this axiomatic principle or that? Is there some deeper principle which lends to each of them its authority, and which may, for cause, withdraw it? There is no hint of such in the treatment of ethics which we are considering, and we seem to have on our hands, not so much a science, as a collection of practical rules, of the scope of which we are more or less in the dark.

The interesting thing to notice is that this view of ethics is very closely akin to that adapted unconsciously by the majority of the persons we meet who have not interested themselves much in ethics as a science.

By the time that we have reached years of discretion we are all in possession of a considerable number of moral maxims. We consider it wrong to steal, to lie, to injure our neighbor. Such maxims lie in our minds side by side, and we do not commonly think of criticising them. But now and then we face a situation in which one maxim seems to urge one course of action and another maxim a contrary one. Shall we tell the truth and the whole truth, when so doing will bring grave misfortune upon an innocent person? And now and then we are brought to the realization that all men do not admit the validity of all our maxims. Judgments differ as to what is right and what is wrong. Who shall be the arbiter? Not infrequently a rough decision is arrived at in the assumption that we have only to interrogate "conscience"—in the assumption, in other words, that we carry a watch which can be counted upon to give the correct time, even if the timepieces of our neighbors are not to be depended upon.

The common sense ethics cannot be regarded as very systematic and consistent, or as very profound. It is a collection of working rules, of practical maxims; and, although it is impossible to overestimate its value as a guide to life, its deficiencies, when it is looked at critically, become evident, I think, even to thoughtful persons who are not scientific at all.

Many writers on ethics have simply tried to turn this collection of working rules into a science, somewhat as Dr. Whewell has done. This is the peculiar weakness of those who have been called the "intuitionalists"—though I must warn the reader against assuming that this term has but the one meaning, and that all those to whom it has been applied should be placed in the same class. Here it is used to indicate those who maintain that we are directly aware of the validity of certain moral principles, must accept them as ultimate, and need only concern ourselves with the problem of their application.

72. ETHICS AND PHILOSOPHY.—When John Locke maintained that there are no "innate practical principles," or innate moral maxims, he pointed in evidence to the "enormities practiced without remorse" in different ages and by different peoples. The list he draws up is a curious and an interesting one.[4]

In our day it has pretty generally come to be recognized by thoughtful men that a man's judgments as to right and wrong reflect the phase of civilization, or the lack of it, which he represents, and that their significance cannot be understood when we consider them apart from their historic setting. This means that no man's conscience is set up as an ultimate standard, but that every man's conscience is regarded as furnishing material which the science of ethics must take into account.

May we, broadening the basis upon which we are to build, and studying the manners, customs, and moral judgments of all sorts and conditions of men, develop an empirical science of ethics which will be independent of philosophy?

It does not seem that we can do this. We are concerned with psychological phenomena, and their nature and significance are by no means beyond dispute. For example, there is the feeling of moral obligation, of which ethics has so much to say. What is this feeling, and what is its authority? Is it a thing to be explained? Can it impel a man, let us say, a bigot, to do wrong? And what can we mean by credit and discredit, by responsibility and free choice, and other concepts of the sort? All this must remain very vague to one who has not submitted his ethical concepts to reflective analysis of the sort that we have a right to call philosophical.

Furthermore, it does not seem possible to decide what a man should or should not do, without taking into consideration the circumstances in which he is placed. The same act may be regarded as benevolent or the reverse according to its context. If we will but grant the validity of the premises from which the medieval churchman reasoned, we may well ask whether, in laying hands violently upon those who dared to form independent judgments in matters of religion, he was not conscientiously doing his best for his fellow-man. He tried by all means to save some, and to what he regarded as a most dangerous malady he applied a drastic remedy. By what standard shall we judge him?

There can be no doubt that our doctrine of the whole duty of man must be conditioned by our view of the nature of the world in which man lives and of man's place in the world. Has ethics nothing to do with religion? If we do not believe in God, and if we think that man's life ends with the death of the body, it is quite possible that we shall set for him an ethical standard which we should have to modify if we adopted other beliefs. The relation of ethics to religion is a problem that the student of ethics can scarcely set aside. It seems, then, that the study of ethics necessarily carries us back to world problems which cannot be approached except by the path of philosophical reflection. We shall see in Chapter XX that the theistic problem certainly belongs to this class.

It is worthy of our consideration that the vast majority of writers on ethics have felt strongly that their science runs out into metaphysics. We can scarcely afford to treat their testimony lightly. Certainly it is not possible for one who has no knowledge of philosophy to understand the significance of the ethical systems which have appeared in the past. The history of ethics may be looked upon as a part of the history of philosophy. Only on the basis of some general view as to nature and man have men decided what man ought to do. As we have seen above, this appears sufficiently reasonable.

73. AESTHETICS.—Of aesthetics, or the science of the beautiful, I shall say little. There is somewhat the same reason for including it among the philosophical sciences that there is for including ethics.

Those who have paid little attention to science or to philosophy are apt to dogmatize about what is and what is not beautiful just as they dogmatize about what is and what is not right. They say unhesitatingly; This object is beautiful, and that one is ugly. It is as if they said: This one is round, and that one square.

Often it quite escapes their attention that what they now regard as beautiful struck them as unattractive a short time before; and will, perhaps, when the ceaseless change of the fashions has driven it out of vogue, seem strange and unattractive once more. Nor do they reflect upon the fact that others, who seem to have as good a right to an opinion as they, do not agree with them in their judgments; nor upon the further fact that the standard of beauty is a thing that has varied from age to age, differs widely in different countries, and presents minor variations in different classes even in the same community.

The dogmatic utterances of those who are keenly susceptible to the aesthetic aspects of things but are not given to reflection stand in striking contrast to the epitome of the popular wisdom expressed in the skeptical adage that there is no disputing about tastes.

We cannot interpret this adage broadly and take it literally, for then we should have to admit that men's judgments as to the beautiful cannot constitute the material of a science at all, and that there can be no such thing as progress in the fine arts. The notion of progress implies a standard, and an approximation to an ideal. Few would dare to deny that there has been progress in such arts as painting and music; and when one has admitted so much as this, one has virtually admitted that a science of aesthetics is, at least, possible.

The science studies the facts of the aesthetic life as ethics studies the facts of the moral life. It can take no man's taste as furnishing a standard: it must take every man's taste as a fact of significance. It is driven to reflective analysis—to such questions as, what is beauty? and what is meant by aesthetic progress? It deals with elusive psychological facts the significance of which is not easily grasped. It is a philosophical science, and is by no means in a position to follow a beaten path, dispensing with a reflective analysis of its materials.

[1] Preface.
[2] section 269.
[3] section 376.
[4] "Essay concerning Human Understanding," Book I, Chapter III.

CHAPTER XIX

METAPHYSICS

74. WHAT IS METAPHYSICS?—The reader has probably already remarked that in some of the preceding chapters the adjectives "metaphysical" and "philosophical" have been used as if they were interchangeable, in certain connections, at least. This is justified by common usage; and in the present chapter I shall be expected by no one, I think, to prove that metaphysics is a philosophical discipline. My task will rather be to show how far the words "metaphysics" and "philosophy" have a different meaning.

In Chapters III to XI, I have given a general view of the problems which present themselves to reflective thought, and I have indicated that they are not problems which can conveniently be distributed among the several special sciences. Is there an external world? What is it? What are space and time? What is the mind? How are mind and body related? How do we know that there are other minds than ours? etc. These have been presented as *philosophical* problems; and when we turn back to the history of speculative thought we find that they are just the problems with which the men whom we agree to call philosophers have chiefly occupied themselves.

But when we turn to our treatises on *metaphysics*, we also find that these are the problems there discussed. Such treatises differ much among themselves, and the problems are not presented in the same form or in the same order; but one who can look beneath the surface will find that the authors are busied with much the same thing—with some or all of the problems above mentioned.

How, then, does metaphysics differ from philosophy? The difference becomes clear to us when we realize that the word philosophy has a broader and looser signification, and that metaphysics is, so to speak, the core, the citadel, of philosophy.

We have seen (Chapter II) that the world and the mind, as they seem to be presented in the experience of the plain man, do not stand forth with such clearness and distinctness that he is able to answer intelligently the questions we wish to ask him regarding their nature. It is not merely that his information is limited; it is vague and indefinite as well. And we have seen, too, that, however the special sciences may increase and systematize his information, they do not clear away such vagueness. The man still uses such concepts as "inner" and "outer," "reality," "the mind," "space," and "time," with no very definite notion of what they mean.

Now, the attempt to clear away this vagueness by the systematic analysis of such concepts—in other words, the attempt to make a thorough analysis of our experience—is metaphysics. The metaphysician strives to limit his task as well as he may, and to avoid unnecessary excursions into the fields occupied by the special sciences, even those which lie nearest to his own, such as psychology and ethics. There is a sense in which he may be said to be working in the field of a special science, though he is using as the material for his investigations concepts which are employed in many sciences; but it is clear that his discipline is not a special science in the same sense in which geometry and physics are special sciences.

Nevertheless, the special sciences stand, as we have already seen in the case of several of them, very near to his own. If he broadens his view, and deliberately determines to take a survey of the field of human knowledge as illuminated by the analyses that he has made, he becomes something more than a *metaphysician*; he becomes a *philosopher*.

This does not in the least mean that he becomes a storehouse of miscellaneous information, and an authority on all the sciences. Sometimes the philosophers have attempted to describe the world of matter and of mind as though they possessed some mysterious power of knowing things that absolved them from the duty of traveling the weary road of observation and experiment that has ended in the sciences as we have them. When they have done this, they have mistaken the significance of their calling. A philosopher has no more right than another man to create information out of nothing.

But it is possible, even for one who is not acquainted with the whole body of facts presented in a science, to take careful note of the assumptions upon which that science rests, to analyze the concepts of which it makes use, to mark the methods which it employs, and to gain a fair idea of its scope and of its relation to other sciences. Such a reflection upon our scientific knowledge is philosophical reflection, and it may result in a classification of the sciences, and in a general view of human knowledge as a whole. Such a view may be illuminating in the extreme; it can only be harmful when its significance is misunderstood.

But, it may be argued, why may not the man of science do all this for himself? Why should he leave it to the philosopher, who is presumably less intimately acquainted with the sciences than he is?

To this I answer: The work should, of course, be done by the man who will do it best. All our subdivision of labor should be dictated by convenience. But I add, that experience has shown that the workers in the special sciences have not as a rule been very successful when they have tried to philosophize.

Science is an imperious mistress; she demands one's utmost efforts; and when a man turns to philosophical reflection merely "by the way," and in the scraps of time at his disposal after the day's work is done, his philosophical work is apt to be rather superficial. Moreover, it does not follow that, because a man is a good mathematician or chemist or physicist, he is gifted with the power of reflective analysis. Then, too, such men are apt to be imperfectly acquainted with what has been done in the past; and those who are familiar with the history of philosophy often have occasion to remark that what is laid before them, in ignorance of the fact that it is neither new nor original, is a doctrine which has already made its appearance in many forms and has been discussed at prodigious length in the centuries gone by.

In certain sciences it seems possible to ignore the past, to a great extent, at least. What is worth keeping has been kept, and there is a solid foundation on which to build for the future. But with reflective thought it is not so. There is no accepted body of doctrine which we have the right to regard as unassailable. We should take it as a safe maxim that the reflections of men long dead *may* be profounder and more worthy of our study than those urged upon our attention by the men of our day.

And this leads me to make a remark upon the titles given to works on metaphysics. It seems somewhat misleading to label them: "Outlines of Metaphysics" or "Elements of Metaphysics." Such titles suggest that we are dealing with a body of doctrine which has met with general acceptance, and may be compared with that found in handbooks on the special sciences. But we should realize that, when we are concerned with the profounder investigations into the nature of our experience, we tread upon uncertain ground and many differences of opinion obtain. We should, if possible, avoid a false semblance of authority.

75. EPISTEMOLOGY.—We hear a great deal at the present day of Epistemology, or the Theory of Knowledge. I have not classed it as a distinct philosophical science, for reasons which will appear below.

We have seen in Chapter XVI that it is possible to treat of logic in a simple way without growing very metaphysical; but we have also seen that when we go deeply into questions touching the nature of evidence and what is meant by truth and falsity, we are carried back to philosophical reflection at once.

We may, for convenience, group together these deeper questions regarding the nature of knowledge and its scope, and call the subject of our study "Epistemology."

But it should be remarked, in the first place, that, when we work in this field, we are exercising a reflective analysis of precisely the type employed in making the metaphysical analyses contained in the earlier chapters of this book. We are treating our experience as it is not treated in common thought and in science.

And it should be remarked, in the second place, that the investigation of our knowledge inevitably runs together with an investigation into the nature of things known, of the mind and the world. Suppose that I give the titles of the chapters in Part III of Mr. Hobhouse's able work on "The Theory of Knowledge." They are as follows: Validity; the Validity of Knowledge; the

Conception of External Reality; Substance; the Conception of Self; Reality as a System; Knowledge and Reality; the Grounds of Knowledge and Belief.

Are not these topics metaphysical? Let us ask ourselves how it would affect our views of the validity and of the limits of our knowledge, if we were converted to the metaphysical doctrines of John Locke, or of Bishop Berkeley, or of David Hume, or of Thomas Reid, or of Immanuel Kant.

We may, then, regard epistemology as a part of logic—the metaphysical part—or as a part of metaphysics; it does not much matter which we call it, since we mean the same thing. But its relation to metaphysics is such that it does not seem worth while to call it a separate discipline.

Before leaving this subject there is one more point upon which I should touch, if only to obviate a possible misunderstanding.

We find in Professor Cornelius's clear little book, "An Introduction to Philosophy" (Leipzig, 1903; it has unhappily not yet been translated into English), that metaphysics is repudiated altogether, and epistemology is set in its place. But this rejection of metaphysics does not necessarily imply the denial of the value of such an analysis of our experience as I have in this work called metaphysical. Metaphysics is taken to mean, not an analysis of experience, but a groping behind the veil of phenomena for some reality not given in experience. In other words, what Professor Cornelius condemns is what many of the rest of us also condemn under another name. What he calls metaphysics, we call bad metaphysics; and what he calls epistemology, we call metaphysics. The dispute is really a dispute touching the proper name to apply to reflective analysis of a certain kind.

As it is the fashion in certain quarters to abuse metaphysics, I set the reader on his guard. Some kinds of metaphysics certainly ought to be repudiated under whatever name they may be presented to us.

CHAPTER XX
THE PHILOSOPHY OF RELIGION

76. RELIGION AND REFLECTION.—A man may be through and through ethical in his thought and feeling, and yet know nothing of the science of ethics. He may be possessed of the finest aesthetic taste, and yet may know nothing of the science of aesthetics. It is one thing to be good, and another to know clearly what goodness means; it is one thing to love the beautiful, and another to know how to define it.

Just so a man may be thoroughly religious, and may, nevertheless, have reflected very little upon his religious belief and the foundations upon which it rests. This does not mean that his belief is without foundation. It may have a firm basis or it may not. But whatever the case may be, he is not in a position to say much about it. He *feels* that he is right, but he cannot prove it. The man is, I think we must admit, rather blind as to the full significance of his position, and he is, in consequence, rather helpless.

Such a man is menaced by certain dangers. We have seen in the chapter on ethics that men are by no means at one in their judgments as to the rightness or wrongness of given actions. And it requires a very little reflection to teach us that men are not at one in their religious notions. God and His nature, the relation of God to man, what the religious life should be, these things are the subject of much dispute; and some men hold opinions regarded by others as not merely erroneous but highly pernicious in their influence.

Shall a man simply assume that the opinions which he happens to hold are correct, and that all who differ with him are in error? He has not framed his opinions quite independently for himself. We are all influenced by what we have inherited from the past, and what we inherit may be partly erroneous, even if we be right in the main. Moreover, we are all liable to prejudices, and he who has no means of distinguishing such from sober truths may admit into his creed many errors. The lesson of history is very instructive upon this point. The fact is that a man's religious notions reflect the position which he occupies in the development of civilization very much as do his ethical notions.

Again. Even supposing that a man has enlightened notions and is living a religious life that the most instructed must approve; if he has never reflected, and has never tried to make clear to himself just what he really does believe and upon what grounds he believes it, how will it be with him when his position is attacked by another? Men are, as I have said, not at one in these matters, and there are few or none of the doctrines put forward as religions that have not been attacked again and again.

Now, those who depend only upon an instinctive feeling may be placed in the very painful position of seeing no answer to the objections brought against them. What is said may seem plausible; it may even seem true, and is it right for a man to oppose what appears to be the truth? One may be shocked and pained, and may feel that he who makes the assault *cannot* be right, and yet may be forced to admit that a relentless logic, or what presents itself as such, has every

91

appearance of establishing the repellent truth that robs one of one's dearest possession. The situation is an unendurable one; it is that of the man who guards a treasure and recognizes that there is no lock on the door.

Surely, if there is error mixed with truth in our religious beliefs, it is desirable that we should have some way of distinguishing between the truth and the error. And if our beliefs really have a foundation, it is desirable that we should know what that foundation is, and should not be at the mercy of every passer-by who takes the notion to throw a stone at us. But these desirable ends, it seems clear, cannot be attained without reflection.

77. THE PHILOSOPHY OF RELIGION.—The reflection that busies itself with these things results in what is called the philosophy of religion. To show that the name is an appropriate one and that we are concerned with a philosophical discipline, I shall take up for a moment the idea of God, which most men will admit has a very important place in our conception of religion.

Does God exist? We may feel very sure that He does, and yet be forced to admit that the evidence of His existence is not so clear and undeniable as to compel the assent of every one. We do not try to prove the existence of the men we meet and who talk to us. No one thinks of denying their existence; it is taken for granted. Even the metaphysician, when he takes up and discusses the question whether we can prove the existence of any mind beyond our own, does not seriously doubt whether there are other minds or not. It is not so much what we know, as how we know it, that interests him.

But with the existence of God it is different. That men do not think that an examination of the evidence can be dispensed with is evident from the books that are written and lectures that are delivered year after year. There seem to be honest differences of opinion, and we feel compelled to offer men proofs—to show that belief is reasonable.

How shall we determine whether this world in which we live is such a world that we may take it as a revelation of God? And of what sort of a Being are we speaking when we use the word "God"? The question is not an idle one, for men's conceptions have differed widely. There is the savage, with a conception that strikes the modern civilized man as altogether inadequate; there is the thoughtful man of our day, who has inherited the reflections of those who have lived in the ages gone by.

And there is the philosopher, or, perhaps, I should rather say, there are the philosophers. Have they not conceived of God as a group of abstract notions, or as a something that may best be described as the Unknowable, or as the Substance which is the identity of thought and extension, or as the external world itself? All have not sinned in this way, but some have, and they are not men whom we can ignore.

If we turn from all such notions and, in harmony with the faith of the great body of religious men in the ages past, some of whom were philosophers but most of whom were not, cling close to the notion that God is a mind or spirit, and must be conceived according to the analogy, at least, of the human mind, the mind we most directly know—if we do this, we are still confronted by problems to which the thoughtful man cannot refuse attention.

What do we mean by a mind? This is a question to which one can scarcely give an intelligent answer unless one has exercised one's faculty of philosophic reflection. And upon what sort of evidence does one depend in establishing the existence of minds other than one's own? This has been discussed at length in Chapter X, and the problem is certainly a metaphysical one. And if we believe that the Divine Mind is not subject to the limitations which confine the human, how shall we conceive it? The question is an important one. Some of the philosophers and theologians who have tried to free the Divine Mind from such limitations have taken away every positive mark by which we recognize a mind to be such, and have left us a naked "Absolute" which is no better than a labeled vacuum.

Moreover, we cannot refuse to consider the question of God's relation to the world. This seems to lead back to the broader question: How are we to conceive of any mind as related to the world? What is the relation between mind and matter? If any subject of inquiry may properly be called metaphysical, surely this may be.

We see, then, that there is little wonder that the thoughtful consideration of the facts and doctrines of religion has taken its place among the philosophical sciences. Aesthetics has been called applied psychology; and I think it is scarcely too much to say that we are here concerned with applied metaphysics, with the attempt to obtain a clear understanding of the significance of the facts of religion in the light of those ultimate analyses which reveal to us the real nature of the world of matter and of minds.

CHAPTER XXI
PHILOSOPHY AND THE OTHER SCIENCES

78. THE PHILOSOPHICAL AND NON-PHILOSOPHICAL SCIENCES.—We have seen in the preceding chapters that certain of the sciences can scarcely be cultivated successfully in complete separation from philosophy. It has also been indicated in various places that the relation of other sciences to philosophy is not so close.

Thus, the sciences of arithmetic, algebra, and geometry may be successfully prosecuted by a man who has reflected little upon the nature of numbers and who has never asked himself seriously what he means by space. The assumptions which he is justified in making, and the kind of operations which he has the right to perform, do not seem, as a rule, to be in doubt.

So it is also in the sciences of chemistry and physics. There is nothing to prevent the chemist or the physicist from being a philosopher, but he is not compelled to be one. He may push forward the investigations proper to his profession regardless of the type of philosophy which it pleases him to adopt. Whether he be a realist or an idealist, a dualist or a monist, he should, as chemist or physicist, treat the same sort of facts in the same sort of a way. His path appears to be laid out for him, and he can do work the value of which is undisputed by traveling quietly along it, and without stopping to consider consciously what kind of a path it is. There are many who work in this way, and they succeed in making important contributions to human knowledge.

Such sciences as these I call the non-philosophical sciences to distinguish them from the group of sciences I have been discussing at length. What marks them out is, that the facts with which the investigator has to deal are known by him with sufficient clearness to leave him usually in little doubt as to the use which he can make of them. His knowledge is clear enough for the purpose in hand, and his work is justified by its results. What is the relation of such sciences as these to philosophy?

79. THE STUDY OF SCIENTIFIC PRINCIPLES AND METHODS.—It is one thing to have the instinct of the investigator and to be able to feel one's way along the road that leads to new knowledge of a given kind, and it is another thing to have the reflective turn of mind that makes one clearly conscious of just what one has been doing and how one has been doing it. Men reasoned before there was a science of logic, and the sciences made their appearance before what may be called the logic of the sciences had its birth.

"It may be truly asserted," writes Professor Jevons,[1] "that the rapid progress of the physical sciences during the last three centuries has not been accompanied by a corresponding advance in the theory of reasoning. Physicists speak familiarly of Scientific Method, but they could not readily describe what they mean by that expression. Profoundly engaged in the study of particular classes of natural phenomena, they are usually too much engrossed in the immense and ever accumulating details of their special sciences to generalize upon the methods of reasoning which they unconsciously employ. Yet few will deny that these methods of reasoning ought to be studied, especially by those who endeavor to introduce scientific order into less successful and methodical branches of knowledge."

Professor Jevons suggests that it is lack of time and attention that prevents the scientific investigator from attaining to a clear conception of what is meant by scientific method. This has something to do with it, but I think we may also maintain that the work of the investigator and that of the critic are somewhat different in kind, and require somewhat different powers of mind. We find a parallel to this elsewhere. Both in literature and in art men may be in the best sense productive, and yet may be poor critics. We are often wofully disappointed when we attend a lecture on poetry by a poet, or one on painting by an artist.

It may be said: If what is maintained above regarding the possibility of prosecuting scientific researches without having recourse to reflective thought is true, why should the man of science care whether the principles and methods of the non-philosophical sciences are investigated or are merely taken for granted?

I answer: It should be observed that the statements made in the last section were somewhat guarded. I have used the expressions "as a rule" and "usually." I have spoken thus because one can work in the way described, without danger of error, only where a beaten track has been attained and is followed. In Chapter XVI it was pointed out that even in the mathematical sciences one may be forced to reflect upon the significance of one's symbols. As I write this, a pamphlet comes to hand which is concerned to prove that "every cause is potentially capable of producing several effects," and proves it by claiming that the square root of four ([square root symbol]4) is a *cause* which may have as *effect* either two (2) or minus two (-2).

Is this mathematical reasoning? Are mathematical relations ever those of cause and effect? And may one on the basis of such reasonings claim that in nature the relation of cause and effect is not a fixed and invariable one?

Even where there is a beaten track, there is some danger that men may wander from it. And on the confines of our knowledge there are fields in which the accepted road is yet to be established. Science makes constant use of hypotheses as an aid to investigation. What hypotheses may one frame, and what are inadmissible? How important an investigation of this question may be to the worker in certain branches of science will be clear to one who will read with attention Professor Poincaré's brilliant little work on "Science and Hypothesis." [2]

There is no field in art, literature, or science in which the work of the critic is wholly superfluous. "There are periods in the growth of science," writes Professor Pearson in his deservedly popular work, "The Grammar of Science," [3] "when it is well to turn our attention from its imposing superstructure and to examine carefully its foundations. The present book is primarily intended as a criticism of the fundamental concepts of modern science, and as such finds its justification in the motto placed upon its title-page." The motto in question is a quotation from the French philosopher Cousin: "Criticism is the life of science."

We have seen in Chapter XVI that a work on logic may be a comparatively simple thing. It may describe the ways in which men reason when they reason correctly, and may not go deep into metaphysical questions. On the other hand, it may be deeply metaphysical.

When we approach the part of logic which deals with the principles and methods of the sciences, this difference is forced upon our attention. One may set forth the assumptions upon which a science rests, and may describe the methods of investigation employed, without going much below the plane of common thought. As a type of such works I may mention the useful treatise by Professor Jevons cited earlier in this chapter.

On the other hand, our investigations may be more profound, and we may scrutinize the very foundations upon which a science rests. Both the other works referred to illustrate this method of procedure.

For example, in "The Grammar of Science," we find our author discussing, under the title "The Facts of Science," such problems as the following: the Reality of Things; Sense-impressions and Consciousness; the Nature of Thought; the External Universe; Sensations as the Ultimate Source of the Materials of Knowledge; and the Futility of "Things-in-themselves." The philosophical character of such discussions does not need to be pointed out at length.

[1] "The Principles Of Science," London, 1874, Preface.

[2] English translation, New York, 1905.

[3] Second edition, London, 1900.

VI. ON THE STUDY OF PHILOSOPHY
CHAPTER XXII

THE VALUE OF THE STUDY OF PHILOSOPHY

80. THE QUESTION OF PRACTICAL UTILITY.—Why should men study philosophy? The question is a natural one, for man is a rational being, and when the worth of a thing is not at once evident to him, he usually calls for proof of its worth. Our professional schools, with the exception of schools of theology, usually pay little attention to philosophical studies; but such studies occupy a strong position in our colleges, and a vast number of persons not students in the technical sense think it worth while to occupy themselves with them more or less. Wherever liberal studies are prosecuted they have their place, and it is an honored place. Is this as it should be?

Before we ask whether any given study is of practical value, it is wise to determine what the word "practical" shall be taken to mean. Shall we say that we may call practical only such learning as can be turned to direct account in earning money later? If we restrict the meaning of the word in this way, we seem to strike a blow at liberal studies in general.

Thus, no one would think of maintaining that the study of mathematics is not of practical value—sometimes and to some persons. The physicist and the engineer need to know a good deal about mathematics. But how is it with the merchant, the lawyer, the clergyman, the physician? How much of their algebra, geometry, and trigonometry do these remember after they have become absorbed in the practice of their several callings, and how often do they find it necessary to use anything beyond certain simple rules of arithmetic?

Sometimes we are tempted to condemn the study of the classics as unpractical, and to turn instead to the modern languages and to the physical sciences. Now, it is, of course, a fair question to ask what should and what should not be regarded as forming part of a liberal education, and I shall make no effort to decide the question here. But it should be borne well in mind that one cannot decide it by determining what studies are practical in the sense of the word under discussion.

If we keep strictly to this sense, the modern languages are to the majority of Americans of little more practical value than are the Latin and Greek. We scarcely need them except when we travel abroad, and when we do that we find that the concierge and the waiter use English with surprising fluency. As for the sciences, those who expect to earn a living through a knowledge of them, seek, as a rule, that knowledge in a technical or professional school, and the rest of us can enjoy the fruit of their labors without sharing them. It is a popular fallacy that because certain studies have a practical value to the world at large, they must necessarily have a practical value to every one, and can be recommended to the individual on that account. It is worth while to sit down quietly and ask oneself how many of the bits of information acquired during the course of a liberal education are directly used in the carrying on of a given business or in the practice of a given profession.

Nevertheless, we all believe that liberal education is a good thing for the individual and for the race. One must not too much restrict the meaning of the word "practical." A civilized state composed of men who know nothing save what has a direct bearing upon their especial work in life is an absurdity; it cannot exist. There must be a good deal of general enlightenment and there must be a considerable number of individuals who have enjoyed a high measure of enlightenment.

This becomes clear if we consider the part played in the life of the state by the humblest tradesman. If he is to be successful, he must be able to read, write, and keep his accounts, and make, let us say, shoes. But when we have said this, we have summed him up as a workman, but not as a man, and he is also a man. He may marry, and make a good or a bad husband, and a good or a bad father. He stands in relations to his neighborhood, to the school, and to the church; and he is not without his influence. He may be temperate or intemperate, frugal or extravagant, law-abiding or the reverse. He has his share, and no small share, in the government of his city and of his state. His influence is indeed far-reaching, and that it may be an influence for good, he is in need of all the intellectual and moral enlightenment that we can give him. It is of the utmost practical utility to the state that he should know a vast number of things which have no direct bearing upon the making and mending of shoes.

And if this is true in the case of the tradesman, it is scarcely necessary to point out that the physician, the lawyer, the clergyman, and the whole army of those whom we regard as the leaders of men and the molders of public opinion have spheres of non-professional activity of great importance to the state. They cannot be mere specialists if they would. They must influence society for good or ill; and if they are ignorant and unenlightened, their influence cannot be good.

When we consider the life of man in a broad way, we see how essential it is that many men should be brought to have a share in what has been gained by the long travail of the centuries past. It will not do to ask at every step whether they can put to direct professional use every bit of information gained. Literature and science, sweetness and light, beauty and truth, these are the heritage of the modern world; and unless these permeate its very being, society must undergo degeneration. It is this conviction that has led to the high appreciation accorded by intelligent men to courses of liberal study, and among such courses those which we have recognized as philosophical must take their place.

81. WHY PHILOSOPHICAL STUDIES ARE USEFUL.—But let us ask a little more specifically what is to be gained by pursuing distinctively philosophical studies. Why should those who go to college, or intelligent persons who cannot go to college, care to interest themselves in logic and ethics, psychology and metaphysics? Are not these studies rather dry, in the first place, and rather profitless, in the second?

As to the first point, I should stoutly maintain that if they are dry, it is somebody's fault. The most sensational of novels would be dry if couched in the language which some philosophers have seen fit to use in expressing their thoughts. He who defines "existence" as "the still and simple precipitate of the oscillation between beginning to be and ceasing to be" has done his best to alienate our affections from the subject of his predilection.

But it is not in the least necessary to talk in this way about matters philosophical. He who is not a slave to tradition can use plain and simple language. To be sure, there are some subjects, especially in the field of metaphysics, into which the student cannot expect to see very deeply at the outset of his studies. Men do not expect to understand the more difficult problems of mathematics without making a good deal of preparation; but, unhappily, they sometimes expect to have the profoundest problems of metaphysics made luminous to them in one or two popular lectures.

Philosophical studies are not dry, when men are properly taught, and are in a position to understand what is said. They deal with the most fascinating of problems. It is only necessary to pierce through the husk of words which conceals the thoughts of the philosopher, and we shall find the kernel palatable, indeed. Nor are such studies profitless, to take up our second point. Let us see what we may gain from them.

Let us begin with logic—the traditional logic commonly taught to beginners. Is it worth while to study this? Surely it is. No one who has not tried to introduce the average undergraduate to logic can realize how blindly he uses his reasoning powers, how unconscious he is of the full meaning of the sentences he employs, how easily he may be entrapped by fallacious reasonings where he is not set on his guard by some preposterous conclusion touching matters with which he is familiar.

And he is not merely unconscious of the lapses in his processes of reasoning, and of his imperfect comprehension of the significance of his statements; he is unconscious also of the mass of inherited and acquired prejudices, often quite indefensible, which he unquestioningly employs as premises.

He fairly represents the larger world beyond the walls of the college. It is a world in which prejudices are assumed as premises, and loose reasonings pass current and are unchallenged until they beget some unpalatable conclusion. It is a world in which men take little pains to think carefully and accurately unless they are dealing with something touching which it is practically inconvenient to make a mistake.

He who studies logic in the proper way is not filling his mind with useless facts; he is simply turning the light upon his own thinking mind, and realizing more clearly what he has always done rather blindly and blunderingly. He may completely forget the

"Barbara, Celarent, Darii, Ferioque prioris,"

and he may be quite unable to give an account of the moods and figures of the syllogism; but he cannot lose the critical habit if he once has acquired it, and he cannot but be on his guard against himself as well as against others.

There is a keen pleasure in gaining such insight. It gives a feeling of freedom and power, and rids one of that horrid sense that, although this or that bit of reasoning is certainly bad, it is impossible to tell just what is the matter with it. And as for its practical utility, if it is desirable to get rid of prejudice and confusion, and to possess a clear and reasonable mind, then anything that makes for this must be of value.

Of the desirability that all who can afford the luxury of a liberal education should do some serious reading in ethics, it seems hardly necessary to speak. The deficiencies of the ethics of the unreflective have already been touched upon in Chapter XVIII.

But I cannot forbear dwelling upon it again. What thoughtful man is not struck with the variety of ethical standards which obtain in the same community? The clergyman who has a strong sense of responsibility for the welfare of his flock is sometimes accused of not sufficiently realizing the importance of a frank expression of the whole truth about things; the man of science, whose duty it seems to be to peer into the mysteries of the universe, and to tell what he sees or what he guesses, is accused of an indifference to the effect which his utterances may have upon the less enlightened who hear him speak; many criticise the lawyer for a devotion to the interests of his client which is at times in doubtful harmony with the interests of justice in the larger sense; in the business world commercial integrity is exalted, and lapses from the ethical code which do not assail this cardinal virtue are not always regarded with equal seriousness.

It is as though men elected to worship at the shrine of a particular saint, and were inclined to overlook the claims of others. For all this there is, of course, a reason; such things are never to be looked upon as mere accident. But this does not mean that these more or less conflicting standards are all to be accepted as satisfactory and as ultimate. It is inevitable that those who study ethics seriously, who really reflect upon ethical problems, should sometimes criticise the judgments of their fellow-men rather unfavorably.

Of such independent criticism many persons have a strong distrust. I am reminded here of an eminent mathematician who maintained that the study of ethics has a tendency to distort the student's judgments as to what is right and what is wrong. He had observed that there is apt to be some divergence of opinion between those who think seriously upon morals and those who do not, and he gave the preference to the unthinking majority.

Now, there is undoubtedly danger that the independent thinker may be betrayed into eccentricities of opinion which are unjustifiable and are even dangerous. But it seems a strange doctrine that it is, on the whole, safer not to think, but rather to drift on the stream of public opinion. In other fields we are not inclined to believe that the ignorant man, who has given no especial attention to a subject, is the one likely to be right. Why should it be so in morals?

That the youth who goes to college to seek a liberal education has a need of ethical studies becomes very plain when we come to a realization of the curious limitations of his ethical training as picked up from his previous experience of the world. He has some very definite notions as to right and wrong. He is as ready to maintain the desirability of benevolence, justice, and veracity, as was Bishop Butler, who wrote the famous "Analogy "; although, to be sure, he is most inarticulate when called upon to explain what constitutes benevolence, justice, or veracity. But the strangest thing is, that he seems to place some of the most important decisions of his whole life quite outside the realm of right and wrong.

He may admit that a man should not undertake to be a clergyman, unless he possesses certain qualifications of mind and character which evidently qualify him for that profession. But he does not see why he has not the right to become a wearisome professor or an incompetent physician, if he chooses to enter upon such a career. Is a man not free to take up what profession he pleases? He must take the risk, of course; but if he fails, he fails.

And when he is asked to consider from the point of view of ethics the question of marriage and its responsibilities, he is at first inclined to consider the whole subject as rather a matter for jest. Has a man not the right to marry or remain single exactly as he pleases? And is he not free to marry any one whom he can persuade to accept him? To be sure, he should be a little careful about marrying quite out of his class, and he should not be hopelessly careless about money matters. Thus, a decision, which may affect his whole life as much as any other that he can be called upon to make, which may practically make it or mar it, is treated as though it were not a matter of grave concern, but a private affair, entailing no serious consequences to any one and calling for no reflection.

I wish it could be said that the world outside of the college regarded these matters in another light. But the student faithfully represents the opinions current in the community from which he comes. And he represents, unhappily, the teachings of the stage and of the world of current fiction. The influence of these is too often on the side of inconsiderate passion, which stirs our sympathy and which lends itself to dramatic effect. With the writers of romance the ethical philosophers have an ancient quarrel.

It may be said: But the world gets along very well as it is, and without brooding too much upon ethical problems. To this we may answer: Does the world get along so very well, after all? Are there no evils that foresight and some firmness of character might have obviated? And when we concern ourselves with the educated classes, at least, the weight of whose influence is enormous, is it too much to maintain that they should do some reading and thinking in the field of ethics? should strive to attain to clear vision and correct judgment on the whole subject of man's duties?

Just at the present time, when psychological studies have so great a vogue, one scarcely feels compelled to make any sort of an apology for them. It is assumed on all hands that it is desirable to study psychology, and courses of lectures are multiplied in all quarters.

Probably some of this interest has its root in the fallacy touched upon earlier in this chapter. The science of psychology has revolutionized educational theory. When those of us who have arrived at middle life look back and survey the tedious and toilsome path along which we were unwillingly driven in our schoolboy days, and then see how smooth and pleasant it has been made since, we are impelled to honor all who have contributed to this result. Moreover, it seems very clear that teachers of all grades should have some acquaintance with the nature of the minds that they are laboring to develop, and that they should not be left to pick up their information for themselves—a task sufficiently difficult to an unobservant person.

These considerations furnish a sufficient ground for extolling the science of psychology, and for insisting that studies in it should form some part of the education of a teacher. But why should the rest of us care for such studies?

To this one may answer, in the first place, that nearly all of us have, or ought to have, some responsibility for the education of children; and, in the second, that we deal with the minds of others every day in every walk in life, and it can certainly do no harm to have our attention called to the way in which minds function. To be sure, some men are by nature tactful, and instinctively conscious of how things strike the minds of those about them. But even such persons may gain helpful suggestions, and, at least, have the habit of attention to the mental processes of others confirmed in them. How often we are impressed at church, at the public lecture, and in private conversations, with the fact that the speaker lives in blissful unconsciousness of what can be understood by or can possibly interest his hearers! For the confirmed bore, there is, perhaps, no cure; but it seems as though something might be done for those who are afflicted to a minor degree.

And this brings me to another consideration, which is that a proper study of psychology ought to be of service in revealing to a man his own nature. It should show him what he is, and this is surely a first step toward becoming something better. It is wonderful how blind men may be with regard to what passes in their own minds and with regard to their own peculiarities. When they learn to reflect, they come to a clearer consciousness of themselves—it is as though a lamp were lighted within them. One may, it is true, study psychology without attaining to any of the good results suggested above; but, for that matter, there is no study which may not be pursued in a profitless way, if the teacher be sufficiently unskilled and the pupil sufficiently thoughtless.

82. METAPHYSICS AND PHILOSOPHY OF RELIGION.—Perhaps it will be said:
For such philosophical studies as the above a good defense may perhaps be made, but can one defend in the same way the plunge into the obscurities of metaphysics? In this field no two men seem to be wholly agreed, and if they were, what would it signify? Whether we call ourselves monists or dualists, idealists or realists, Lockians or Kantians, must we not live and deal with the things about us in much the same way?

Those who have dipped into metaphysical studies deeply enough to see what the problems discussed really are; who have been able to reach the ideas concealed, too often, under a rather forbidding terminology; who are not of the dogmatic turn of mind which insists upon unquestioned authority and is repelled by the uncertainties which must confront those who give themselves to reflective thought,—these will hardly need to be persuaded that it is desirable to give some attention to the question: What sort of a world, after all, is this world in which we live? What is its meaning?

To many men the impulse to peer into these things is over-powering, and the pleasure of feeling their insight deepen is extremely keen. What deters us in most instances is not the conviction that such investigations are not, or should not be, interesting, but rather the difficulty of the approach. It is not easy to follow the path which leads from the world of common thought into the world of philosophical reflection. One becomes bewildered and discouraged at the outset. Sometimes, after listening to the directions of guides who disagree among themselves, we are tempted to believe that there can be no certain path to the goal which we have before us.

But, whatever the difficulties and uncertainties of our task, a little reflection must show that it is not one which has no significance for human life.

Men can, it is true, eat and sleep and go through the routine of the day, without giving thought to science or religion or philosophy, but few will defend such an existence. As a matter of fact, those who have attained to some measure of intellectual and moral development do assume, consciously or unconsciously, some rather definite attitude toward life, and this is not independent of their conviction as to what the world is and means.

Metaphysical speculations run out into the philosophy of religion; and, on the other hand, religious emotions and ideals have again and again prompted men to metaphysical construction. A glance at history shows that it is natural to man to embrace some attitude toward the system of things, and to try to justify this by reasoning. Vigorous and independent minds have given birth to theories, and these have been adopted by others. The influence of such theories upon the evolution of humanity has been enormous.

Ideas have ruled and still rule the world, some of them very abstract ideas. It does not follow that one is uninfluenced by them, when one has no knowledge of their source or of their original setting. They become part of the intellectual heritage of us all, and we sometimes suppose that we are responsible for them ourselves. Has not the fact that an idealistic or a materialistic type of thought has been current at a particular time influenced the outlook on life of many who have themselves devoted little attention to philosophy? It would be interesting to know how many, to whom Spencer is but a name, have felt the influence of the agnosticism of which he was the apostle.

I say this without meaning to criticise here any of the types of doctrine referred to. My thesis is only that philosophy and life go hand in hand, and that the prying into the deeper mysteries of the universe cannot be regarded as a matter of no practical moment. Its importance ought to be admitted even by the man who has little hope that he will himself be able to attain to a doctrine wholly satisfactory and wholly unshakable.

For, if the study of the problems of metaphysics does nothing else for a given individual, it, at least, enables him to comprehend and criticise intelligently the doctrines which are presented for his acceptance by others. It is a painful thing to feel quite helpless in the face of plausible reasonings which may threaten to rob us of our most cherished hopes, or may tend to persuade us of the vanity of what we have been accustomed to regard as of highest worth. If we are quite unskilled in the examination of such doctrines, we may be captured by the loosest of arguments—witness the influence of Spencer's argument for the "Unknowable," in the "First Principles"; and if we are ignorant of the history of speculative thought, we may be carried away by old and exploded notions which pose as modern and impressive only because they have been given a modern dress.

We can, of course, refuse to listen to those who would talk with us. But this savors of bigotry, and the world will certainly not grow wiser, if men generally cultivate a blind adherence to the opinions in which they happen to be brought up. A cautious conservatism is one thing, and blind obstinacy is another. To the educated man (and it is probable that others will have to depend on opinions taken at second hand) a better way of avoiding error is open.

Finally, it will not do to overlook the broadening influence of such studies as we are discussing. How dogmatically men are in the habit of expressing themselves upon those obscure and difficult problems which deal with matters that lie on the confines of human knowledge! Such an assumption of knowledge cannot but make us uncomprehending and unsympathetic.

There are many subjects upon which, if we hold an opinion at all, we should hold it tentatively, waiting for more light, and retaining a willingness to be enlightened. Many a bitter and fruitless quarrel might be avoided, if more persons found it possible to maintain this philosophical attitude of mind. Philosophy is, after all, reflection, and the reflective man must realize that he is probably as liable to error as are other men. He is not infallible, nor has the limit of human knowledge been attained in his day and generation. He who realizes this will not assume that his neighbor is always wrong, and he will come to have that wide, conscientious tolerance, which is not indifference, but which is at the farthest remove from the zeal of mere bigotry.

CHAPTER XXIII

WHY WE SHOULD STUDY THE HISTORY OF PHILOSOPHY

83. THE PROMINENCE GIVEN TO THE SUBJECT.—When one reflects upon the number of lecture courses given every year at our universities and colleges on the history of philosophy, one is struck by the fact that philosophy is not treated as are most other subjects with which the student is brought into contact.

If we study mathematics, or chemistry, or physics, or physiology, or biology, the effort is made to lay before us in a convenient form the latest results which have been attained in those sciences. Of their history very little is said; and, indeed, as we have seen (section 6), lectures on the history of the inductive sciences are apt to be regarded as philosophical in their character and aims rather than as merely scientific.

The interest in the history of philosophy is certainly not a diminishing one. Text-books covering the whole field or a part of it are multiplied; extensive studies are made and published covering the work of individual philosophers; innumerable historical discussions make their appearance in the pages of current philosophical journals. No student is regarded as fairly acquainted with philosophy who knows nothing of Plato and Aristotle, Descartes and Spinoza, Berkeley and Hume, Kant and Hegel, and the rest. We should look upon him as having a very restricted outlook if he had read only the works of the thinkers of our own day; indeed, we should not expect him to have a proper comprehension even of these, for their chapters must remain blind and meaningless to one who has no knowledge of what preceded them and has given birth to the doctrines there set forth.

It is a fair question to ask: Why is philosophy so bound up with the study of the past? Why may we not content ourselves with what has up to the present been attained, and omit a survey of the road along which our predecessors have traveled?

84. THE ESPECIAL IMPORTANCE OF HISTORICAL STUDIES TO REFLECTIVE THOUGHT.—In some of the preceding chapters dealing with the various philosophical sciences, it has been indicated that, in the sciences we do not regard as philosophical, men may work on the basis of certain commonly accepted assumptions and employ methods which are generally regarded as trustworthy within the given field. The value both of the fundamental assumptions and of the methods of investigation appear to be guaranteed by the results attained. There are not merely observation and hypothesis; there is also verification, and where this is lacking, men either abandon their position or reserve their judgment.

Thus, a certain body of interrelated facts is built up, the significance of which, in many fields at least, is apparent even to the layman. Nor is it wholly beyond him to judge whether the results of scientific investigations can be verified. An eclipse, calculated by methods which he is quite unable to follow, may occur at the appointed hour and confirm his respect for the astronomer. The efficacy of a serum in the cure of diseases may convince him that work done in the laboratory is not labor lost.

It seems evident that the several sciences do really rise on stepping stones of their dead selves, and that those selves of the past are really dead and superseded. Who would now think of going back for his science to Plato's "Timaeus," or would accept the description of the physical world contained in the works of Aristotle? What chemist or physicist need busy himself with the doctrine of atoms and their clashings presented in the magnificent poem of Lucretius? Who can forbear a smile—a sympathetic one—when he turns over the pages of Augustine's "City of God," and sees what sort of a world this remarkable man believed himself to inhabit?

It is the historic and human interest that carries us back to these things. We say: What ingenuity! what a happy guess! how well that was reasoned in the light of what was actually known about the world in those days! But we never forget that what compels our admiration does so because it makes us realize that we stand in the presence of a great mind, and not because it is a foundation-stone in the great edifice which science has erected.

But it is not so in philosophy. It is not possible to regard the philosophical reflections of Plato and of Aristotle as superseded in the same sense in which we may so regard their science. The reason for this lies in the difference between scientific thought and reflective thought.

The two have been contrasted in Chapter II of this volume. It was there pointed out that the sort of thinking demanded in the special sciences is not so very different from that with which we are all familiar in common life. Science is more accurate and systematic, it has a broader outlook, and it is free from the imperfections which vitiate the uncritical and fragmentary knowledge which experience of the world yields the unscientific. But, after all, the world is much the same sort of a world to the man of science and to his uncritical neighbor. The latter can, as we have seen, understand what, in general, the former is doing, and can appropriate many of his results.

On the other hand, it often happens that the man who has not, with pains and labor, learned to reflect, cannot even see that the philosopher has a genuine problem before him. Thus, the plain man accepts the fact that he has a mind and that it knows the world. That both mental phenomena and physical phenomena should be carefully observed and classified he may be ready to admit. But that the very conceptions of mind and of what it means to know a world are vague and indefinite in the extreme, and stand in need of careful analysis, he does not realize.

In other words, he sees that our knowledge needs to be extended and rendered more accurate and reliable, but he does not see that, if we are to think clearly and consciously, all our knowledge needs to be gone over in a different way. In common life it is quite possible to use in the attainment of practical ends knowledge which has not been analyzed and of the full meaning of which we are ignorant. I hope it has become evident in the course of this volume that something closely analogous is true in the field of science. The man of science may measure space and time, and may study the phenomena of the human mind, without even attempting to answer all the questions which may be raised as to what is meant, in the last analysis, by such concepts as space, time, and the mind.

That such concepts should be analyzed has, I hope, been made clear, if only that erroneous and misleading notions as to these things should be avoided. But when a man with a genius for metaphysical analysis addresses himself to this task, he cannot simply hand the results attained by his reflections over to his less reflective fellow-man. His words are not understood; he seems to be dealing with shadows, with unrealities; he has passed from the real world of common thought into another world which appears to have little relation to the former.

Nor can verification, indubitable proof, be demanded and furnished as it can in many parts of the field cultivated by the special sciences. We may judge science fairly well without ourselves being scientists, but it is not possible to judge philosophy without being to some extent a philosopher.

In other words, the conclusions of reflective thought must be judged by following the process and discovering its cogency or the reverse. Thus, when the philosopher lays before us an argument to prove that we must regard the only ultimate reality in the world as unknowable, and must abandon our theistic convictions, how shall we make a decision as to whether he is right or is wrong? May we expect that the day will come when he will be justified or condemned as is the astronomer on the day predicted for an eclipse? Neither the philosophy of Locke, nor that of Descartes, nor that of Kant, can be vindicated as can a prediction touching an eclipse of the sun. To judge these men, we must learn to think with them, to survey the road by which they travel; and this we cannot do until we have learned the art.

Whether we like to admit it or not, we must admit, if we are fair-minded and intelligent, that philosophy cannot speak with the same authority as science, where science has been able to verify its results. There are, of course, scientific hypotheses and speculations which should be regarded as being quite as uncertain as anything brought forward by the philosophers. But, admitting this, the fact remains that there is a difference between the two fields as a whole, and that the philosopher should learn not to speak with an assumption of authority. No final philosophy has been attained, so palpably firm in its foundation, and so admittedly trustworthy in its construction, that we are justified in saying: Now we need never go back to the past unless to gratify the historic interest. It is a weakness of young men, and of older men of partisan temper, to feel very sure of matters which, in the nature of things, must remain uncertain.

Since these things are so, and since men possess the power of reflection in very varying degree, it is not surprising that we find it worth while to turn back and study the thoughts of those who have had a genius for reflection, even though they lived at a time when modern science was awaiting its birth. Some things cannot be known until other things are known; often there must be a vast collection of individual facts before the generalizations of science can come into being. But many of the problems with which reflective thought is still struggling have not been furthered in the least by information which has been collected during the centuries which have elapsed since they were attacked by the early Greek philosophers.

Thus, we are still discussing the distinction between "appearance" and "reality," and many and varied are the opinions at which philosophers arrive. But Thales, who heads the list of the Greek philosophers, had quite enough material, given in his own experience, to enable him to solve this problem as well as any modern philosopher, had he been able to use the material. He who is familiar with the history of philosophy will recognize that, although one may smile at Augustine's accounts of the races of men, and of the spontaneous generation of small animals, no one has a right to despise his profound reflections upon the nature of time and the problems which arise out of its character as past, present, and future.

The fact is that metaphysics does not lag behind because of our lack of material to work with. The difficulties we have to face are nothing else than the difficulties of reflective thought. Why can we not tell clearly what we mean when we use the word "self," or speak of "knowledge," or insist that we know an "external world"? Are we not concerned with the most familiar of experiences? To be sure we are—with experiences familiarly, but vaguely and unanalytically, known and, hence, only half known. All these experiences the great men of the past had as well as we; and if they had greater powers of reflection, perhaps they saw more deeply into them than we do. At any rate, we cannot afford to assume that they did not.

One thing, however, I must not omit to mention. Although one man cannot turn over bodily the results of his reflection to another, it by no means follows that he cannot give the other a helping hand, or warn him of dangers by himself stumbling into pitfalls, as the case may be. We have an indefinite advantage over the solitary thinkers who opened up the paths of reflection, for we have the benefit of their teaching. And this brings me to a consideration which I must discuss in the next section.

85. THE VALUE OF DIFFERENT POINTS OF VIEW.—The man who has not read is like the man who has not traveled—he is not an intelligent critic, for he has nothing with which to compare what falls within the little circle of his experiences. That the prevailing architecture of a town is ugly can scarcely impress one who is acquainted with no other town. If we live in a community in which men's manners are not good, and their standard of living not the highest, our attention does not dwell much upon the fact, unless some contrasted experience wakes within us a clear consciousness of the difference. That to which we are accustomed we accept uncritically and unreflectively. It is difficult for us to see it somewhat as one might see it to whom it came as a new experience.

Of course, there may be in the one town buildings of more and of less architectural beauty; and there may be in the one community differences of opinion that furnish intellectual stimulus and keep awake the critical spirit. Still, there is such a thing as a prevalent type of architecture, and there is such a thing as the spirit of the times. He who is carried along by the spirit of the age may easily conclude that what is, is right, because he hears few raise their voices in protest.

To estimate justly the type of thought in which he has been brought up, he must have something with which to compare it. He must stand at a distance, and try to judge it as he would judge a type of doctrine presented to him for the first rime. And in the accomplishment of this task he can find no greater aid than the study of the history of philosophy.

It is at first something of a shock to a man to discover that assumptions which he has been accustomed to make without question have been frankly repudiated by men quite as clever as he, and, perhaps, more critical. It opens the eyes to see that his standards of worth have been weighed by others and have been found wanting. It may well incline him to reexamine reasonings in which he has detected no flaw, when he finds that acute minds have tried them before, and have declared them faulty.

Nor can it be without its influence upon his judgment of the significance of a doctrine, when it becomes plain to him that this significance can scarcely be fully comprehended until the history of the doctrine is known. For example, he thinks of the mind as somehow in the body, as interacting with it, as a substance, and as immaterial. In the course of his reading it begins to dawn upon his consciousness that he has not thought all this out for himself; he has taken these notions from others, who in turn have had them from their predecessors. He begins to realize that he is not resting upon evidence independently found in his own experience, but has upon his hands a sheaf of opinions which are the echoes of old philosophies, and whose rise and development can be traced over the stretch of the centuries. Can he help asking himself, when he sees this, whether the opinions in question express the truth and the whole truth? Is he not forced to take the critical attitude toward them?

And when he views the succession of systems which pass in review before him, noting how a truth may be dimly seen by one writer, denied by another, taken up again and made clearer by a third, and so on, how can he avoid the reflection that, as there was some error mixed with the truth presented in earlier systems, so there probably is some error in whatever may happen to be the form of doctrine generally received in his own time? The evolution of humanity is not yet at an end; men still struggle to see clearly, and fall short of the ideal; it must be a good thing to be freed from the dogmatic assumption of finality natural to the man of limited outlook. In studying the history of philosophy sympathetically we are not merely calling to our aid critics who possess the advantage of seeing things from a different point of view, but we are reminding ourselves that we, too, are human and fallible.

86. PHILOSOPHY AS POETRY, AND PHILOSOPHY AS SCIENCE.—The recognition of the truth that the problems of reflection do not admit of easy solution and that verification can scarcely be expected as it can in the fields of the special sciences, need not, even when it is brought home to us, as it is apt to be, by the study of the history of philosophy, lead us to believe that philosophies are like the fashions, a something gotten up to suit the taste of the day, and to be dismissed without regret as soon as that taste changes.

Philosophy is sometimes compared with poetry. It is argued that each age must have its own poetry, even though it be inferior to that which it has inherited from the past. Just so, it is said, each age must have its own philosophy, and the philosophy of an earlier age will not satisfy its demands. The implication is that in dealing with philosophy we are not concerned with what is true or untrue in itself considered, but with what is satisfying to us or the reverse.

Now, it would sound absurd to say that each age must have its own geometry or its own physics. The fact that it has long been known that the sum of the interior angles of a plane triangle is equal to two right angles, does not warrant me in repudiating that truth; nor am I justified in doing so, and in believing the opposite, merely because I find the statement uninteresting or distasteful. When we are dealing with such matters as these, we recognize that truth is truth, and that, if we mistake it or refuse to recognize it, so much the worse for us.

Is it otherwise in philosophy? Is it a perfectly proper thing that, in one age, men should be idealists, and in another, materialists; in one, theists, and in another, agnostics? Is the distinction between true and false nothing else than the distinction between what is in harmony with the spirit of the times and what is not?

That it is natural that there should be such fluctuations of opinion, we may freely admit. Many things influence a man to embrace a given type of doctrine, and, as we have seen, verification is a difficult problem. But have we here, any more than in other fields, the right to assume that a doctrine was true at a given time merely because it *seemed* to men true at that time, or because they found it pleasing? The history of science reveals that many things have long been believed to be true, and, indeed, to be bound up with what were regarded as the highest interests of man, and that these same things have later been discovered to be false—not false merely for a later age, but false for all time; as false when they were believed in as when they were exploded and known to be exploded. No man of sense believes that the Ptolemaic system was true for a while, and that then the Copernican became true. We say that the former only *seemed* true, and that the enthusiasm of its adherents was a mistaken enthusiasm.

It is well to remember that philosophies are brought forward because it is believed or hoped that they are true. A fairy tale may be recited and may be approved, although no one dreams of attaching faith to the events narrated in it. But a philosophy attempts to give us some account of the nature of the world in which we live. If the philosopher frankly abandons the attempt to tell us what is true, and with a Celtic generosity addresses himself to the task of saying what will be agreeable to us, he loses his right to the title. It is not enough that he stirs our emotions, and works up his unrealities into something resembling a poem. It is not primarily his task to please, as it is not the task of the serious worker in science to please those whom he is called upon to instruct. Truth is truth, whether it be scientific truth or philosophical truth. And error, no matter how agreeable or how nicely adjusted to the temper of the times, is always error. If it is error in a field in which the detection and exposure of error is difficult, it is the more dangerous, and the more should we be on our guard against it.

We may, then, accept the lesson of the history of philosophy, to wit, that we have no right to regard any given doctrine as final in such a sense that it need no longer be held tentatively and as subject to possible revision; but we need not, on that account, deny that philosophy is, what it has in the past been believed to be, an earnest search for truth. A philosophy that did not even profess to be this would not be listened to at all. It would be regarded as too trivial to merit serious attention. If we take the word "science" in the broad sense to indicate a knowledge of the truth more exact and satisfactory than that which obtains in common life, we may say that every philosophy worthy of the name is, at least, an attempt at scientific knowledge. Of course, this sense of the word "science" should not be confused with that in which it has been used elsewhere in this volume.

87. HOW TO READ THE HISTORY OF PHILOSOPHY.—He who takes up the history of philosophy for the first time is apt to be impressed with the fact that he is reading something that might not inaptly be called the history of human error.

It begins with crude and, to the superficial spectator, seemingly childish attempts in the field of physical science. There are clever guesses at the nature of the physical world, but the boldest of speculations are entered upon with no apparent recognition of the difficulty of the task undertaken, and with no realization of the need for caution. Somewhat later a different class of problems makes its appearance—the problems which have to do with the mind and with the nature of knowledge, reflective problems which scarcely seem to have come fairly within the horizon of the earliest thinkers.

These problems even the beginner may be willing to recognize as philosophical; but he may conscientiously harbor a doubt as to the desirability of spending time upon the solutions which are offered. System rises after system, and confronts him with what appear to be new questions and new answers. It seems as though each philosopher were constructing a world for himself independently, and commanding him to accept it, without first convincing him of his right to assume this tone of authority and to set up for an oracle. In all this conflict of opinions where shall we seek for truth? Why should we accept one man as a teacher rather than another? Is not the lesson to be gathered from the whole procession of systems best summed up in the dictum of Protagoras: "Man is the measure of all things"—each has his own truth, and this need not be truth to another?

This, I say, is a first impression and a natural one. I hasten to add: this should not be the last impression of those who read with thoughtful attention.

One thing should be emphasized at the outset: nothing will so often bear rereading as the history of philosophy. When we go over the ground after we have obtained a first acquaintance with the teachings of the different philosophers, we begin to realize that what we have in our hands is, in a sense, a connected whole. We see that if Plato and Aristotle had not lived, we could not have had the philosophy which passed current in the Middle Ages and furnished a foundation for the teachings of the Church. We realize that without this latter we could not have had Descartes, and without Descartes we could not have had Locke and Berkeley and Hume. And had not these lived, we should not have had Kant and his successors. Other philosophies we should undoubtedly have had, for the busy mind of man must produce something. But whatever glimpses at the truth these men have vouchsafed us have been guaranteed by the order of development in which they have stood. They could not independently have written the books that have come down to us.

This should be evident from what has been said earlier in this chapter and elsewhere in this book. Let us bear in mind that a philosopher draws his material from two sources. First of all, he has the experience of the mind and the world which is the common property of us all. But it is, as we have seen, by no means easy to use this material. It is vastly difficult to reflect. It is fatally easy to misconceive what presents itself in our experience. With the most earnest effort to describe what lies before us, we give a false description, and we mislead ourselves and others.

In the second place, the philosopher has the interpretations of experience which he has inherited from his predecessors. The influence of these is enormous. Each age has, to a large extent, its problems already formulated or half formulated for it. Every man must have ancestors, of some sort, if he is to appear upon this earthly stage at all; and a wholly independent philosopher is as impossible a creature as an ancestorless man. We have seen how Descartes (section 60) tried to repudiate his debt to the past, and how little successful he was in doing so.

Now, we make a mistake if we overlook the genius of the individual thinker. The history of speculative thought has many times taken a turn which can only be accounted for by taking into consideration the genius for reflective thought possessed by some great mind. In the crucible of such an intellect, old truths take on a new aspect, familiar facts acquire a new and a richer meaning. But we also make a mistake if we fail to see in the writings of such a man one of the stages which has been reached in the gradual evolution of human thought, if we fail to realize that each philosophy is to a great extent the product of the past.

When one comes to understand these things, the history of philosophy no longer presents itself as a mere agglomeration of arbitrary and independent systems. And an attentive reading gives us a further key to the interpretation of what seemed inexplicable. We find that there may be distinct and different streams of thought, which, for a while, run parallel without commingling their waters. For centuries the Epicurean followed his own tradition, and walked in the footsteps of his own master. The Stoic was of sterner stuff, and he chose to travel another path. To this day there are adherents of the old church philosophy, Neo-Scholastics, whose ways of thinking can only be understood when we have some knowledge of Aristotle and of his influence upon men during the Middle Ages. We ourselves may be Kantians or Hegelians, and the man at our elbow may recognize as his spiritual father Comte or Spencer.

It does not follow that, because one system follows another in chronological order, it is its lineal descendant. But some ancestor a system always has, and if we have the requisite learning and ingenuity, we need not find it impossible to explain why this thinker or that was influenced to give his thought the peculiar turn that characterizes it. Sometimes many influences have conspired to attain the result, and it is no small pleasure to address oneself to the task of disentangling the threads which enter into the fabric.

Moreover, as we read thus with discrimination, we begin to see that the great men of the past have not spoken without appearing to have sufficient reason for their utterances in the light of the times in which they lived. We may make it a rule that, when they seem to be speaking arbitrarily, to be laying before us reasonings that are not reasonings, dogmas for which no excuse seems to be offered, the fault lies in our lack of comprehension. Until we can understand how a man, living in a certain century, and breathing a certain moral and intellectual atmosphere, could have said what he did, we should assume that we have read his words, but not his real thought. For the latter there is always a psychological, if not a logical, justification.

And this brings me to the question of the language in which the philosophers have expressed their thoughts. The more attentively one reads the history of philosophy, the clearer it becomes that the number of problems with which the philosophers have occupied themselves is not overwhelmingly great. If each philosophy which confronts us seems to us quite new and strange, it is because we have not arrived at the stage at which it is possible for us to recognize old friends with new faces. The same old problems, the problems which must ever present themselves to reflective thought, recur again and again. The form is more or less changed, and the answers which are given to them are not, of course, always the same. Each age expresses itself in a somewhat different way. But sometimes the solution proposed for a given problem is almost the same in substance, even when the two thinkers who are contrasting belong to centuries which lie far apart. In this case, only our own inability to strip off the husk and reach the fruit itself prevents us from seeing that we have before us nothing really new.

Thus, if we read the history of philosophy with patience and with discrimination, it grows luminous. We come to feel nearer to the men of the past. We see that we may learn from their successes and from their failures; and if we are capable of drawing a moral at all, we apply the lesson to ourselves.

CHAPTER XXIV
SOME PRACTICAL ADMONITIONS
88. BE PREPARED TO ENTER UPON A NEW WAY OF LOOKING AT THINGS.—We have seen that reflective thought tries to analyze experience and to attain to a clear view of the elements that make it up—to realize vividly what is the very texture of the known world, and what is the nature of knowledge. It is possible to live to old age, as many do, without even a suspicion that there may be such a knowledge as this, and nevertheless to possess a large measure of rather vague but very serviceable information about both minds and bodies.

It is something of a shock to learn that a multitude of questions may be asked touching the most familiar things in our experience, and that our comprehension of those things may be so vague that we grope in vain for an answer. Space, time, matter, minds, realities,—with these things we have to do every day. Can it be that we do not know what they are? Then we must be blind, indeed. How shall we set about enlightening our ignorance?

Not as we have enlightened our ignorance heretofore. We have added fact to fact; but our task now is to gain a new light on all facts, to see them from a different point of view; not so much to extend our knowledge as to deepen it.

It seems scarcely necessary to point out that our world, when looked at for the first time in this new way, may seem to be a new and strange world. The real things of our experience may appear to melt away, to be dissolved by reflection into mere shadows and unrealities. Well do I remember the consternation with which, when almost a schoolboy, I first made my acquaintance with John Stuart Mill's doctrine that the things about us are "permanent possibilities of sensation." To Mill, of course, chairs and tables were still chairs and tables, but to me they became ghosts, inhabitants of a phantom world, to find oneself in which was a matter of the gravest concern.

I suspect that this sense of the unreality of things comes often to those who have entered upon the path of reflection. It may be a comfort to such to realize that it is rather a thing to be expected. How can one feel at home in a world which one has entered for the first time? One cannot become a philosopher and remain exactly the man that one was before. Men have tried to do it,—Thomas Reid is a notable instance (section 50); but the result is that one simply does not become a philosopher. It is not possible to gain a new and a deeper insight into the nature of things, and yet to see things just as one saw them before one attained to this.

If, then, we are willing to study philosophy at all, we must be willing to embrace new views of the world, if there seem to be good reasons for so doing. And if at first we suffer from a sense of bewilderment, we must have patience, and must wait to see whether time and practice may not do something toward removing our distress. It may be that we have only half understood what has been revealed to us.

89. BE WILLING TO CONSIDER POSSIBILITIES WHICH AT FIRST STRIKE ONE AS ABSURD.—It must be confessed that the philosophers have sometimes brought forward doctrines which seem repellent to good sense, and little in harmony with the experience of the world which we have all our lives enjoyed. Shall we on this account turn our backs upon them and refuse them an impartial hearing?

Thus, the idealist maintains that there is no existence save psychical existence; that the material things about us are really mental things. One of the forms taken by this doctrine is that alluded to above, that things are permanent possibilities of sensation.

I think it can hardly be denied that this sounds out of harmony with the common opinion of mankind. Men do not hesitate to distinguish between minds and material things, nor do they believe that material things exist only in minds. That dreams and hallucinations exist only in minds they are very willing to admit; but they will not admit that this is true of such things as real chairs and tables. And if we ask them why they take such a position, they fall back upon what seems given in experience.

Now, as the reader of the earlier chapters has seen, I think that the plain man is more nearly right in his opinion touching the existence of a world of non-mental things than is the idealistic philosopher. The latter has seen a truth and misconceived it, thus losing some truth that he had before he began to reflect. The former has not seen the truth which has impressed the idealist, and he has held on to that vague recognition that there are two orders of things given in our experience, the physical and the mental, which seems to us so unmistakable a fact until we fall into the hands of the philosophers.

But all this does not prove that we have a right simply to fall back upon "common sense," and refuse to listen to the idealist. The deliverances of unreflective common sense are vague in the extreme; and though it may seem to assure us that there is a world of things non-mental, its account of that world is confused and incoherent. He who must depend on common sense alone can find no answer to the idealists; he refuses to follow them, but he cannot refute them. He is reduced to dogmatic denial.

This is in itself an uncomfortable position. And when we add to this the reflection that such a man loses the truth which the idealist emphasizes, the truth that the external world of which we speak must be, if we are to know it at all, a world revealed to our senses, a world given in our experience, we see that he who stops his ears remains in ignorance. The fact is that the man who has never weighed the evidence that impresses the idealist is not able to see clearly what is meant by that external world in which we all incline to put such faith. We may say that he *feels* a truth blindly, but does not see it.

Let us take another illustration. If there is one thing that we feel to be as sure as the existence of the external world, it is that there are other minds more or less resembling our own. The solipsist may try to persuade us that the evidence for such minds is untrustworthy. We may see no flaw in his argument, but he cannot convince us. May we ignore him, and refuse to consider the matter at all?

Surely not, if we wish to substitute clear thinking for vague and indefinite opinion. We should listen with attention, strive to understand all the reasonings laid before us, and then, if they seem to lead to conclusions really not in harmony with our experience, go carefully over the ground and try to discover the flaw in them. It is only by doing something like this that we can come to see clearly what is meant when we speak of two or more minds and the relation between them. The solipsist can help us, and we should let him do it.

We should, therefore, be willing to consider seriously all sorts of doctrines which may at first strike us as unreasonable. I have chosen two which I believe to contain error. But the man who approaches a doctrine which impresses him as strange has no right to assume at the outset that it contains error. We have seen again and again how easy it is to misapprehend what is given in experience. The philosopher may be in the right, and what he says may repel us because we have become accustomed to certain erroneous notions, and they have come to seem self-evident truths.

90. DO NOT HAVE TOO MUCH RESPECT FOR AUTHORITY.—But if it is an error to refuse to listen to the philosopher, it is surely no less an error to accord him an authority above what he has a right to demand. Bear in mind what was said in the last chapter about the

difference between the special sciences and philosophy. There is in the latter field no body of doctrine that we may justly regard as authoritative. There are "schools" of philosophy, and their adherents fall into the very human error of feeling very sure that they and those who agree with them are right; and the emphasis with which they speak is apt to mislead those who are not well informed. I shall say a few words about the dangers of the "school."

If we look about us, we are impressed by the fact that there are "schools" of philosophy, somewhat as there are religious sects and political parties. An impressive teacher sets the mark of his personality and of his preferences upon those who come under his influence. They are not at an age to be very critical, and, indeed, they have not as yet the requisite learning to enable them to be critical. They keep the trend which has been given them early in life, and, when they become teachers, they pass on the type of thought with which they have been inoculated, and the circle widens. "Schools" may arise, of course, in a different way. An epoch-making book may sweep men off of their feet and make of them passionate adherents. But he who has watched the development of the American universities during the last twenty-five years must be impressed with the enormous influence which certain teachers have had in giving a direction to the philosophic thought of those who have come in contact with them. We expect the pupils of a given master to have a given shade of opinion, and very often we are not disappointed in our guess.

It is entirely natural that this should be so. Those who betake themselves to the study of philosophy are men like other men. They have the same feelings, and the bending of the twig has the same significance in their case that it has in that of others. It is no small compliment to a teacher that he can thus spread his influence, and leave his proxies even when he passes away.

But, when we strive to "put off humanity" and to look at the whole matter under the cold light of reason, we may well ask ourselves, whether he who unconsciously accepts his philosophy, in whole or in part, because it has been the philosophy of his teacher, is not doing what is done by those persons whose politics and whose religion take their color from such accidental circumstances as birth in a given class or family traditions?

I am far from saying that it is, in general, a bad thing for the world that men should be influenced in this way by one another. I say only that, when we look at the facts of the case, we must admit that even our teachers of philosophy do not always become representatives of the peculiar type of thought for which they stand, merely through a deliberate choice from the wealth of material which the history of speculative thought lays before them. They are influenced by others to take what they do take, and the traces of this influence are apt to remain with them through life. He who wishes to be entirely impartial must be on his guard against such influences as these, and must distrust prejudices for or against certain doctrines, when he finds that he imbibed them at an uncritical age and has remained under their influence ever since. Some do appear to be able to emancipate themselves, and to outgrow what they first learned.

It is, as I have said, natural that there should be a tendency to form "schools" in philosophy. And there are certain things that make this somewhat uncritical acceptance of a doctrine very attractive.

In the first place, if we are willing to take a system of any sort as a whole, it saves us a vast amount of trouble. We seem to have a citadel, a point of vantage from which we can look out upon life and interpret it. If the house we live in is not in all respects ideal, at least it is a house, and we are not homeless. There is nothing more intolerable to most men than the having of no opinions. They will change one opinion for another, but they will rarely consent to do without altogether. It is something to have an answer to offer to those who persist in asking questions; and it is something to have some sort of ground under one's feet, even if it be not very solid ground.

Again. Man is a social creature, and he is greatly fortified in his opinions by the consciousness that others share them with him. If we become adherents of a "school," we have the agreeable consciousness that we are not walking alone through the maze of speculations that confronts those who reflect. There appears to be a traveled way in which we may have some confidence. Are we not following the crowd, or, at least, a goodly number of the pilgrims who are seeking the same goal with ourselves? Under such circumstances we are not so often impelled to inquire anxiously whether we are after all upon the right road. We assume that we have made no mistake.

Under such circumstances we are apt to forget that there are many such roads, and that these have been traveled in ages past by troops very much like our own, who also cherished the hope that they were upon the one and only highway. In other words, we are apt to forget the lesson of the history of philosophy. This is a serious mistake.

And what intensifies our danger, if we belong to a school which happens to be dominant and to have active representatives, is that we get very little real criticism. The books that we write are usually criticised by those who view our positions sympathetically, and who are more inclined to praise than to blame. He who looks back upon the past is struck with the fact that books which have been lauded to the skies in one age have often been subjected to searching criticism and to a good deal of condemnation in the next. Something very like this is to be expected of books written in our own time. It is, however, a pity that we should have to wait so long for impartial criticism.

This leads me to say a word of the reviews which fill our philosophical journals, and which we must read, for it is impossible to read all the books that come out, and yet we wish to know something about them.

To the novice it is something of a surprise to find that books by men whom he knows to be eminent for their ingenuity and their learning are condemned in very offhand fashion by quite young men, who as yet have attained to little learning and to no eminence at all. One sometimes is tempted to wonder that men admittedly remarkable should have fathered such poor productions as we are given to understand them to be, and should have offered them to a public that has a right to be indignant.

Now, there can be no doubt that, in philosophy, a cat has the right to look at a king, and has also a right to point out his misdoings, if such there be. But it seems just to indicate that, in this matter, certain cautions should be observed.

If a great man has been guilty of an error in reasoning, there is no reason why it should not be pointed out by any one who is capable of detecting it. The authority of the critic is a matter of no moment where the evidence is given. In such a case, we take a suggestion and we do the criticising for ourselves. But where the evidence is not given, where the justice of the criticism is not proved, the case is different. Here we must take into consideration the authority of the critic, and, if we follow him at all, we must follow him blindly. Is it safe to do this?

It is never safe in philosophy, or, at any rate, it is safe so seldom that the exceptions are not worth taking into account. Men write from the standpoint of some school of opinion; and, until we know their prepossessions, their statements that this is good, that is bad, the third thing is profound, are of no significance whatever. We should simply set them aside, and try to find out from our reviewer what is contained in the book under criticism.

One of the evils arising out of the bias I am discussing is, that books and authors are praised or condemned indiscriminately because of their point of view, and little discrimination is made between good books and poor books. There is all the difference in the world between a work which can be condemned only on the ground that it is realistic or idealistic in its standpoint, and those feeble productions which are to be condemned from every point of view. If we consistently carry out the principle that we may condemn all those who are not of our party, we must give short shrift to a majority of the great men of the past.

So I say, beware of authority in philosophy, and, above all, beware of that most insidious form of authority, the spirit of the "school." It cannot but narrow our sympathies and restrict our outlook.

91. REMEMBER THAT ORDINARY RULES OF EVIDENCE APPLY.—What I am going to say in this section is closely related to what has been said just above. To the disinterested observer it may seem rather amusing that one should think it worth while to try to show that we have not the right to use a special set of weights and measures when we are dealing with things philosophical. There was a time when men held that a given doctrine could be philosophically false, and, at the same time, theologically true; but surely the day of such twists and turnings is past!

I am by no means sure that it is past. With the lapse of time, old doctrines take on new aspects, and come to be couched in a language that suits the temper of the later age. Sometimes the doctrine is veiled and rendered less startling, but remains essentially what it was before, and may be criticised in much the same way.

I suppose we may say that every one who is animated by the party spirit discussed above, and who holds to a group of philosophical tenets with a warmth of conviction out of proportion to the authority of the actual evidence which may be claimed for them, is tacitly assuming that the truth or falsity of philosophical dogmas is not wholly a matter of evidence, but that the desires of the philosopher may also be taken into account.

This position is often taken unconsciously. Thus, when, instead of proving to others that a given doctrine is false, we try to show them that it is a dangerous doctrine, and leads to unpalatable consequences, we assume that what seems distasteful cannot be true, and we count on the fact that men incline to believe what they like to believe.

May we give this position the dignity of a philosophical doctrine and hold that, in the somewhat nebulous realm inhabited by the philosopher, men are not bound by the same rules of evidence that obtain elsewhere? That this is actually done, those who read much in the field of modern philosophy are well aware. Several excellent writers have maintained that we need not, even if there seems to be evidence for them, accept views of the universe which do not satisfy "our whole nature."

We should not confuse with this position the very different one which maintains that we have a right to hold tentatively, and with a willingness to abandon them should evidence against them be forthcoming, views which we are not able completely to establish, but which seem reasonable. One may do this with perfect sincerity, and without holding that philosophical truth is in any way different from scientific truth. But the other position goes beyond this; it assumes that man must be satisfied, and that only that can be true which satisfies him.

I ask, is it not significant that such an assumption should be made only in the realm of the unverifiable? No man dreams of maintaining that the rise and fall of stocks will be such as to satisfy the whole nature even of the elect, or that the future history of man on this planet is a thing to be determined by some philosopher who decides for us what would or would not be desirable.

Surely all truths of election—those truths that we simply choose to have true—are something much less august than that Truth of Evidence which sometimes seems little to fall in with our desires, and in the face of which we are humble listeners, not dictators. Before the latter we are modest; we obey, lest we be confounded. And if, in the philosophic realm, we believe that we may order Truth about, and make her our slave, is it not because we have a secret consciousness that we are not dealing with Truth at all, but with Opinion, and with Opinion that has grown insolent because she cannot be drawn from her obscurity and be shown to be what she is?

Sometimes it is suddenly revealed to a man that he has been accepting two orders of truth. I once walked and talked with a good scholar who discoursed of high themes and defended warmly certain theses. I said to him: If you could go into the house opposite, and discover unmistakably whether you are in the right or in the wrong,—discover it as unmistakably as you can discover whether there is or is not furniture in the drawing-room,—would you go? He thought over the matter for a while, and then answered frankly; No! I should not go; I should stay out here and argue it out.

92. AIM AT CLEARNESS AND SIMPLICITY.—There is no department of investigation in which it is not desirable to cultivate clearness and simplicity in thinking, speaking, and writing. But there are certain reasons why we should be especially on our guard in philosophy against the danger of employing a tongue "not understood of the people." There are dangerous pitfalls concealed under the use of technical words and phrases.

The value of technical expressions in the special sciences must be conceded. They are supposed to be more exact and less ambiguous than terms in ordinary use, and they mark an advance in our knowledge of the subject. The distinctions which they indicate have been carefully drawn, and appear to be of such authority that they should be generally accepted. Sometimes, as, for example, in mathematics, a conventional set of symbols may quite usurp the function of ordinary language, and may enormously curtail the labor of setting forth the processes and results of investigation.

But we must never forget that we have not in philosophy an authoritative body of truth which we have the right to impose upon all who enter that field. A multitude of distinctions have been made and are made; but the representatives of different schools of thought are not at one touching the value and significance of these distinctions. If we coin a word or a phrase to mark such, there is some danger that we fall into the habit of using such words or phrases, as we use the coins in our purse, without closely examining them, and with the ready assumption that they must pass current everywhere.

Thus, there is always a possibility that our technical expressions may be nothing less than crystallized error. Against this we should surely be on our guard.

Again. When we translate the language of common life into the dialect of the learned, there is danger that we may fall into the error of supposing that we are adding to our knowledge, even though we are doing nothing save to exchange one set of words for another. Thus, we all know very well that one mind can communicate with another. One does not have to be a scholar to be aware of this. If we choose to call this "intersubjective intercourse," we have given the thing a sounding name; but we know no more about it than we did before. The problem of the relation between minds, and the way in which they are to be conceived as influencing each other, remains just what it was. So, also, we recognize the everyday fact that we know both ourselves and what is not ourselves. Shall we call this knowledge of something not ourselves "self-transcendence"? We may do so if we wish, but we ought to realize that this bestowal of a title makes no whit clearer what is meant by knowledge.

Unhappily, men too often believe that, when they have come into the possession of a new word or phrase, they have gained a new thought. The danger is great in proportion to the breadth of the gulf which separates the new dialect from the old language of common life in which we are accustomed to estimate things. Many a philosopher would be bereft, indeed, were he robbed of his vocabulary and compelled to express his thoughts in ordinary speech. The theories which are implicit in certain recurring expressions would be forced to come out into the open, and stand criticism without disguise.

But can one write philosophical books without using words which are not in common use among the unphilosophic? I doubt it. Some such words it seems impossible to avoid. However, it does seem possible to bear in mind the dangers of a special philosophical terminology and to reduce such words to a minimum.

Finally, we may appeal to the humanity of the philosopher. The path to reflection is a sufficiently difficult one as it is; why should he roll rocks upon it and compel those who come after him to climb over them? If truths are no truer for being expressed in a repellent form, why should he trick them out in a fantastic garb? What we want is the naked truth, and we lose time and patience in freeing our mummy from the wrappings in which learned men have seen fit to encase it.

93. DO NOT HASTILY ACCEPT A DOCTRINE.—This brings me to the last of the maxims which I urge upon the attention of the reader. All that has been said so far may be regarded as leading up to it.

The difficulty that confronts us is this: On the one hand, we must recognize the uncertainty that reigns in this field of investigation. We must ever weigh probabilities and possibilities; we do not find ourselves in the presence of indubitable truths which all competent persons stand ready to admit. This seems to argue that we should learn to suspend judgment, and should be most wary in our acceptance of one philosophical doctrine and our rejection of another.

On the other hand, philosophy is not a mere matter of intellectual curiosity. It has an intimate connection with life. As a man thinks, so is he, to a great extent, at least. How, then, can one afford to remain critical and negative? To counsel this seems equivalent to advising that one abandon the helm and consent to float at the mercy of wind and tide.

The difficulty is a very real one. It presents itself insistently to those who have attained to that degree of intellectual development at which one begins to ask oneself questions and to reflect upon the worth and meaning of life. An unreflective adherence to tradition no longer satisfies such persons. They wish to know why they should believe in this or that doctrine, and why they should rule their lives in harmony with this or that maxim. Shall we advise them to lay hold without delay of a set of philosophical tenets, as we might advise a disabled man to aid himself with any staff that happens to come to hand? Or shall we urge them to close their eyes to the light, and to go back again to the old unreflective life?

Neither of these counsels seems satisfactory, for both assume tacitly that it does not much matter what the *truth* is, and that we can afford to disregard it.

Perhaps we may take a suggestion from that prudent man and acute philosopher, Descartes. Discontented with the teachings of the schools as they had been presented to him, he resolved to set out upon an independent voyage of discovery, and to look for a philosophy of his own. It seemed necessary to him to doubt, provisionally at least, all that he had received from the past. But in what house should he live while he was reconstructing his old habitation? Without principles of some sort he could not live, and without reasonable principles he could not live well. So he framed a set of provisional rules, which should guide his life until he had new ground beneath his feet.

When we examine these rules, we find that, on the whole, they are such as the experience of mankind has found prudent and serviceable. In other words, we discover that Descartes, until he was in a position to see clearly for himself, was willing to be led by others. He was a unit in the social order, and he recognized that truth.

It does not seem out of place to recall this fact to the consciousness of those who are entering upon the reflective life. Those who are rather new to reflection upon philosophical matters are apt to seize single truths, which are too often half-truths, and to deduce their consequences remorselessly. They do not always realize the extreme complexity of society, or see the full meaning of the relations in which they stand to the state and to the church. Breadth of view can only come with an increase of knowledge and with the exercise of reflection.

For this reason I advise patience, and a willingness to accept the established order of things until one is very sure that one has attained to some truth—some real truth, not a mere truth of election—which may serve as the basis of a reconstruction. The first glimpses of truth cannot be depended upon to furnish such a foundation.

Thus, we may suspend judgment, and, nevertheless, be ready to act. But is not this a mere compromise? Certainly. All life is a compromise; and in the present instance it means only that we should keep our eyes open to the light, whatever its source, and yet should nourish that wholesome self-distrust that prevents a man from being an erratic and revolutionary creature, unmindful of his own limitations. Prudent men in all walks in life make this compromise, and the world is the better for it.

NOTES

CHAPTER I, sections 1-5. If the student will take a good history of philosophy, and look over the accounts of the different systems referred to, he will see the justice of the position taken in the text, namely, that philosophy was formerly synonymous with universal knowledge. It is not necessary, of course, to read the whole history of philosophy to attain this end. One may take such a text-book as Ueberweg's "History of Philosophy," and run over the summaries contained in the large print. To see how the conception of what constitutes universal knowledge changed in successive ages, compare Thales, the Sophists, Aristotle, the Schoolmen, Bacon, and Descartes. For the ancient philosophy one may consult Windelband's "History of the Ancient Philosophy," a clear and entertaining little work (English translation, N.Y., 1899).

In Professor Paulsen's "Introduction to Philosophy" (English translation, N.Y., 1895), there is an interesting introductory chapter on "The Nature and Import of Philosophy" (pp. 1-41). The author pleads for the old notion of philosophy as universal knowledge, though he does not, of course, mean that the philosopher must be familiar with all the details of all the sciences.

Section 6. In justification of the meaning given to the word "philosophy" in this section, I ask the reader to look over the list of courses in philosophy advertised in the catalogues of our leading universities at home and abroad. There is a certain consensus of opinion as to what properly comes under the title, even among those who differ widely as to what is the proper definition of philosophy.

CHAPTER II, sections 7-10. Read the chapter on "The Mind and the World in Common Thought and in Science" (Chapter I) in my "System of Metaphysics," N.Y., 1904.

One can be brought to a vivid realization of the fact that the sciences proceed upon a basis of assumptions which they do not attempt to analyze and justify, if one will take some elementary work on arithmetic or geometry or psychology and examine the first few chapters, bearing in mind what philosophical problems may be drawn from the materials there treated. Section 11. The task of reflective thought and its difficulties are treated in the chapter entitled "How Things are Given in Consciousness" (Chapter III), in my "System of Metaphysics."

CHAPTER III, sections 12-13. Read "The Inadequacy of the Psychological Standpoint," "System of Metaphysics," Chapter II. I call especial attention to the illustration of "the man in the cell" (pp. 18 ff.). It would be a good thing to read these pages with the class, and to impress upon the students the fact that those who have doubted or denied the existence of the external material world have, if they have fallen into error, fallen into a very natural error, and are not without some excuse.

Section 14. See "The Metaphysics of the Telephone Exchange," "System of Metaphysics," Chapter XXII, where Professor Pearson's doctrine is examined at length, with quotations and references.

It is interesting to notice that a doubt of the external world has always rested upon some sort of a "telephone exchange" argument; naturally, it could not pass by that name before the invention of the telephone, but the reasoning is the same. It puts the world at one remove, shutting the mind up to the circle of its ideas; and then it doubts or denies the world, or, at least, holds that its existence must be proved in some roundabout way. Compare Descartes, "Of the Existence of Material Things," "Meditations," VI.

CHAPTER IV, sections 15-18. See Chapters VI and VII, "What we mean by the External World," and "Sensations and 'Things,'" in my "System of Metaphysics." In that work the discussion of the distinction between the objective order of experience and the subjective order is completed in Chapter XXIII, "The Distinction between the World and the Mind." This was done that the subjective order might be treated in the part of the book which discusses the mind and its relation to matter.

As it is possible that the reader may be puzzled by differences of expression which obtain in the two books, a word of explanation is not out of place.

In the "Metaphysics," for example, it is said that sensations so connect themselves together as to form what we call the system of material things (p. 105). It is intimated in a footnote that this is a provisional statement and the reader is referred to later chapters. Now, in the present book (sections 16-17), it is taught that we may not call material things groups of sensations.

The apparent contradiction is due to the fact that, in this volume, the full meaning of the word "sensation" is exhibited at the outset, and sensations, as phenomena of the subjective order, are distinguished from the phenomena of the objective order which constitute the external world. In the earlier work the word "sensation" was for a while used loosely to cover all our experiences that do not belong to the class called imaginary, and the distinction between the subjective and objective in this realm was drawn later (Chapter XXIII).

I think the present arrangement is the better one, as it avoids from the outset the suggestion that the real world is something subjective—our sensations or ideas—and thus escapes the idealistic flavor which almost inevitably attaches to the other treatment, until the discussion is completed, at least.

CHAPTER V, sections 10-21. See Chapters VIII and IX, "System of Metaphysics," "The Distinction between Appearance and Reality" and "The Significance of the Distinction."

Section 22. See Chapter XXVI, "The World as Unperceived, and the 'Unknowable,'" where Spencer's doctrine is examined at length, and references are given. I think it is very important that the student should realize that the "Unknowable" is a perfectly useless assumption in philosophy, and can serve no purpose whatever.

CHAPTER VI, sections 23-25. See Chapters X and XI, "System of Metaphysics," "The Kantian Doctrine of Space" and "Difficulties connected with the Kantian Doctrine of Space."

It would be an excellent thing for the student, after he has read the above chapters, to take up Kant's "Critique of Pure Reason," and read and analyze the argument of Antinomies I and II, with the Observations appended. One can understand these arguments without being familiar with the "Critique" as a whole; at any rate, the account of Kant's philosophy contained in section 51 of this book will serve to explain his use of certain terms, such as "the laws of our sensibility."

Kant's reasonings are very curious and interesting in this part of his book. It seems to be proved that the world must be endless in space and without a beginning or end in time, and just as plausibly proved that it cannot be either. It seems to be proved that finite spaces and times are infinitely divisible, and at the same time that they cannot be infinitely divisible. The situation is an amusing one, and rendered not the less amusing by the seriousness with which the mutually destructive arguments are taken.

When the student meets such a tangle in the writings of any philosopher, I ask him to believe that it is not the human reason that is at fault—at least, let him not assume that it is. The fault probably lies with a human reason.

Section 26. See Chapter XII, "The Berkeleian Doctrine of Space," in my "System of Metaphysics." The argument ought not to be difficult to one who has mastered Chapter V of this volume.

CHAPTER VII, sections 27-29. Compare Chapter XIII, "System of Metaphysics," "Of Time."

With the chapters on Space and Time it would be well for the student to read Chapter XIV, "The Real World in Space and Time," where it is made clear why we have no hesitation in declaring space and time to be infinite, although we recognize that it seems to be an assumption of knowledge to declare the material world infinite.

CHAPTER VIII, sections 30-32. Read, in the "System of Metaphysics," Chapters V and XVII, "The Self or Knower" and "The Atomic Self."

Section 33. The suggestions, touching the attitude of the psychologist toward the mind, contained in the preface to Professor William James's "Psychology" are very interesting and instructive.

CHAPTER IX, sections 35-36. For a strong argument in favor of interactionism see James's "Psychology," Chapter V. I wish the student would, in reading it, bear in mind what is said in my chapter on "The Atomic Self," above referred to. The subject should be approached with an open mind, and one should suspend judgment until both sides have been heard from.

Section 37. Descartes held that the lower animals are automata and that their actions are not indicative of consciousness; he regarded their bodies as machines lacking the soul in the "little pineal gland." Professor Huxley revived the doctrine of animal automatism and extended it so as to include man. He regarded consciousness as a "collateral product" of the working of the body, related to it somewhat as is the steam-whistle of a locomotive engine to the working of the machine. He made it an effect, but not a cause, of motions. See "System of Metaphysics," Chapter XVIII, "The Automaton Theory: its Genesis."

We owe the doctrine of parallelism, in its original form, to Spinoza. It was elaborated by W. K. Clifford, and to him the modern interest in the subject is largely due. The whole subject is discussed at length in my "System of Metaphysics," Chapters XIX-XXI. The titles are: "The Automaton Theory: Parallelism," "What is Parallelism?" and "The Man and the Candlestick." Clifford's doctrine is presented in a new form in Professor Strong's recent brilliant work, "Why the Mind has a Body" N.Y., 1903.

Section 38. See "System of Metaphysics," Chapter XXIV, "The Time and Place of Sensations and Ideas."

CHAPTER X, sections 40-42. See "System of Metaphysics," Chapters XXVII and XXVIII, "The Existence of Other Minds," and "The Distribution of Minds."

Writers seem to be divided into three camps on this question of other minds.

(1) I have treated our knowledge of other minds as due to an inference. This is the position usually taken.

(2) We have seen that Huxley and Clifford cast doubts upon the validity of the inference, but, nevertheless, made it. Professor Strong, in the work mentioned in the notes to the previous chapter, maintains that it is not an inference, and that we do not directly perceive other minds, but that we are assured of their existence just the same. He makes our knowledge an "intuition" in the old-fashioned sense of the word, a something to be accepted but not to be accounted for.

(3) Writers who have been influenced more or less by the Neo-Kantian or Neo-Hegelian doctrine are apt to speak as though we had the same direct evidence of the existence of other minds that we have of the existence of our own. I have never seen a systematic and detailed exposition of this doctrine. It appears rather in the form of hints dropped in passing. A number of such are to be found in Taylor's "Elements of Metaphysics."

Section 43. The "Mind-stuff" doctrine is examined at length and its origin discussed in Chapter XXXI of the "System of Metaphysics," "Mental Phenomena and the Causal Nexus." It is well worth while for the student to read the whole of Clifford's essay "On the Nature of Things-in-themselves," even if he is pressed for time.

CHAPTER XI, section 44. See "System of Metaphysics," Chapter XV, "The World as Mechanism."

Section 45. See Chapter XXXI, "The Place of Mind in Nature."

Section 46. For a definition of Fatalism, and a description of its difference from the scientific doctrine of Determinism, see Chapter XXXIII, "Fatalism, 'Freewill' and Determinism." For a vigorous defense of "Freewill" (which is not, in my opinion, free will at all, in the common acceptation of the word) see Professor James's Essay on "The Dilemma of the Determinist," in his volume, "The Will to Believe."

Fatalism and Determinism are constantly confused, and much of the opposition to Determinism is attributable to this confusion.

Section 47. See Chapter XXXII, "Mechanism and Teleology."

CHAPTER XII, section 48. The notes to Chapter III (see above) are in point here. It is well worth the student's while to read the whole of Chapter XI, Book IV, of Locke's "Essay." It is entitled "Of our Knowledge of the Existence of Other Things." Notice the headings of some of his sections:—

Section 1. "It is to be had only by sensation."

Section 2. "Instance whiteness of this paper."

Section 3. "This, though not so certain as demonstration, yet may be called 'Knowledge,' and proves the existence of things without us."

Locke's argument proceeds, as we have seen, on the assumption that we perceive external things directly,—an assumption into which he slips unawares,—and yet he cannot allow that we really do perceive directly what is external. This makes him uncomfortably conscious that he has not absolute proof, after all. The section that closes the discussion is entitled: "Folly to expect demonstration in everything."

Section 49. I wish that I could believe that every one of my readers would sometime give himself the pleasure of reading through Berkeley's "Principles of Human Knowledge" and his "Three Dialogues between Hylas and Philonous." Clearness of thought, beauty of style, and elevation of sentiment characterize them throughout.

The "Principles" is a systematic treatise. If one has not time to read it all, one can get a good idea of the doctrine by running through the first forty-one sections. For brief readings in class, to illustrate Berkeley's reasoning, one may take sections 1-3, 14, 18-20, and 38.

The "Dialogues" is a more popular work. As the etymology of the names in the title suggests, we have in it a dispute between a man who pins his faith to matter and an idealist. The aim of the book is to confute skeptics and atheists from the standpoint of idealism.

For Hume's treatment of the external world, see his "Treatise of Human Nature," Part IV, section 2. For his treatment of the mind, see Part IV, section 6.

Section 50. Reid repeats himself a great deal, for he gives us asseveration rather than proof. One can get the gist of his argument by reading carefully a few of his sections. It would be a good exercise to read in class, if time permitted, the two sections of his "Inquiry" entitled "Of Extension" (Chapter V, section 5), and "Of Perception in General" (Chapter VI, section 20).

Section 51. For an account of the critical Philosophy, see Falckenberg's "History of Modern Philosophy" (English translation, N.Y., 1893). Compare with this the accounts in the histories of philosophy by Ueberweg and Höffding (English translation of the latter, London, 1900). Full bibliographies are to be found especially in Ueberweg.

It is well to look at the philosophy of Kant through more than one pair of eyes. Thus, if one reads Morris's "Kant's Critique of Pure Reason" (Chicago, 1882), one should read also Sidgwick's "Lectures on the Philosophy of Kant" (N.Y., 1905).

CHAPTER XIII, section 52. It is difficult to see how Hamilton could regard himself as a "natural" realist (the word is employed by him). See his "Lectures on Metaphysics," VIII, where he develops his doctrine. He seems to teach, in spite of himself, that we can know directly only the impressions that things make on us, and must infer all else: "Our whole knowledge of mind and matter is, thus, only relative; of existence, absolutely and in itself, we know nothing."

Whom may we regard as representing the three kinds of "hypothetical realism" described in the text? Perhaps we may put the plain man, who has not begun to reflect, in the first class. John Locke is a good representative of the second; see the "Essay concerning Human Understanding," Book II, Chapter VIII. Herbert Spencer belonged to the third while he wrote Chapter V of his "First Principles of Philosophy."

Section 53. I have said enough of the Berkeleian idealism in the notes on Chapter XII. As a good illustration of objective idealism in one of its forms I may take the doctrine of Professor Royce; see his address, "The Conception of God" (N.Y., 1902).

Mr. Bradley's doctrine is criticised in Chapter XXXIV (entitled "Of God"), "System of Metaphysics."

CHAPTER XIV, section 55. See "System of Metaphysics," Chapter XVI, "The Insufficiency of Materialism."

Section 56. Professor Strong's volume, "Why the Mind has a Body" (N.Y., 1903), advocates a panpsychism much like that of Clifford. It is very clearly written, and with Clifford's essay on "The Nature of Things-in-themselves," ought to give one a good idea of the considerations that impel some able men to become panpsychists.

Section 57. The pantheistic monism of Spinoza is of such importance historically that it is desirable to obtain a clear notion of its meaning. I have discussed this at length in two earlier works: "The Philosophy of Spinoza" (N.Y., 1894) and "On Spinozistic Immortality." The student is referred to the account of Spinoza's "God or Substance" contained in these. See, especially, the "Introductory Note" in the back of the first-mentioned volume.

Professor Royce is a good illustration of the idealistic monist; see the volume referred to in the note above (section 53). His "Absolute," or God, is conceived to be an all-inclusive mind of which our finite minds are parts.

Section 58. Sir William Hamilton's dualism is developed in his "Lectures on Metaphysics," VIII. He writes: "Mind and matter, as known or knowable, are only two different series of phenomena or qualities; as unknown and unknowable, they are the two substances in which these two different series of phenomena or qualities are supposed to inhere. The existence of an unknown substance is only an inference we are compelled to make, from the existence of known phenomena; and the distinction of two substances is only inferred from the seeming incompatibility of the two series of phenomena to coinhere in one."

CHAPTER XV, section 60. The reader will find Descartes's path traced in the "Meditations." In I, we have his sweeping doubt; in II, his doctrine as to the mind; in III, the existence of God is established; in VI, he gets around to the existence of the external world. We find a good deal of the "natural light" in the first part of his "Principles of Philosophy."

Section 61. We have an excellent illustration of Locke's inconsistency in violating his own principles and going beyond experience, in his treatment of "Substance." Read, in his "Essay," Book I, Chapter IV, section 18, and Book II, Chapter XXIII, section 4. These sections are not long, and might well be read and analyzed in class.

Section 62. See the note to section 51.

Section 64. I write this note (in 1908) to give the reader some idea of later developments of the doctrine called pragmatism. There has been a vast amount printed upon the subject in the last two or three years, but I am not able to say even yet that we have to do with "a clear-cut doctrine, the limits and consequences of which have been worked out in detail." Hence, I prefer to leave section 64 as I first wrote it, merely supplementing it here.

We may fairly consider the three leaders of the pragmatic movement to be Professor William James, Dr. F. C. S. Schiller, and Professor John Dewey. The first has developed his doctrine at length in his volume entitled "Pragmatism" (London, 1907); the second, who calls his doctrine "Humanism," but declares himself a pragmatist, and in essential agreement with Professor James, has published two volumes of philosophical essays entitled "Humanism" (London, 1903) and "Studies in Humanism" (London, 1907); the third has developed his position in the first four chapters of the "Studies in Logical Theory" (Chicago, 1903).

Professor James, in his "Pragmatism" (Lecture II), says that pragmatism, at the outset, at least, stands for no particular results. It has no dogmas, and no doctrines save its method. This method means:

"The attitude of looking away from first things, principles, 'categories,' supposed necessities; and of looking towards last things, fruits, consequences, facts." He remarks further, however, that pragmatism has come to be used also in a wider sense, as signifying a certain theory of truth (pp. 54-55). This theory is brought forward in Lecture VI.

The theory maintains that: "True ideas are those that we can assimilate, validate, corroborate, and verify. False ideas are those that we can not" (p. 201). This sounds as though Professor James abandoned his doctrine touching the Turk and the Christian mentioned in section 64.

But what do the words "verification" and "validation" pragmatically mean? We are told that they signify certain practical consequences of the verified and validated idea. Our ideas may be said to "agree" with reality when they lead us, through acts and other ideas which they instigate, up to or towards other parts of experience with which we feel that the original ideas remain in agreement. "The connections and transitions come to us from point to point as being progressive, harmonious, satisfactory. This function of agreeable leading is what we mean by an idea's verification" (p. 202).

Thus, we do not seem to be concerned with verification in the sense in which the word has usually been employed heretofore. The tendency to take as true what is useful or serviceable has not been abandoned. That Professor James does not really leave his Turk in the lurch becomes clear to any one who will read his book attentively and note his reasons for taking the various pragmatic attitudes which he does take. See, for example, his pragmatic argument for "free-will." The doctrine is simply assumed as a doctrine of "relief" (pp. 110-121).

Briefly stated, Dr. Schiller's doctrine is that truths are man-made, and that it is right for man to consult his desires in making them. It is in substantial harmony with the pragmatism of Professor James, and I shall not dwell upon it. Dr. Schiller's essays are very entertainingly written.

Professor Dewey's pragmatism seems to me sufficiently different from the above to merit another title. In the "Journal of Philosophy, Psychology, and Scientific Methods," Volume IV, No. 4, Professor Dewey brings out the distinction between his own position and that of Professor James.

To the periodical literature on pragmatism I cannot refer in detail. Professor James defends his position against misconceptions in the

"Philosophical Review," Volume XVII, No. 1. See, on the other side, Professor Perry, in the "Journal of Philosophy, Psychology, and Scientific Methods," Volume IV, pp. 365 and 421; Professor Hibben, "Philosophical Review," XVII, 4; and Dr. Carus, "The Monist," July, 1908.

CHAPTER XVI, sections 65-68. To see how the logicians have regarded their science and its relation to philosophy, see; Keynes's "Formal Logic" (London, 1894), Introduction; Hobhouse's "Theory of Knowledge" (London, 1896), Introduction; Aikins's "The Principles of Logic" (N.Y., 1902), Introduction; and Creighton's "Introductory Logic" (N.Y., 1898), Preface.

Professor Aikins writes: "Thus, in so far as logic tries to make us reason correctly by giving us correct conceptions of things and the way in which their relations involve each other, it is a kind of simple metaphysics studied for a practical end."

Professor Creighton says, "Although in treating the syllogistic logic I have followed to a large extent the ordinary mode of presentation, I have both here, and when dealing with the inductive methods, endeavored to interpret the traditional doctrines in a philosophical way, and to prepare for the theoretical discussions of the third part of the book."

John Stuart Mill tried not to be metaphysical; but let the reader examine, say, his third chapter, "Of the Things denoted by Names," or look over Book VI, in his "System of Logic."

Professor Sigwart's great work, "Logik" (Freiburg, 2d edition, Volume I, 1889, Volume II, 1893), may almost be called a philosophy of logic.

CHAPTER XVII, section 69. Compare with Professor James's account of the scope of psychology the following from Professor Baldwin: "The question of the relation of psychology to metaphysics, over which a fierce warfare has been waged in recent years, is now fairly settled by the adjustment of mutual claims. . . . The terms of the adjustment of which I speak are briefly these: on the one hand, empirical investigation must precede rational interpretation, and this empirical investigation must be absolutely unhampered by fetters of dogmatism and preconception; on the other hand, rational interpretation must be equally free in its own province, since progress from the individual to the general, from the detached fact to its universal meaning, can be secured only by the judicious use of hypotheses, both metaphysical and speculative. Starting from the empirical we run out at every step into the metempirical." "Handbook of Psychology," Preface, pp. iii and iv.

CHAPTER XVIII, section 71. The teacher might very profitably take extracts from the two chapters of Whewell's "Elements of Morality" referred to in the text, and read them with the class. It is significant of the weakness of Whewell's position that he can give us advice as long as we do not need it, but, when we come to the cross-roads, he is compelled to leave the matter to the individual conscience, and gives us no hint of a general principle that may guide us.

Section 72. Wundt, in his volume "The Facts of the Moral Life" (N.Y., 1897), tries to develop an empirical science of ethics independent of metaphysics; see the Preface.

Compare with this: Martineau's "Types of Ethical Theory" (London, 1885), Preface; T. H. Green's "Prolegomena to Ethics," Introduction; Muirhead's "The Elements of Ethics" (N.Y., 1892); Mackenzie's "A Manual of Ethics" (London, 1893); Jodl's "Gesduchte der Ethik" (Stuttgart, 1882), Preface. I give but a few references, but they will serve to illustrate how close, in the opinion of ethical writers, is the relation between ethics and philosophy.

CHAPTER XIX, section 74. The student who turns over the pages of several works on metaphysics may be misled by a certain superficial similarity that is apt to obtain among them. One sees the field mapped out into Ontology (the science of Being or Reality), Rational Cosmology, and Rational Psychology. These titles are mediaeval landmarks which have been left standing. I may as well warn the reader that two men who discourse of Ontology may not be talking about the same thing at all. Bear in mind what was said in section 57 of the different ways of conceiving the "One Substance"; and bear in mind also what was said in Chapter V of the proper meaning of the word "reality."

I have discarded the above titles in my "System of Metaphysics," because I think it is better and less misleading to use plain and unambiguous language.

Section 75. See the note to Chapter XVI.

CHAPTER XX, sections 76-77. One can get an idea of the problems with which the philosophy of religion has to deal by turning to my "System of Metaphysics" and reading the two chapters entitled "Of God," at the close of the book. It would be

interesting to read and criticise in class some of the theistic arguments that philosophers have brought forward. Quotations and references are given in Chapter XXXIV.

CHAPTER XXI, sections 78-79. What is said of the science of logic, in Chapter XVI, has, of course, a bearing upon these sections. I suggest that the student examine a few chapters of "The Grammar of Science"; the book is very readable.

CHAPTER XXII, sections 80-82. The reader will find in lectures I and II in Sir William Hamilton's "Lectures on Metaphysics" a discussion of the utility of philosophy. It has a pleasant, old-fashioned flavor, and contains some good thoughts. What is said in Chapters XVI-XXI of the present volume has a good deal of bearing upon the subject. See especially what is said in the chapters on logic, ethics, and the philosophy of religion.

CHAPTER XXIII, sections 83-87. There is a rather brief but good and thoughtful discussion of the importance of historical study to the comprehension of philosophical doctrines in Falckenberg's "History of Modern Philosophy" (English translation, N.Y., 1893); see the Introduction.

We have a good illustration of the fact that there may be parallel streams of philosophic thought (section 87) when we turn to the Stoics and the Epicureans. Zeno and Epicurus were contemporaries, but they were men of very dissimilar character, and the schools they founded differed widely in spirit. Zeno went back for his view of the physical world to Heraclitus, and for his ethics to the Cynics. Epicurus borrowed his fundamental thoughts from Democritus.

On the other hand, philosophers may sometimes be regarded as links in the one chain. Witness the series of German thinkers: Kant, Fichte, Schelling, Hegel, Schopenhauer; or the series of British thinkers: Locke, Berkeley, Hume, Mill. Herbert Spencer represents a confluence of the streams. The spirit of his doctrine is predominantly British; but he got his "Unknowable" from Kant, through Hamilton and Mansel.

At any point in a given stream there may be a division. Thus, Kant was awakened to his creative effort by Hume. But Mill is also the successor of Hume, and more truly the successor, for he carries on the traditional way of approaching philosophical problems, while Kant rebels against it, and heads a new line.

CHAPTER XXIV, sections 88-93. I hardly think it is necessary for me to comment upon this chapter. The recommendations amount to this: that a man should be fair-minded and reasonable, free from partisanship, cautious, and able to suspend judgment where the evidence is not clear; also that where the light of reason does not seem to him to shine brightly and to illumine his path as he could wish, he should be influenced in his actions by the reflection that he has his place in the social order, and must meet the obligations laid upon him by this fact. When the pragmatist emphasizes the necessity of accepting ideals and living by them, he is doing us a service. But we must see to it that he does not lead us into making arbitrary decisions and feeling that we are released from the duty of seeking for evidence. Read together sections 64, 91, and 93.

116